Encour

and Journeys

Jane Coates

Unless indicated otherwise, Scripture quotations are taken from the Holy Bible,
New International Version, NIV, or
The Message, MSG
New Living Translation, NLT
The Amplified Bible, AMP
King James Version, KJV
Good News Translation, GNT
The Living Bible, TLV

ISBN 978-1-3999-5777-9

Printed and bound in Great Britain by InPrint & Design

Contents

Introduction

When the Covid Pandemic occurred and the first Covid Lockdown happened in April 2020, most of us found ourselves at home each day and every day, which was a new and challenging experience for us all. School children, students and University students were required to be at home, and working from home, home schooling, and study became the new norm. This was particularly challenging for parents who were able to go to their place of work or office and yet had the responsibility and care of home schooling their school aged children, and college students. It was a time of change, and challenge, and many readjustments were needed. Families with children needed to find new ways to be family together, especially as in the first 'lockdown' only one hour per day of outside physical activity was prescribed and permitted. My husband, my grandson, Sam, and I had to develop a new daily routine of activity, work, recreation, and on-line lessons, with a cycle ride every day, board games and social activities each evening and discovering the joys of baking- along with just about everyone else. So, any excess weight that we lost with cycling was soon added back on again with the calories gained from eating the numerous cakes, muffins, scones, biscuits, and puddings. We all discovered and developed new skills and activities. It was a difficult journey for all of us.

During the three Covid Lockdown periods, I wrote letters and cards to friends, church members and contacts, to keep in touch, to support them from a distance, and to help them to feel that they were not so isolated. At the beginning of April 2020, coinciding with the first Lockdown, I started to write a Monday morning devotional email called Monday Thoughts and Prayers for the Pastoral Care Team that was connected to my church. I was the Pastoral Care Coordinator, with a Team of twelve Pastoral Carers, who each supported friends and members in the church. During the Lockdown periods we supported over eighty elderly and vulnerable members of the congregation with regular phone calls, emails, walks, garden visits and gifts, in addition to those people who were supported by our Seniors Worker and the Lunch Club members. The weekly Monday Thoughts and Prayers was a way of keeping the team connected, and supported, and was intended to be an encouragement to the team at such a difficult time in addition to sharing matters of concern for prayer. Every Monday morning, I would send out the email, as meeting face to face was almost impossible. It is hard to imagine that my Monday devotional messages and reflections have continued for three years. They continue to be well received by many people and not just by the original

Pastoral Care Team as was the intention in the beginning. As other people began to hear about the Monday Thoughts or had received forwarded copies from friends, then the circulation list grew and become far wider. Many of the devotionals made their way on to the church's website.

When my small writing venture began, the devotionals were needed for connection and the encouragement of a group of people at a very difficult time. I had never written in this way before. I am not a trained Bible teacher or scholar, although I studied Theology for a two-year period as part of my university degree. But I have been on my personal journey with Christ from being a teenager, and so I have been able to speak and reflect from my personal, Christian, family, church experience and life experience in general.

I believe that the Holy Spirit gives a nudge, a prompt, or in my words a bit of a 'niggle' in the back of the mind that just won't go away, when He wants to initiate something new. My writing began in just that way- with a gentle push. I never imagined that I could be a writer. But often, I would wake in the night with just a single word or a phrase that would be the heart of a new Monday Thought. In the strange times that we experienced because of Covid, it seemed that God was perhaps doing new things in surprisingly new and different ways with each of us, and that He wanted to use each person in perhaps an unexpected way. God has a purpose for each one of us-and that 'new' thing may be something different and surprising that you or I could not have anticipated. That new thing may be a fresh encounter or an exciting new journey with God.

My three years' worth of weekly devotionals have been gathered and presented in book form for a wider audience. The devotionals are here presented in separate chapters under the title of Encounters and Journeys. The series called Encounters, explores how Jesus encountered different individuals in the Gospel accounts. In each of these episodes and narratives, I have attempted to step into the life and mind of the individual and to write from their perspective- what they might have thought, felt, or experienced. I imagined that I was the person that Jesus was meeting, or the bystander, and so I wrote the account in the first person. This experience was a little like 'hot seating', a technique that I had often used with school children to help them to understand the character in a story. This way of 'stepping into the story or the account,' or 'getting between the pages' helped me to appreciate more the perspective and experience of the character of each person that Jesus encountered, and to see in a deeper way how Jesus responded to each one.

The series called Lessons in the Desert, is based on Bible accounts of groups or individuals who had the hard experience of wandering or being in a desert place. The desert can be a harsh place, but it can also be a very beautiful place. Abram, Moses, Elijah, David, Jonah, John the Baptist and of course Jesus, all experienced desert life, experiences, and times, and had their own journeys in the desert.

Many of the early devotionals were personal experiences from family and personal life but reflections linked with Bible passages. These Monday Thoughts followed experiences such as a dislocated shoulder, a memory jar, a piece of knitting, sunflowers, the baobab tree, the need for oil, roots, a song, and a range of other unconnected things. A random collection of thoughts to dip in and out of.

I loved writing 'thoughts' about real objects, such as a dry-stone wall, a cushion, a lump of clay, a walking stick or a set of oars and drawing out some key lessons from them. We had recently moved to a converted old barn and looking out of my window I could see an ancient, imperfect, dry-stone wall. I loved the imagery of the old wall with its odd, shaped stones placed and built together by a master builder to form a wonderful structure. It spoke to me of God the master builder, Jesus the chief cornerstone, and the church with its living stones-people of different identities, cultures, backgrounds, shapes, and sizes. Imperfect people, with rough edges, that sometimes rubbed against each other, but each one needed and carefully placed.

Some sections of the book have connected thoughts and themes following a series. The Beatitudes of Jesus- or the beautiful attitudes; the names of God, Songs of Significance, Advent, Christmas, Easter, and my key words of life.

This is a book that is not intended to be read from the beginning to the end in any formal way. I hope that you will read sections and pages in any order that you choose. In this book, Encounters and Journeys, I hope that it will help you to encounter Jesus in new and fresh ways and that your journey with Him will take you to new places that perhaps were never on your itinerary. I trust that you will be blessed and encouraged by these pages.

Jane Coates

First Thoughts

My yoke fits perfectly

There is a cycle route around the area where I live that regularly takes me past open spaces and the farmer's fields. I love to watch the changes in the fields. The picture shows one of my favourite fields where the farmer has meticulously prepared the ground for his crop - using a tractor of course. But many years ago, the same perfectly furrowed field would have been done using cattle or horses pulling a plough, to prepare the ground for seed. I love the following verses.

"Come to me, all you who are weary and burdened, and I will give you rest. Take my yoke upon you and learn from me, for I am gentle and humble in heart, and you will find rest for your souls. For my yoke is easy and my burden is light." Matthew 11v 28-30

Walk with me and work with me—watch how I do it. Learn the unforced rhythms of grace. I won't lay anything heavy or ill-fitting on you. Keep company with me and you'll learn to live freely and lightly." Matthew 11v 28-30 MSG

The field, Jesus the Gardener and the plough made me reflect on these words of Jesus. Many of us may be feeling heavy, burdened, weary and that the responsibilities that we carry are too much. So, these wonderful words of Jesus will be very familiar and may be our lifeline.

The yoke is the wooden bar that joins two oxen or cattle, or nowadays two Shire horses, to each other and to the weight or farm machinery they pull. The yoke is placed on the neck of the animals so that when the two animals pull, the yoke settles down in the right place. There are several types of yoke but perhaps Jesus is here referring to the bow type of wooden yoke which needs to be the correct size and fit for the animal, and where new ones are often made as the animal grows. I wonder if Jesus as a carpenter made such items. When pulling heavy loads, often, one of the animals would be heavier and more experienced and used to teach and support the younger animal. Pairs of cattle often worked together in this way for many years.

The image that Jesus is using here is powerful. Jesus is saying that the yoke that He has made is unique, just for you. It will fit perfectly, be comfortable and pleasant for you. There will be nothing harsh or pressing or sharp, it will not chafe or rub. Jesus is saying that you will be linked up with Him and together with Him, you will do whatever is required. The burden that you carry will not be too much to bear. You will not be bowed down or broken. Jesus is saying, "I am gentle and full of grace. I will walk with you step by step, side by side, bearing the weight of the burden and together we will do the task. You will have my strength, companionship and support."

These words give us hope that we can feel free, be joyful and walk lightly in our homes and neighbourhoods again. May we link up with Jesus again in fresh, new ways. The ways that He intended for us.

I am the Lord your God, who brought you out of Egypt so that you would no longer be slaves to the Egyptians; I broke the bars of your yoke and enabled you to walk with heads held high. Leviticus 26 v 13

"Is not this the kind of fasting I have chosen: to loose the chains of injustice and untie the cords of the yoke, to set the oppressed free and break every yoke." Isaiah 58 v 6 NIV

Pray

Jesus, we are heavy and tired. We are carrying unnecessary burdens. Our souls are weary. We lack energy and passion. But You have planned for us to live lightly, freely, joyfully, peacefully. Show us the tasks that You have designed for us. May we walk at the pace that you have set. May we travel with You, step by step, with our heads held high, facing forwards, following that path. May we not run on ahead or pull away. May we work in the garden and the field that you have chosen for us. For You are gentle and gracious.

One more step along the world I go,
One more step along the world I go;
From the old things to the new
Keep me traveling along with you

Round the corners of the world I turn,
More and more about the world I learn;
And the new things that I see
You'll be looking at along with me

As I travel through the bad and good,
Keep me traveling the way I should;
Where I see no way to go
You'll be telling me the way, I know

Give me courage when the world is rough,
Keep me loving though the world is tough;
Leap and sing in all I do,
Keep me traveling along with you.

Sydney Carter (1915-2004) - A familiar Primary School Song:

How are your roots?

I have been following a series on the topic of 'rootfulness' and 'fruitfulness'. In one sermon, the speaker used this wonderful image of the giant redwood trees and their interconnecting roots. So, I make no apology for pinching the imagery which I have found to be so helpful and needed at this time, researching the topic, and now sharing the information about the trees and some lessons that we can perhaps learn.

The sequoia redwood trees located in California, are some of the biggest trees in the world. It could be assumed that trees this huge must have an incredible root system and yet that is not the case at all. These trees have a unique root system that is shallow and often without a central tap root to anchor them deep into the soil. The roots only go down about 6-12 feet, and yet, these trees rarely fall over. They can cope with strong winds, storms, earthquakes, fires, and prolonged flooding.

Although the root system of the redwood is shallow, it is intertwined with the root systems of other redwood trees. These trees grow very close together and literally hold each other up. Only redwoods have the strength and ability to support other redwoods. Redwoods are dependent on each other for support and for nutrients. So, beneath the surface of these enormous trees are roots that are intertwined, interlocked and supportive of each other. The trees literally need each other.

If you know the film Avatar, then you will appreciate that this image of interconnectedness is a key element of the storyline. In the story, there is a Tree of Souls and also an important Home tree and the destruction of these two vital structures would damage the biological neural network native and essential to Pandora.

I believe that there is a wonderful principle to be found here. In a church fellowship we are linked in, dependent, inter-connected and supportive of each other. We encourage others, we celebrate with others, and we come alongside others in rough and hard times. Some have been rooted here for a long time and others are relatively young saplings. We welcome new people into the circle. I need my brothers and sisters in Christ to help me in my faith and growth. I cannot do this alone. You cannot do this alone. We need each other to be stronger together. We are to be rooted in love. It is so important that at this difficult time in the life of our church that we stay connected and intertwined.

They shall be like a tree planted by water, sending out its roots by the stream. It shall not fear when heat comes, and its leaves shall stay green; in the year of drought, it is not anxious, and it does not cease to bear fruit. Jeremiah 17 v 8

As you therefore have received Christ Jesus the Lord, continue to live your lives in Him, rooted and built up in Him and established in the faith, just as you were taught, abounding in thanksgiving.   Colossians 2 v 7

"From Him the whole body, joined and held together by every supporting ligament, grows, and builds itself up in love, as each part does its work. Ephesians 4 v 16

Paul's prayer: For this reason, I bow my knees before the Father, from whom every family in heaven and on earth takes its name. I pray that, according to the riches of his glory, He may grant that you may be strengthened in your inner being with power through His Spirit, and that Christ may dwell in your hearts through faith, as you are being rooted and grounded in love. I pray that you may have the power to comprehend, with all the saints, what is the breadth and length and height and depth, and to know the love of Christ that surpasses knowledge, so that you may be filled with all the fullness of God. *Ephesians 3 v 14-19*

Circling prayers have their origins in Celtic Christian spirituality. They are simple prayers which speak of God's protective 'circling' presence. They can help us invite God's encompassing presence into the circumstances we face and the issues we care about.

Circle us, Lord: keep love within and anger without.
Circle us, Lord: keep pardon within and injury without.
Circle us, Lord: keep faith within and doubt without.
Circle us, Lord: keep hope within and despair without.
Circle us, Lord: keep light within and dark without.
Circle us, Lord: keep joy within and sadness without.
Circle us, Lord: keep peace within and fear without.
Circle us, Sacred Three, now and forever. Amen.

Those who trust in the Lord are like Mount Zion, which can never be shaken, never be moved. As the mountains surround Jerusalem, so the Lord surrounds his people, now and forever. Psalm 125:1-2

Letting go: Lessons from a tree

In the winter period, deciduous trees and shrubs shed their leaves as a way of conserving water and ensuring future growth. By losing leaves in the cold days of winter, trees and plants significantly reduce water loss and by doing this are also protected against wind damage and frost. The leaf litter that forms on the floor of the forest provides the growth medium for the many new and varied plants of the future and so the cycle goes on. I am sure that this is all part of Gods wonderful plan.

We have just moved house from a very large house to a significantly smaller house, and this has involved a great deal of reduction, shedding items and possessions, and letting go of many things that we have held over many years. After a fifty-year marriage and four children, along with treasured artefacts, the family archive, and a vast array of belongings from parents, family members and children, we have had to make some deliberate and sometimes difficult decisions about what to keep and what to let go. Many things have had to go.

Sometimes God in His pruning process may direct or cause things to change or lead us into a period where reduction is necessary to ensure future fruitfulness and growth. Sometimes getting rid of the excess, the things that we have held on to and perhaps which, on reflection, might be considered unnecessary, is a challenging but can be a very helpful process. Reduction and displacement, shedding and disturbance can often herald in a new season and new growth. God in His love, compassion and wisdom assures us that He has unlimited resources and that whatever change comes, He will be with us.

So then, just as you received Christ Jesus as Lord, continue to live your lives in him, rooted and built up in him, strengthened in the faith as you were taught, and overflowing with thankfulness.   Colossians 2 v 6-7

For this reason, I kneel before the Father, from whom every family in heaven and on earth derives its name. I pray that out of his glorious riches he may strengthen you with power through his Spirit in your inner being, so that Christ may dwell in your hearts through faith. And I pray that you, being rooted and established in love, may have power, together with all the Lord's holy people, to grasp how wide and long and high and deep is the love of Christ, and to know this love that surpasses knowledge—that you may be filled to the measure of all the fullness of God. Now to him who is able to do immeasurably more than all we ask or imagine, according to his power that is at work within us, to him be glory in the church and in Christ Jesus throughout all generations, for ever and ever! Amen. Paul's prayer for the Ephesian church   Ephesians 3 v 14-17

Pray

Lord, change of any kind is challenging. Sometimes it is hard to let go of the things that we hang on to. Sometimes we find it hard to let go of thoughts, griefs, pain, and guilt. You hold my hand, and you never let go. Your hand will always hold mine tight. If I hold your hand, my hand might slip, or I may choose to let go but even then, you will hold on tight. Thank you for your faithful love.

Knitted together into a garment of praise

I am not a great knitter. I once knitted a beautiful sweater for my husband, Phil, with elaborate cabling down the front and when I had finished it, it looked admirable. But when Phil tried it on, it was clear that I had not followed the instructions as accurately as I should have. The sleeves were far too long, and the body of the sweater was perhaps a little short and a fraction tight. I am an impatient, erratic knitter who fails to follow the pattern exactly and who adds a few extra lines of knitting here and a few extra stiches on the needle there. I have no patience to read what the tension should be and to knit a sample swatch to see if I have got the tension correct. You experienced knitters will tell me that the tension is crucial and controls the right amount of 'stretch'. The tension makes sure that you do not knit loosely (which would result in the work becoming too big) or too tight (which would result in your work becoming too small). So, it is important before starting any knitting project, we are told, that you check the tension at the beginning of the pattern. But I tend to ignore this!

If you look at a piece of knitting you will see that the individual stitches are knitted together perfectly. You can add stitches and decrease your stitches almost imperceptibly to create the given shape that you need. But the stitches are held together and together they make the garment stretch, move, and 'give'. The tension and stretching will provide the ability to get the garment over your head! There are simple stitches-knit, purl, but there are also fancy stitches, stocking stitch, cable stitches, moss stitch etc.

When knitting, you carefully follow the patterns instructions, your stitches need to be connected perfectly and you need the correct tension. Your completed, new wool garment will be amazing, provide warmth, comfort and with care will last for a very long time.

This could almost be an analogy for the church. Our Heavenly Father sets the pattern, the Bible provides instructions for us to follow, and we are the stitches held together in perfect tension by the work of the Holy Spirit. Every stitch is needed, to be knit together by strong ties of love, to produce something of value, usefulness, warmth, and beauty that is to be admired. The growth and expansion are given by God, who wants us to have and to be a garment of praise. One day in Heaven, we will be clothed quite differently and given new garments to wear.

I want you to know how much I have agonized for you and for the church at Laodicea, and for many other believers who have never met me personally. I want them to be encouraged and knit together by strong ties of love. I want them to have complete confidence that they understand God's mysterious plan, which is Christ himself. In him lie hidden all the treasures of wisdom and knowledge. Colossians 2 v 1-3 holding fast to the Head, from Whom the entire body, supplied and knit together by means of its joints and ligaments, grows with a growth that is from God. Colossians 2 v 19

He has sent me to bind up the broken-hearted, to proclaim freedom for the captives and release from darkness for the prisoners, to proclaim the year of the Lord's favour and the day of vengeance of our God, to comfort all who mourn, and provide for those who grieve in Zion – to bestow on them a crown of beauty instead of ashes, the oil of joy instead of mourning, and a garment of praise instead of a spirit of despair. Isaiah 61 v 2-3

I will rejoice greatly in the LORD, My soul will exult in my God; For He has clothed me with garments of salvation, He has covered me with a robe of righteousness, Isaiah 61v3 and v 10 A.V

"Are you tired? Worn out? Burned out on religion? Come to me. Get away with me and you'll recover your life. I'll show you how to take a real rest. Walk with me and work with me—watch how I do it. Learn the unforced rhythms of grace. I won't lay anything heavy or ill-fitting on you. Keep company with me and you'll learn to live freely and lightly." Matthew 11v 28-30 MSG

Pray

We are your church. We have not followed the example of Jesus to love one another as you have loved. We confess our strife, division, tensions, pain, conflict, hurt feelings, unhelpful words, and opinions. We want to come back to Jesus and to allow Him to guide us forward in love, wisdom, and grace. May we listen for your words and silence our own. Bind us together in love with cords that cannot be broken that we may be one family.

Those of you of a certain age may remember this old chorus by John Keys:

Bind us together, Lord, Bind us together
With cords that cannot be broken
Bind us together, Lord, Bind us together
Bind us together in love.
There is only one God, There is only one King
There is only one body, That is why we sing.

Made for the glory of God, Purchased by His precious Son;
Born with the right to be clean, For Jesus the victory has won.

Dislocation

A couple of weeks ago my husband fell and dislocated his shoulder. He concluded that he had not broken his arm, but it was clear that there was a major dislocation. It was extremely painful and needed a hospital visit and two medics who had several attempts to relocate the arm and shoulder. A sling was put in place to support the arm and he was returned home. Surgery was required to repair the torn and damaged muscles and this was followed by physiotherapy and exercises. The shoulder joint may never be restored to full function after such a major trauma and so chances are that there will be little niggles of discomfort and small frustrations at the inability to accomplish certain movements that were once done with ease- like right arm bowling at cricket! But recovery is now a real hope.

Any dislocation is damaging, causes dysfunction and distress, and prolonged dislocation may cause a measure of disappointment. Dislocation is frustrating, annoying and places an additional burden on the other who accepts additional responsibilities that were once equally shared.

In life we can experience different kinds of dislocation, disconnections, and disappointments. We may be temporarily dislocated from our building, office, or home. We may be disconnected from our family and unable to meet face to face. Our normal everyday lives may be disrupted. There are many people who are displaced from their homeland and are seeking refuge and asylum. There are those who are separated from family in Care Homes and are unable to meet easily with them.

There are many accounts in the Bible of those who were displaced. Ruth left her Moab homeland, culture, and family connections behind to go to a land and culture that she would not know. It would lead to an uncertain future. But God had her future in hand.

So Naomi said, 'See, your sister-in-law has gone back to her people and to her gods; return after your sister-in-law.' But Ruth said, 'Do not press me to leave you or to turn back from following you! Where you go, I will go; where you lodge, I will lodge; your people shall be my people and your God my God. Where you die, I will die there will I be buried. May the Lord do thus and so to me, and more as well, if even death parts me from you!' When Naomi saw that she was determined to go with her, she said no more to her.

God had an amazing plan for Ruth.

There were 70 years of Exile in Babylon for the people of Judah. Those displaced were instructed to settle and adjust to a new life until the Lord would bring them back to a new and bright future. God gives this amazing and familiar promise in the book of Jeremiah.

For surely, I know the plans I have for you, says the LORD, plans for your welfare and not for harm, to give you a future with hope. Then when you call upon me and come and pray to me, I will hear you. When you search for me, you will find me; if you seek me with all your heart, I will let you find me, says the Lord, and I will restore your fortunes and gather you from all the nations and all the places where I have driven you, says the Lord, and I will bring you back to the place from which I sent you into exile. Jeremiah 29

An Ancient Prayer

Alone with none but thee, my God, I journey on my way.
What need I fear, when thou art near O king of night and day?
More safe am I within thy hand Than if a host did round me stand.
Columba, c.521 - 597

Come and stay

A while ago we holidayed in this log cabin near to the East coast of Yorkshire. My husband described it as a 'human hen hut'. It had everything that you needed -a bathroom, small kitchen, a double bed, and a double bed settee, table and four chairs inside, electricity, water and even a T.V. set. It was perfectly formed but very compact. It was small enough for a family for a short period of time. It is only meant to be a temporary dwelling or 'luxury glamping 'as they called it. It can only be a temporary arrangement. You stay for a while and then leave. We loved it but it was lovely to come home to a bigger space and home comforts. We could return to the familiar, the safe and our permanent home here on earth. It has made me consider those words in John where Jesus invites us to come and dwell with Him- to abide.

"As the father has loved me, so have I loved you. Now remain in my love."
John 15 v 9

Jesus invites us to come and stay, not just for a brief time but for good. He invites us to come and remain, to dwell with Him permanently, to reside with Him. ("make your home in my love" Peterson version). Jesus wants us to settle into this place of stability and peace. It is the place where I can kick off my shoes and put my slippers on. It is where I am restored, known, and loved. It is the place where I am connected and in relationship- a place of love and acceptance.

So, when things seem crazy, and when there are so many changes and unknowns, it is more important than ever to come home and to rest in Him – to settle and to stay. To find times to just 'be' with Him. In times of physical separation from family and friends it is even more important to come to this safe dwelling place where there is room for all who come.

He who dwells in the shelter of the Most High, who abides in the shadow of the Almighty will say to the Lord, "My refuge and my fortress; my God, in whom I trust." Because you have made the Lord your refuge, the Most High your habitation, no evil shall befall you, no scourge come near your tent.

Psalm 91 v 2 RSV

"Thou hast made us for thyself o Lord and our hearts are restless until they find their rest in Thee." Augustine

A new wardrobe

We are in the season of the January sales- the sales that started in December! Folk are shopping online or venturing into the shops to grab the best bargains. When our teenage grandson became fourteen years of age, we felt that it would be a good time for him to choose his own clothes rather than have clothes chosen for him. So, we ventured into the stores, and our grandson, with his Christmas gift money in hand, was invited to wander around the store, try things on and choose the style of things that he wanted to wear. We left him to it! He chose three sports wear garments that he was pleased with- nothing dramatic- and left the store hot and exhausted. He had been trusted to buy his own things.

This first independent shopping outing reminded me of those words in Colossians about putting on, clothing ourselves, with the character of Jesus- love, kindness, humility, gentleness, forgiveness, and patience. These are the values that we are to have and to put on each day. Jesus has given us a whole new wardrobe that has been picked out and custom made for us- perfectly fitting, attractive and pleasing to others. We have been given the designer label, to be the trendsetters, the fashion leaders of the day. Love is to be the basic, all-purpose garment that we should never be without. We should never leave the house without getting dressed in this essential garment.

Don't lie to one another. You're done with that old life. It's like a filthy set of ill-fitting clothes you've stripped off and put in the fire. Now you're dressed in a new wardrobe. Every item of your new way of life is custom-made by the Creator, with his label on it. All the old fashions are now obsolete. Colossians 3 v 9-11 MSG

So, chosen by God for this new life of love, dress in the wardrobe God picked out for you: compassion, kindness, humility, quiet strength, discipline. Be even-tempered, content with second place, quick to forgive an offense. Forgive as quickly and completely as the Master forgave you. And regardless of what else you put on, wear love. It's your basic, all-purpose garment. Never be without it. Beyond all these things put on and wrap yourselves in unselfish love, which is the perfect bond of unity [for everything is bound together in agreement when each one seeks the best for others]. Colossians 3 v 14 AMP

put on the clean fresh clothes of the new life which was made by God's design for righteousness and the holiness which is no illusion. Ephesians 4 v 24 JBP

I am overwhelmed with joy in the Lord my God For he has dressed me with the clothing of salvation and draped me in a robe of righteousness. Isaiah 61 v 10 NIV

Pray

Jesus, there's a lot of stuff that I need to get rid of and things that I've kept for far too long. I need a de-clutter and to look for the things that you want me to wear. Help me to start the change and to put on your garments of grace and love. Your love is perfect, never fails, and nothing can separate me from your love. Help me to love you and to choose to love others. Thank you that your love bears all things, believes all things, hopes all things, endures all things, and that your love never fails.

A new pathway

Your road led through the sea, your pathway through the mighty waters- a pathway no-one knew was there! You led your people along that road like a flock of sheep with Moses and Aaron as their shepherds. Psalm 77 v 19-20

I will lead blind Israel down a new path, guiding them along an unfamiliar way. I will brighten the darkness before them and smooth out the road ahead of them. Yes, I will indeed do these things; I will not forsake them. Isaiah 42 v 16

Some years ago, I was recommended a book by Dr. Spencer Johnson called Who moved my Cheese? The story, of Who moved my Cheese? is a simple parable that reveals profound truths. It is an amusing story about four characters, four mice, Sniff, Scurry, Haw and Hem, who live in a maze and who every day look in the maze for cheese to nourish them and make them happy. Cheese is the metaphor for what we want to have in life, whether it is a good job, a loving relationship, money, a possession, purpose, health or spiritual peace of mind and the maze is where we look for what we desire. The maze is-perhaps the organisation that we might work in, the family, the community or church.

The four imaginary characters, the four mice, go to the maze every day and go to the cheese station looking for cheese which always seems to be there. But one day, the supply of cheese has gone, never to return. Hem, one of the mice is immobile, frozen, and determinedly sticks to the old paths. Hem is afraid to leave the comfort zone and continually goes back to the same place trying to look for cheese. However, two of the mice, Sniff and Scurry, determinedly go off to find new cheese. One mouse, Haw, knows that he must go off in search of new cheese, in new places in the maze, places that he has never been before. He knows that there is always new cheese out there to be found and sure enough he does find the source of new cheese.

This book has four key themes or lessons: anticipate change, adapt to change quickly, enjoy change and do not be afraid of it, be ready to change quickly, again and again.

The book asks us to look at how to deal with change and maybe how to deal with loss, failure, or disappointment. It also points out that change can sometimes lead to something better. How we deal with change is a key secret and help us to keep moving forward.

Make me to know your ways, O Lord teach me your paths. Lead me in your truth and teach me for you are the God of my salvation; for you I wait all day long. Psalm 25 v 4,5

You chart the path ahead of me and tell me where to stop and rest. Every moment you know where I am. You both precede and follow me. Psalm 139 v 3,5.

Resilience and the rubber band

There are two words that have often come to my mind when I think about the difficult period of the Covid-19 Pandemic of 2020-2021 and its effects on our lives- stress and resilience. Many have experienced and felt the consequences of prolonged stress, uncertainty and tension caused by Covid, its consequences and restrictions on our lives and perhaps our resilience has been severely stretched. We have lost our stretch. We are like a rubber band that has been continually stretched. A rubber band can be stretched and stretched to its maximum length and then return to its precise original form. But after prolonged use it may weaken or break until it snaps. You may attempt to fasten the two ends of the rubber band together again, but this is never ultimately successful, and the band will often break at another point. Sometimes the rubber band will become brittle and hard with overuse and age and begin to lose its stretch. For us, perhaps resilience is one key factor in how well we can live successfully during times of pressure, confusion, uncertainty, and emotional strain. Can we return quickly to our original shape without weakening after being twisted and over stretched? We may know those who have felt over stretched, and who have attempted to tie the ends back together until they feel as if they are tied in knots physically and emotionally, inside, and out.

School children and students found that the days and weeks of home learning and study that their store of resilience was very much stretched. Working parents and families were also put under additional strain. I am aware, as an experienced teacher, that one of the key factors for the success of young people is their store of resilience. Those students who have a generous store of resilience cope better with the challenges that they face academically.

So how are we doing in terms of resilience, stickability and patience?

The Book of James opens with these words.

Consider it pure joy, my brothers, and sisters, whenever you face trials of many kinds, because you know that the testing of your faith produces perseverance. Let perseverance finish its work so that you may be mature and complete, not lacking anything. James 1 v 2-4

I am to be joyful, as these times of stretching are intended to produce endurance, steadfastness, maturity, a reworking of my faith and inner peace. But I do not always consider these tough times "as nothing but joy!" I do not want to be stretched and re-worked. I would much prefer a comfortable, peaceful, and easy life.

Thankfully, there is a wonderful counterbalance to these words from James. One section of Psalm 23 encourages me.

"He makes me lie down in green pastures. He leads me beside quiet waters. He refreshes my soul."

When our soul is tired our Father, God knows we are overstretched and weary. He knows when we need to change pace and go to the fresh green meadows for refreshment, quietness, and rest. He knows when we need to lay down and rest so that once again, we can spring back and spring into action. We need to seek His pace for our life so that we do not become overstretched, brittle and snap.

Fear not [there is nothing to fear], for I am with you; do not look around you in terror and be dismayed, for I am your God. I will strengthen and harden you to difficulties, yes, I will help you; yes, I will hold you up and retain you with My [victorious] right hand of rightness and justice. Isaiah 41 v 10 AMP

Pray

Dear Father God, my mind, body, and spirit feel tired and worn down. I ask for the strength that I need to not give up. Things in my life may feel impossible but your word says that all things are possible with you. By your grace, may I find rest in your shadow and shelter from any storms that I am facing. Give me wisdom so that I can take the next step forward. You are my ever-present help. May I find your rhythm of rest. Amen.

In heavenly love abiding, No change my heart shall fear;
And safe is such confiding, For nothing changes here.
The storm may roar without me, My heart may low be laid
But God is round about me, And can I be dismayed?

Wherever He may guide me, No want shall turn me back;
My Shepherd is beside me, And nothing can I lack.
His wisdom ever waketh, His sight is never dim;
He knows the way He taketh, And I will walk with Him.

Green pastures are before me, Which yet I have not seen;
Bright skies will soon be o'er me, Where darkest clouds have been.
My hope I cannot measure, My path to life is free;
My Saviour has my treasure, And He will walk with me.

Anna Letitia Waring (1850)

Right-handed

I am the Lord your God who takes hold of your right hand. Isaiah 41:13

I am predominantly right-handed. In fact, there is little that I can easily do with my left hand. About the only thing that I accomplish, where my left hand needs to have some strength in it and be useful, is to untwist the lid from a jar of jam- both hands are needed in this instance. As I get older, I am beginning to be troubled with some arthritis in the fingers of my right hand and this has affected the strength of this hand- especially when I need to lift a heavy pan of boiled potatoes from the cooker!

I remember when I was a young Probationary Teacher a supervisor repeatedly telling me to move my hands away from the task that a child was attempting. The child had to do it on their own, even if the task was unsuccessful, the product or the piece of clay work incomplete or not aesthetic to my eyes- they must do it on their own. It had to be their work. I was often too quick to jump in and to remedy the piece of art, rescue the clay model, repair the wobbly box structure or redesign the Lego house. I knew how it should look, stand, match the brief given, and successfully complete the task in hand. I still grapple with the inclination to dive in and do it.

When I read the above words it suddenly and powerfully hit me that this was why God needed to hold my hand. I am a meddler! I can't help myself from attempting to take over to take control, interfering and thinking that I know what to do and know how it should turn out. God was holding my right hand so that I couldn't meddle! Yes, it is His powerful right hand, His victorious right hand, that protects, keeps me safe and guides me, but it is also the hand that keeps me from doing something crazy. He keeps a firm grip of my hand, to help, and to guide, so that I will not be moved, but also, so that I am not tempted to meddle.

"For I the Lord your God keep hold of your right hand; [I am the Lord, Who says to you, 'Do not fear, I will help you.' AMP

Because I, your God, have a firm grip on you and I'm not letting go. I'm telling you, 'Don't panic. I'm right here to help you.' MSG

I am holding you by your right hand—I, the Lord your God—and I say to you, Don't be afraid; I am here to help you. TLB

You love me! You are holding my right hand! You will keep on guiding me all my life with your wisdom and counsel, and afterwards receive me into the glories of heaven. Psalm 73 v 23

I have set the Lord always before me: because he is at my right hand, I shall not be moved. Psalm 16 v 8

"You are my servant, I have chosen you and not cast you off"; do not fear, for I am with you, do not be afraid, for I am your God;

I will strengthen you, I will help you, I will uphold you with my victorious right hand. Isaiah 41 v 10

Pray

Your Hand is powerful to save, to guide, to strengthen and to protect. May we learn that it is Your work and not ours. May we learn that we do not have the answers. In any task, role, or mission, will You lead and direct us. May we resist the attempts to meddle and learn to follow and not to lead.

Support and Growth

Every year, my grandson and I plant sunflower seeds. Our friends, family, and colleagues around the country and far off places in the world, New Zealand, Australia, also plant sunflower seeds and then send us images. This year we planted 15 giraffe sunflower seeds that would grow to perhaps 2 to 3 metres tall. It always amazes me that from a small seed we can end up with a plant that is 3 metres tall! We never know how many of the seeds will germinate and thrive and observing our plants this year, we can see that some have already grown tall and strong, and some are not growing as well. We need to water them regularly, feed them generous amounts of Growmore and fertilizer, transplant them into larger pots with good compost so that their roots can spread and develop and as they are growing we need to secure them to garden canes and supports on a sunny wall. Our neighbours walk past our garden and smile at the dinner plate sized sunflower heads nodding at them over the wall. By the time they reach one metre tall, they need to have support which we do with string and garden canes. They are secured safely to the canes and the wall to protect them against the wind.

Our sunflower plants are a useful picture of our growth as Christians. There are many things that are helpful or essential to me as I grow. There are also things that might limit my growth. I need warmth as I get going- this is a new beginning. I need water and nourishment. I need sunshine, light and the right temperature. I need time and the right environment- this process cannot be hurried or fast tracked. I need a space to expand, stretch and grow if I am to reach my full potential. I occasionally need protection in the days of wind and storm. I need air above and below ground - below ground is just as important so that my roots can grow and spread- or they may fail. I need to be secure and tied into those things that will hold me up and help me to be strong. If any of these things go wrong then this can be a 'limiting factor' and my growth can be stunted, I may not reach my potential or I may give up altogether. This would be sad as I would never produce flower or fruit – and with it that potential to start new seed and life.

And so, I need a nurturing fellowship, Bible teaching, the Holy Spirit and prayer to breathe through my being, a space to develop my strengths and work out my gifts, skills, and potentials. A place to be rooted and the support of others who will help me to be strong. I need those who are strong when I am in that vulnerable place so that I can be held up. I need to be given time to develop and grow- growth cannot be hurried! I need fellowship and fun, companionship and challenge, networks, and inspiration. I need role models and prayer supporters. With His help I will grow tall.

Let your roots grow down into him and draw up nourishment from him. See that you go on growing in the Lord and become strong and vigorous in the truth you were taught. Let your lives overflow with joy and thanksgiving for all he has done. Colossians 2 v7

And I pray that Christ will be more and more at home in your hearts, living within you as you trust in him. May your roots go down deep into the soil of God's marvellous love. Ephesians 3v 17

The UK Blessing-Turn to the Son

I love to see our giant sunflowers growing tall and to watch the huge flower heads regularly turn to face the sun. The Italian word for sunflower is 'girasole' which literally means' turn to the sun.' I was pleased to be reminded of the words 'The Lord make His face to shine upon you' in the UK Blessing. The UK Blessing is the video of singers from 65 UK churches who have joined together to sing the words based on Numbers 6:24-27- the Aaronic or Priestly Blessing. This video has received many millions of views on YouTube. The song begins with these words:

The Lord bless you and keep you, make his face shine upon you and be gracious to you, the Lord turn his face toward you, and give you peace.
I just love the idea of God turning His face to shine upon me. I am told that the Hebrew word *panim* (face) can also mean "countenance" or "presence." It perhaps could be translated as, "may God smile at you." It communicates God's great love and affection for us and His pleasure as He looks at us and hears our prayers - and as we turn towards Him. The idea behind these words is of God giving his full and complete attention to us and listening deeply to our concerns and prayers. Think of how a person's face "lights up" when they see a loved one. When we see our smallest grandchildren after a long absence, our faces light up as we rush to greet them. May we turn our face to the Son.

May His favour be upon you and a thousand generations
And your family and your children and their children, and their children
May His favour be upon you and a thousand generations
And your family and your children and their children, and their children
May His presence go before you and behind you, and beside you
All around you, and within you He is with you, He is with you.
In the morning, in the evening in your coming, and your going
In your weeping, and rejoicing He is for you, He is for you
He is for you, He is for you He is for you, He is for you
He is for you, He is for you.

"The Blessing" by Cody Carnes, Kari Jobe and Elevation Worship.
Written by Chris Brown, Cody Carnes, Kari Jobe and Steven Furtick

The Baobab Tree- the upside-down tree

Some years ago, I had the opportunity to spend three months in Angola with a Charity Organisation supporting pre-school education projects. It was a very valuable and challenging experience at times as travelling on the Angolan roads was far from an enjoyable experience. But one thing that I loved on those two hour plus long journeys around Luanda every day, was appreciating the red earth of the landscape and spotting the Baobab tress.

The Baobab trees are crazy, weird, amazing and look like upside down trees. Sometimes they can be so huge that men are able to make a home within the trunk of the tree. When the tree is bare of leaves, the spreading branches of the Baobab tree look like roots sticking up into the air, rather as if it had been planted upside down. The African bushmen have a legend that tells of the god Thora who took a dislike to the Baobab growing in his garden, so he threw it out over the wall of paradise on to Earth below. Although the tree landed upside down it continued to grow. This tree is certainly very different to any other. The trunk is smooth, shiny and a pinkish grey colour. The tree has large white flowers which open at night and the fruit, which looks like rats hanging upside down by their tails, can be used to make a range of different health drinks. The craziness goes on!

I have just started studying a series on 'being rooted' in Christ, or 'rootfulness' as the speaker likes to call it, alongside ideas of fruitfulness. In times of stress, trouble, and confusion it can sometimes feel that our lives are topsy turvy, thrown upside down, as if we are no longer rooted, our roots are exposed and in danger of shrivelling. We are in a dry, parched place and struggling for refreshment and nourishment. It is during these times that we need to go back to the love of God and to fix ourselves in Him.

May your roots go down deep into the soil of God's marvellous love. Ephesians 3 v 17

Let your roots go down into Him and draw up nourishment from Him, so you will grow in faith, strong and vigorous in the truth you were taught. Let your lives overflow with thanksgiving for all He has done. Colossians 2 v7

We need to remind ourselves of who we are in Christ- to fix ourselves in His truth and His love. If we 'put down roots' somewhere then we make ourselves feel at home – it is where we belong, where we are settled and comfortable. It is also our strong base from which to reach out and to bear fruit. May we dig down deep into His love for ourselves and as we support others who are feeling vulnerable, may we bring His love to them.

"The righteous will flourish like the palm trees- but palm trees do not grow in the beautiful, lush forest but in the desert."

"God does His best work in the most difficult of circumstances". Tim Hansel 'You gotta keep dancing'

The Film, The Secret Garden, and the Memory Jar

The story of The Secret Garden, by Frances Burnett, described as a 'pastoral story of 'self-healing', is a children's classic and has now just been turned into a new film version. In this story, the main character, Mary Lennox, 10 years old, is sent back to the UK from India after the death of her parents to cholera. She is cared for by her maternal uncle at Misselthwaite Manor, Yorkshire, and his young son, Colin. Mary uncovers the secret garden that belonged to the late wife of her uncle, her mother's sister. Mary had always believed that her mother had no time for her and did not love her, until she discovered some hidden letters written by her mother to the sister and found photographs of the two sisters in the secret garden. The letters transform Mary's understanding of her mother and make it clear to her that her mother loved her very much.

Watching the film made me consider my grandson and his knowledge of his mum and dad. Richard, the father of our grandson, died aged 40 when Sam had just reached his 5th birthday and had started in Reception at school. Consequently, his memories of his dad can be sometimes sketchy. At Richard's funeral friends and contacts from around the world were asked to contribute to a 'Jar of Memories' for Charlotte and Sam. Inside the jar there are over150 personal letters, often with photographs, which portray a very clear picture of the kind of man that Richard was. Recently, at every mealtime, Sam has been selecting out three or so letters that we read out together. This has helped Sam to learn more of the character, strengths, passions, travels, Christian faith, loves, careers and sheer devotion of his dad to Charlotte, his mum, and to himself and to Jesus His

Lord. It has enabled Sam to see his dad more clearly. Many of the stories and memories are very funny and very personal. We have laughed and sometimes been very teary as we have read the memories. When Charlotte died only a year after Richard, aged 36, we asked for friends and contacts to do the same for Sam, so that he had a jar of memories of his mum, and we kept the cards that were given to us at that time. So, we have plenty of wonderful memories that will keep us going for quite some time.

This made me think again about that phrase "an observable love". Richard's passions were obvious and clear for all to see- his family, walking, mountain biking, camping in Scotland, the Lake District and Wales, photography, and his Christian family. People spoke of his enthusiastic faith and witness and his sharing of that faith naturally and openly to anyone he contacted. He spoke about Jesus to all who would listen. He gossiped the gospel.

The beautiful phrase, 'an observable love', comes from a book The Mark of a Christian by Francis Schaeffer who wrote many other books such as Escape from Reason. This is how we are to be known and this is how Jesus is to be known.

"A new commandment I give to you, that you love one another; even as I have loved you, that you also love one another. By this all men will know that you are my disciples, if you have love for one another." John 13.v 34

The Shepherds Oil

I am approaching a significant birthday and I am being aware that my body is beginning to tell me that some parts need extra care! Like my skin. I have never had to worry about lotions and creams apart from sun protection, but I have now taken the plunge and purchased skin care lotions and serums. This made me think about those beautiful verses from Psalm 23, the Shepherd Psalm," you anoint my head with oil" v 5. In Bible times, as today, oil was much in use as a lotion for skin and hair, for healing with its medicinal properties, for oil lamps and light, for consecration and anointing and for food.

David, as a shepherd, would know so well about caring for his sheep. The shepherd would always carry oil with him and would use it generously on his sheep for very specific purposes. By spreading the oil on to the sheep's head it would protect the sheep from the insects and bugs that would annoy them. The oil was a protective covering. The shepherd would apply the oil to cuts, grazes scratches and even wounds. Even the greenest of pastures sometimes had dangers- thorns, thistles, rocks, predators and so the oil would be used as a healing ointment- it had a medicinal use. Sometimes the sheep would clash with each other and fight for position and so the shepherd knew that the **oil** or grease on the head would protect the heads of his squabbling sheep- their heads would slide off each other and both would be protected. The shepherd was careful to check on his sheep every day looking for cuts and bites and the healing oil would be applied.

Jesus is our good shepherd, and we can come to Him each day. He will pour the oil of the gentle, healing Holy Spirit on to our heads. All the daily irritations, hurts, conflicts, harmful and negative thoughts, anger, and disagreements can be eased by the fragrant oil. Some wounds may need a generous application of oil, both morning and evening. I need the Shepherd's oil every day. Each day I need to come to Him so that He can check for those scratches and hurts and apply the oil. Each day I need to have the protective coating of the oil to guard my thoughts and words.

The Lord is my shepherd; I shall not want.
He maketh me to lie down in green pastures:
he leadeth me beside the still waters.
He restoreth my soul:
he leadeth me in the paths of righteousness for his name's sake.
Yea, though I walk through the valley of the shadow of death,
I will fear no evil: for thou art with me;
Thy rod and thy staff they comfort me.
Thou preparest a table before me in the presence of mine enemies:
thou anointest my head with oil; my cup runneth over.
Surely goodness and mercy shall follow me all the days of my life:
and I will dwell in the house of the Lord for ever.

Psalm 23 A Psalm of David. KJV

The Spirit of the Lord GOD is upon me; because the LORD hath anointed me to preach good tidings unto the meek; he hath sent me to bind up the broken hearted, to proclaim liberty to the captives, and the opening of the prison to them that are bound; to proclaim the acceptable year of the LORD, and the day of vengeance of our God; to comfort all that mourn; to appoint unto them that mourn in Zion, to give unto them beauty for ashes, the oil of joy for mourning, the garment of praise for the spirit of heaviness; that they might be called trees of righteousness, the planting of the LORD, that he might be glorified. Isaiah 61

He went to him and bandaged his wounds, having poured oil and wine on them. Then he put him on his own animal, brought him to an inn, and took care of him. Luke 10 v 34

You did not anoint my head with oil, but she has anointed my feet with ointment. Luke 7 v46

Weariness

As I have been speaking with people this week I have listened to a new note of weariness in their voices. There are many people who may have good reason to be weary and disheartened. There are those people who are isolated, lonely, or struggling to make ends meet. There are those suffering financial stress and hardship, coping with family pressures or family breakdown, or with mental ill health. There are carers, family carers, and young carers, looking after vulnerable members of the family, who may feel isolated from sources of support and so feel jaded and weary because of their circumstances. There are many synonyms for the word weary-listless, sluggish, inertia, spent, diminished, eroded, lethargic and jaded. We may all have periods of time when we have felt jaded and weary, and any energy or spark of creativity has left us.

We turn to the Bible for words of encouragement, and we are given fresh hope and reassurance.

And let us not grow weary in well-doing, for in due season we shall reap if we do not lose heart. So then, as we have opportunity, let us do good to all men, and especially to those who are of the household of faith. Galatians 6 v 9-10

Have you not known? Have you not heard? The Lord is the everlasting God, the Creator of the ends of the earth. He does not faint or grow weary, his understanding is unsearchable. He gives power to the faint, and to him who has no might he increases strength. Even youths shall faint and be weary, and young men shall fall exhausted; but they who wait for the Lord shall renew their strength, they shall mount up with wings like eagles, they shall run and not be weary, they shall walk and not faint. *Isaiah 40*

Pray

Teach us good Lord, to serve Thee as Thou deserves: To give and not to count the cost; To fight and not to heed the wounds; To toil and not to seek for rest; To labour and not to ask for any reward, save that of knowing that we do Thy will. Ignatius of Loyola

Thoughts from the Forest

Show me the right path, O Lord; point out the road for me to follow. Lead me by your truth and teach me, for you are the God who saves me. All day long I put my hope in you. Psalm 25 v 3-4

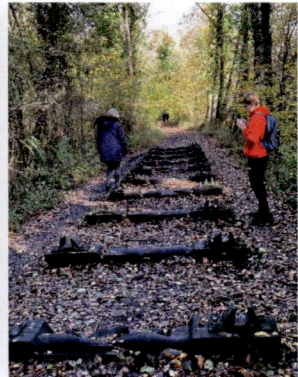

We have just spent a week in the beautiful Forest of Dean, Gloucestershire, walking next to the River Wye and spending time in the oak and beech forests in this special part of the countryside. We visited Symonds Yat (gate) on the River Wye, which is a place for canoeists, paddle boarders and kayakers. From Symonds Yat there is a very steep climb up from the very bottom of the valley to the very top, where you reach Symonds Rock. I did not make or even attempt the climb! The path was incredibly steep and not for me. The Forestry Commission have a sculpture trail through a section of the forest where the paths, although occasionally steep, are well laid out, clearly signposted and manageable. There were other paths where the track was obvious and very direct with no risk of getting lost. There were climbs, where the tree roots, which had become exposed because of natural weather erosion, had turned into ladders and where you could comfortably and securely place your feet upon them as if climbing up a set of steps. I thought again about those important lessons of 'root-fullness'. Along the trail we were able to follow the blue arrows that marked our route.

Sometimes the path may be wide- it is broad, beautiful, and clear. Sometimes the path is so direct that you can clearly see the way ahead and on into the future. At other times, the path may seem to be obscured and almost concealed- but God is the Guide still. Sometimes it is hard for us to detect where the blue arrows of direction are, but we can be sure that Jesus will make the path clear for us.

We long to be able to see our way ahead. Often, we want to be in control of the map and think that we can navigate the route. God longs to guide us and our peace will come when we hand the navigation over to Him. The route may be steep, clear, concealed, rugged, easy, in plain sight- but He knows best. We need to let him be the guide. Do not attempt to follow another's path. It is not for you.

God is our Guide and He has a wonderful path for us to follow. That path is unique to each of us. I cannot walk your path- it might be too hard for me and the climb too steep. You cannot walk my path.

Those of us of a certain age may remember the old chorus that was very popular:

When the road is rough and steep, fix your eyes upon Jesus.
He alone has power to keep, fix your eyes upon Him.
Jesus is the greatest friend, One on whom we can depend.
He is faithful to the end - fix your eyes upon Him.

"How do you make God laugh? Answer. Tell Him the plans you've got for your life."

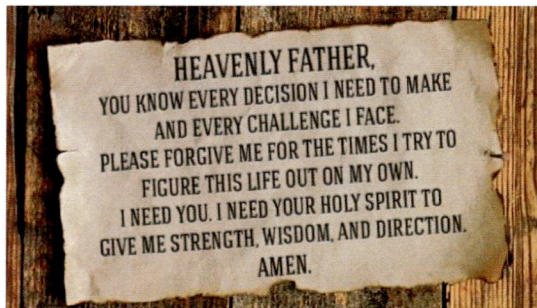

HEAVENLY FATHER,
YOU KNOW EVERY DECISION I NEED TO MAKE
AND EVERY CHALLENGE I FACE.
PLEASE FORGIVE ME FOR THE TIMES I TRY TO
FIGURE THIS LIFE OUT ON MY OWN.
I NEED YOU. I NEED YOUR HOLY SPIRIT TO
GIVE ME STRENGTH, WISDOM, AND DIRECTION.
AMEN.

Be Thou my Vision

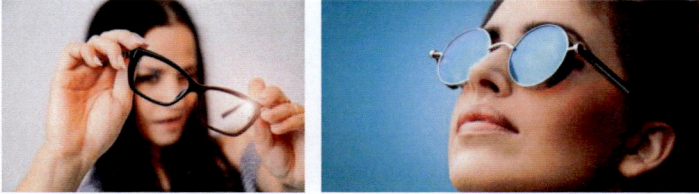

Some years ago, I needed to have surgery to remove the cataracts that had formed in both of my eyes. Having less than perfect vision was a real problem for me as a teacher and a car driver and I knew that the problem had to be addressed. My appreciation of colours was affected, my vision was blurry and inadequate even with glasses, and I had trouble with bright lights especially when driving at night. My cataract surgery involved replacing the cloudy, faulty lenses inside my eyes with perfectly clear artificial ones that would give me perfect vision again.

The difference was dramatic. In fact, it was quite shocking. The first thing that I noticed was how bright the colours were. Everything literally looked like Blackpool illuminations! For the first time in my adult life, I had no worries about taking a sight test! I would of course need reading glasses-it's an age thing! Over time now, my vision has changed again, and I miss those first heady days of wonderful, sharp vision-the clarity, the colours, the focus and of reading the small print effortlessly!

We can often be troubled by blurred or distorted vision when we look at ourselves, when we look at other people and situations and in our Christian walk. Over time we are beginning to see through cloudy lenses. This may affect us almost without fully realising it as with a developing cataract. The change is gradual and sometimes imperceptible.

How do I see myself? How do I want others to see me? How does God see me? I need to remind myself that I belong, that I am His, that I am intentionally designed by God to be who I am and to do what He wants me to do.

How do I see others? Is my view distorted? I need to see that together; we are His children purposely placed together.

How do I see my future? Am I affected by concerns and anxieties that may disturb my peace? Do I know that Jesus is with me at every point? Do I see a glorious future that is prepared for me?

I ask—ask the God of our Master, Jesus Christ, the God of glory—to make you intelligent and discerning in knowing him personally, your eyes focused and clear, so that you can see exactly what it is he is calling you to do, grasp the immensity of this glorious way of life he has for his followers, oh, the utter extravagance of his work in us who trust him— endless energy, boundless strength! Ephesians 1v 17-18 MSG

I pray that your hearts will be flooded with light so that you can see something of the future he has called you to share. 2 Corinthians 4:18

For now, we see through a glass, darkly; but then face to face: now I know in part; but then shall I know even as also I am known. 1 Corinthians 13

Paul boldly acknowledged that "we fix our eyes not on what is seen, but on what is unseen, since what is seen is temporary, but what is unseen is eternal".

Be thou my vision, O Lord of my heart.
Naught be all else to me, save that thou art.
Thou my best thought, by day or by night,
Waking or sleeping, thy presence my light, my light.

We believe that the words of this hymn are based on an old Irish poem, attributed to an Irish saint, Dallan Forgaill, born in530 A.D. who experienced blindness later in life. In 1905 the words were translated into English by Mary Byrne and then seven years later Eleanor Hull put the words into verse for the hymn.

The following was one of my school prayers which we would sing every week. It is from the 1558 Sarum Primer, which was a collection of prayers and worship resources from the 13th century.

God be in my head, and in my understanding;
God be in mine eyes, and in my looking;
God be in my mouth, and in my speaking;
God be in my heart, and in my thinking;
God be at mine end, and at my departing.

An Observable Love

For eleven consecutive years, I spent a part of every summer teaching English as a foreign language to the Chinese Teachers of English in various parts of China with a Chinese Christian organisation called Amity. The Chinese word for Amity means 'love in action'. Teaching in China as a Christian is an interesting and challenging experience. There could be no outward sign of being a Christian. That means no jewellery crosses, no Bible or Christian books in the classroom and very careful teaching surrounding Christian festivals and stories. However, the Chinese teachers knew that we were with Amity and therefore observed us very carefully over the four weeks of the teaching programme. Therefore, how did we share our faith in the classroom when there was always a member of the Communist Party present in the lessons and accompanying us on visits and shopping trips? When I was preparing candidates and volunteers for this challenge my advice was to always 'be authentic'. The teachers will be observing you every day- your manner, speech, your attitude, how you cope with pressure, the quality of your relationships, the quality of your teaching- and so be real, be authentic, be open, be personal and let them into your life. Let them see the person that you are with your vagaries, problems, and faults. Do not hide. In seeing you they will come to see something of the person of Jesus in you. Then they will ask their questions and want to know why you have travelled from the UK to China to support them with their teaching. Then you can explain about the love of Jesus. This is truly love in action- an observable love. I take this beautiful phrase from Francis Schaeffer who wrote many books such as Escape from Reason and The Mark of a Christian. This is how we are to be known and this is how Jesus is to be known.

A new commandment I give to you, that you love one another; even as I have loved you, that you also love one another. By this all men will know that you are my disciples, if you have love for one another." John 13.v 34

"An 'if' is involved. If you obey, you will wear the badge that Christ gave you. If we expect others to know that we are Christians, we must show the mark." Francis Schaeffer

I need this" observable love" and it must be of the same quality as the love of Jesus- "as I have loved you". This is a very tall order and one that I repeatedly and miserably fail at. The standard is so high, and I make so many glaring mistakes. But I aim for this observable love because for others to come to share this faith they need to see it in action.

That they all may be one; as thou, Father, art in me, and I in thee, that they also may be one in us: that the world may believe that thou hast sent me. John 17 v 21

Pray

We pray that by our connections, concern, contacts, and every small act that we do that we will reflect His love.

Lord, bless our journey through this coming week. May the pace be steady, paths made safe, no obstacles impede, and conversations with fellow travellers be fruitful and uplifting. Lord, bless our journey through this coming week.

Are you a thermometer or a thermostat?

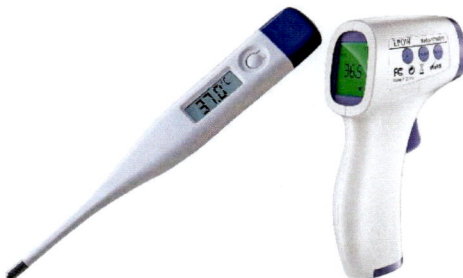

I recently attended a conference and during one session, we were asked the question, "Are you a thermometer or a thermostat? It struck me quite powerfully! A thermostat maintains the correct temperature and warms things up. It regulates the temperature and steps up to set a new temperature. We were challenged to not just reflect the temperature around us but to have the courage to set a new temperature-to create a new climate that reflects God's values. I want to be a thermostat!

It also made me consider that there are those people who seem to be 'thermostat people' and who can enter a room and immediately warm up the temperature in the room and for those with whom they engage. I felt that I was more of a 'thermometer' than a 'thermostat' and I very much wanted to be the 'thermostat! I would love to be that someone with the warmth of personality, attractiveness, engaging gregarious nature and humorous chatter to whom others instantly warm. But we are not all like that – nor were we meant to be. We are uniquely designed to be who we are- different temperament, abilities, skills, hopes and dreams.

But we can all still be 'thermostats. We should never underestimate the influence that we have at home, work, neighbourhood, community, house group, church etc. We can all demonstrate the grace of God in our lives and bring His gracious presence into each encounter. It should be our aim to bring warmth, comfort, care, comfortableness, security, continuity, and connection wherever we are, and so raise the temperature for those around us.

May we live and go in the grace and beauty of our living Lord this week.

The son is the radiance of God's glory Hebrews 1 v 3

It is in Christ we find out who we are and what we are living for. Long before we first heard of Christ and got our hopes up, He had his eye on us, had designs on us for glorious living, part of the overall purpose He is working out. Ephesians 1 v 4

May the mind of Christ, my Saviour, Live in me from day to day,
By His love and power controlling All I do and say.

May the Word of God dwell richly In my heart from hour to hour,
So that all may see I triumph Only through His power.

May the peace of God my Father Rule my life in everything.
That I may be calm to comfort Sick and sorrowing.

May the love of Jesus fill me, As the waters fill the sea;
Him exalting, self-abasing, This is victory.

K Barclay Wilkinson and M Peterson

The Eternal Wall of Answered Prayer

Prayer has always been a bit of a challenge for me. I am not practised in the rhythm of prayer. But as I have reached more senior years and have often been wakeful for a short time in the early hours of the morning, just before first light, I have found that this quiet time of the day when my mind is more relaxed and perhaps has processed the other matters that has occupied it, that this is a good time to reflect and pray. It is also the time when I sometimes have a flow of ideas too. If I remember them in the morning, well that is another matter! Jesus needed time in prayer and his disciples would have regularly witnessed Him going to the garden, mountain or quiet place alone to be with his Father. Prayer and being with Father God was part of His rhythm of life. This led to the disciples to ask Him to teach them how to pray.

So, it was with great interest that I read about Richard Gamble, who was planning for and has been awarded planning permission for an enormous Christian prayer monument, taking the shape of a continuous loop known as the Mobius strip. The Eternal Wall of Answered Prayer was to be more than twice the size of the Anthony Gormley, Angel of the North sculpture. It was to be built on the outskirts of Birmingham, constructed using a million bricks, each representing an answered prayer from a member of the public. The Eternal Wall of Answered prayer will have three aims: to encourage prayer, to proclaim Jesus for the country and to preserve the Christian heritage of the nation. The site was designed to have a visitor centre, café and bookshop to cater for an estimated 3,000 visitors a year, who would be able to use an app to access the database, for the stories of hope of a million people whose prayers were answered.

The aim of the Eternal Wall is to make hope visible to the nation, to be a monument of remembrance to our faithful God who hears and answers prayer, as was Joshua's Gilgal stones.

Joshua told them, *"Go into the middle of the Jordan, in front of the Ark of the Lord your God. Each of you must pick up one stone and carry it out on your shoulder—twelve stones in all, one for each of the twelve tribes of Israel. We will use these stones to build a memorial. In the future your children will ask you, 'What do these stones mean?' Then you can tell them, 'They remind us that the Jordan River stopped flowing when the Ark of the Lord's Covenant went across.' These stones will stand as a memorial among the people of Israel forever." Joshua 4 v 5-7*

"We're trying to make the largest database of hope stories in the world visible and provoke a conversation about prayer. Everyone goes through storms in life, and hope is one of the greatest antidotes to anxiety and fear". Richard Gamble

The Eternal Wall will stand for hundreds of years and will hold a million testimonies of answered prayer. Eternalwall.org.uk/testimony

Together

We have been playing two cooperative board games. The game, Forbidden Desert-Thirst for Survival is a game based around a mission to excavate an ancient desert city and recover a legendary flying machine powered by the sun. Six adventurers, stranded in a vast desert and exposed to unrelenting sandstorms must work together to excavate the city, find the parts of the flying machine, and rebuild it for their escape. Their only hope for survival is to work together before a team member expires from thirst or the storm gets too intense. Each adventurer has a different role to play and each must know and use their teammates individual strengths and capabilities. One person cannot do it on their own. Along the way valuable bits of equipment can be collected, shared, agreed upon and used.

Our other cooperative game is called Pandemic. In this board game, the players are skilled members of a disease fighting team who must keep four deadly diseases at bay while discovering their cures. The players each take a different role and have unique functions and skills which must be shared. Teammates travel across the globe along agreed routes treating infections while finding resources for the cures. Once again, it is essential that players work as a team. Players win or lose together. Outbreaks and epidemics fuel four spreading diseases but the players must work to find all four cures in time.

The key elements in each game are knowing each other's role, strengths, and abilities, sharing resources, communicating with each other, working out the plans and routes together, and working to a common aim. There are no Lone Rangers.

Jesus has given us a mission. Our God loves diversity and creativity, and He has gifted each of us with a role to carry out in His mission. He has given each of us unique temperaments, personalities, character strengths, abilities, skills, gifts, and spiritual gifts. He has placed us together to work together. He does the work in and through all of us, but we are in it together.

Never feel that you do not have anything to offer. Never try to imitate someone else or do what they do. God has His place and space for you. You are essential, God has chosen you to do what only you can do. He has the equipment cards for us to share and use. We need to communicate and support each other in His work.

God's various gifts are handed out everywhere; but they all originate in God's Spirit. God's various ministries are carried out everywhere; but they all originate in God's Spirit. God's various expressions of power are in action everywhere; but God himself is behind it all. Each person is given something to do that shows who God is: Everyone gets in on it, everyone benefits. All kinds of things are handed out by the Spirit, and to all kinds of people! The variety is wonderful. I Corinthians 1 v 4-11 MSG

To one person the Spirit gives the ability to give wise advice; someone else may be especially good at studying and teaching, and this is his gift from the same Spirit. He gives special faith to another, and to someone else the power to heal the sick. He gives power for doing miracles to some, and to others power to prophesy and preach. He gives someone else the power to know whether evil spirits are speaking through those who claim to be giving God's messages—or whether it is really the Spirit of God who is speaking. Still another person is able to speak in languages he never learned; and others, who do not know the language either, are given power to understand what he is saying. It is the same and only Holy Spirit who gives all these gifts and powers, deciding which each one of us should have.   1 Corinthians 12 v 4-11 TLB

We are confident of all this because of our great trust in God through Christ. It is not that we think we are qualified to do anything on our own. Our qualification comes from God. 2 Corinthians 3 v 4-5

Pray

It is from your hand that we have received all we have, and are, and will be.

Help us always to use your gifts wisely and to share them generously. By working together may we bear witness to the love of Christ in our lives, our church, and our community. May we value each person, their unique gifts, and their special role. We pray with grateful hearts.

Be filled and flow

In Him, you also, when you heard the word of truth, the good news of your salvation, and as a result, believed in Him, were stamped with the seal of the promised Holy Spirit, the One promised by Christ, as owned, and protected by God. The Spirit is the guarantee, the first instalment, the pledge, a foretaste of our inheritance until the redemption of God's own purchased possession, His believers, to the praise of His glory. Ephesians 1 v 13-14 AMP

Don't drink too much wine, for many evils lie along that path; be filled instead with the Holy Spirit and controlled by him. Ephesians 5 v 18

Paul wrote his letter to the Ephesians from his prison cell in Rome in about AD 60. Ephesus was a very large, influential, and cosmopolitan city in what is Turkey today, and was the centre of worship for the Goddess Artemis. In writing to the Ephesians, Paul was seeking to give clear guidance and teaching to Christians as to who they were in Christ and how they should live. Christians were under great pressure from the influences of their surrounding cultures. Greek culture at the time, included pagan gatherings called symposiums which often involved a lot of drinking in addition to their discussions and gatherings, and Paul would have been very familiar with these kinds of drinking parties. He wanted to warn the Ephesians against joining in with this style of gathering, which could often lead to excesses and so he encourages them to be filled, to be continually, constantly filled with the Holy Spirit. Paul wanted to show that the filling and flow of the Holy Spirit would lead to change, give a greater self-awareness and self-control not less, and an enhanced performance not reduced effectiveness. The filling and flowing were to be continuous. As

God's love flows into every part of our being, it is intended to flow out, fully, and freely to others around us and in our sphere of influence.

"Let love in and let it out. You are destined to be a channel for God to flow through and not a reservoir that merely sits and collects things. You are special and God has special plans for you." Joyce Meyer

In Him, you also, when you heard the word of truth, the good news of your salvation, and as a result, believed in Him, were stamped with the seal of the promised Holy Spirit, the One promised by Christ, as owned, and protected by God. The Spirit is the guarantee, the first instalment, the pledge, a foretaste of our inheritance until the redemption of God's own purchased possession, His believers, to the praise of His glory. Ephesians 1 v 13-14 AMP

I remember listening to a talk by Joel Holm, United Christian Broadcasters entitled The Fluence Principle, and he used the scientific principles of 'flow' using the key words of fluence, affluence, influence, and confluence. He asked his Christian listeners to evaluate their 'fluence factor.' He was referring to fluence being our outward 'flow' of Christian love and care. Affluence being God's abundant, generous supply and flow of love and grace to us and through us. Influence was that love flowing out, the direction of that flow, and who we shared that love with. Who is in my sphere of influence? Confluence was about flowing together and delighting to work with others. As a church and teams, we can be compelling forces with greater influence as we work together.

The Holy Spirit is God's mark on our life, His blessing and grace, His transformation energy, which we should not hold tightly to ourselves. His love and grace are to flow out for others.

Pray

Just as the owner's seal is pressed into soft wax as a sign of ownership, I ask for your Holy Spirit to make His mark on my heart and my life. May my life reflect His love and may that love be evident to those around me and in my sphere of influence. May we delight to join together and work for your kingdom here.

Gracious Spirit, dwell with me! I myself would gracious be,
And with words that help and heal would thy life in mine reveal;
And with actions bold and meek would for Christ my Saviour speak.
Truthful Spirit, dwell with me! I myself would truthful be,
And with wisdom kind and clear let thy life in mine appear;
And with actions brotherly speak my Lord's sincerity.   Charles Wesley

Stand firm

Be on guard. Stand firm in the faith. Be courageous and strong and do everything with love. 1 Corinthians 16 v 13-14

It is God who enables us, along with you, to stand firm for Christ. He has commissioned us and He has identified us as his own by placing the Holy Spirit in our hearts as the first instalment that guarantees everything He has promised us. 2 Corinthians 1 v 21-22

When tragedy hits and our circumstances are unstable, challenging, uncertain, scary, isolating and bleak- what can we do? Where do we go for strength, perspective and understanding? What is there to keep us on track and to prevent us folding and crumpling?

When my husband and I experienced a very bleak time in our family we held on to the knowledge that God is faithful, that God is constant and loving and that God is completely trustworthy. We stood firm in the knowledge that He had always been our faithful God through the many years that we had walked with him. This was the foundation stone on which we planted our feet. As He had been with us in the past- He would be with us now and on into the future. We planted our feet and we stood firm.

There are days when we feel isolated and anxious. It is hard to meet with family, friends, and church friends. We may know of those who may have received a difficult diagnosis, an uncertain time with employment, a financial concern, tensions in a relationship, a troubling family situation or mental wellbeing issues. How do we stand firm during these times and help others to stand firm?

Chadwick Boseman, was an actor who took on the role of the Black Panther Marvel star, but who died suddenly, at the age of 43, after a four-year battle with cancer. During those 4 years he was able to stand firm. He had never discussed his illness publicly and had continued to work on blockbuster films throughout his treatment and surgeries during that period. He was standing firm without drawing attention to his very real concerns. For that, he is a superhero.

Chadwick had openly spoken about his faith in God during difficult times. On one occasion, he had been selected for a role in a soap opera that involved playing the role of a stereotypical black man. After questioning the producers on the portrayal of the character he was dismissed from the role. He trusted that his disappointment would lead to other opportunities. When he addressed a group of graduating students at Howard University in 2018, he spoke of his faith, quoted Jeremiah 29 v 11, and spoke of God's purpose being the essential element of who you are. "You are on this planet, at this particular time in history and your very existence is wrapped up in the things you are here to fulfil. Whatever you choose for your career path, remember the struggles along the way are only meant to shape you for your purpose."

After his death, the NAACP one of the leading civil rights groups in the US wrote, " for showing us how to conquer adversity with grace, for showing us how to 'say it loud', for showing us how to walk as a king without losing the common touch, for showing us just how powerful we are. Thank you."

The encouragement in these difficult days is to stand firm but not in our own strength but in God's strength. To fix your feet. Instead of giving us strength to face whatever situation we need to face, He becomes our strength. It is His strength. Strength made perfect in weakness.

Deer

A few weeks ago, I took a walk in the Harewood House grounds from the Muddy Boots Café along the road which forms part of the perimeter of the estate, and I was delighted to witness the movement of the whole Harewood herd of deer immediately in front of me. It was a bitterly cold day and the herd, of 60 to 80 strong of beautiful deer, were in search of water. They were heading to the water troughs where they knew that they would find a source of water and I would guess a source of supplementary

food as it was a bitterly cold period for them, with snow and ice on the ground. It naturally made me think of those beautiful verses in the Psalms which are a cry of longing for help.

In Psalm 42 the writer describes his sense of great need, discouragement, and desperate longing for God. He compares the deer longing for water with his desperate longing for God. He is distanced from the house of God and unable to worship with others and feels distant from God Himself. He remembers happier times when he was able to meet with others in joyful worship but now, he is taunted by questions about 'where is his god'? Although there is discouragement and even despair, yet the writer looks to the future with hope, recognising that God will be with him again, and knowing that God will once again meet with him.

We too need to look to the future with hope. When we are isolated, discouraged and even despondent about our present situation or the future may we trust that as God has intervened in the past He will do so again in the future. I am encouraged by the thought that God does not lead us to a water trough- a source of standing water- but that He leads us to a river of water flowing free fresh and abundant- a constant source that can never run dry. I can take this water freely and frequently and Jesus can lead me safely and securely to the high places.

Longing for God and His Help in Distress Psalm 42:

As a deer longs for flowing streams, so my soul longs for you, O God. My soul thirsts for God, for the living God. When shall I come and behold the face of God? Why are you cast down, O my soul, and why are you disquieted within me? Hope in God; for I shall again praise him, my help and my God.

Jesus answered, "Everyone who drinks this water will be thirsty again, but whoever drinks the water I give them will never thirst. Indeed, the water I give them will become in them a spring of water welling up to eternal life." John 4 v 13-14

He said to me: "It is done. I am the Alpha and the Omega, the Beginning, and the End. To the thirsty I will give water without cost from the spring of the water of life Revelation 21 v 6

17 The Spirit and the bride say, "Come!" And let the one who hears say, "Come!" Let the one who is thirsty come; and let the one who wishes take the free gift of the water of life. Revelation 22 v 17

He makes my feet like the feet of a deer. And He sets me on my high places. Psalm 18 v 33

The Lord God is my strength. He has made my feet like the feet of a deer, and He makes me walk on high places. Habbakuk 3 v 19

All who are thirsty, All who are weak
Just come to the fountain Dip your heart in the stream of life.
Let the pain and the sorrow Be washed away
In the waves of His mercy As deep cries out to deep!
We sing, come Lord Jesus come. Come Lord Jesus, come
Come Lord Jesus, come, Come Lord Jesus, come.
Come Lord Jesus come
Nothing but your will for me I am only free in you.

All Who Are Thirsty, Brenton Brown

What a friend we have in Jesus

We once had a wonderful holiday in a log cabin in a Forest Retreat, in Norfolk. We were connecting again, face to face, with our longest and closest friends, who have shared and stood with us for well over forty years.

When I was teaching in China, one of the questions that I used to ask my Chinese students in one of my teaching sessions was-" who is your best friend and what are the qualities that you look for in a friend?" I would often begin by describing my closest friend so that they would begin to formulate ideas of their own.

My best friend has been my consistent supporter. We have brought up our young families together, we have shared happy times and struggles, we have worked together in mum's and toddler's groups, house groups and church groups. We have shared our thoughts, trials, worries, and concerns. When I have wanted to be distant and not connect or communicate, she has been the one to call, text, send a card, a small gift and let me know that she is still there. She is the one who takes the initiative to arrange things, the meet up's, the weekend visits. Though we are now separated by many miles she is faithful and an ever- present strength in my life, my marriage, and my family. She has supported my children and she has prayed for us all. She is consistently thoughtful, generous, and kind. She has the uncanny ability to anticipate my needs and to know what I am thinking. She does not need to ask me "how has your day been?" or" how are you feeling today?" as she is able to read my face, my eyes, my body language, my words and mood. We have a shared history and understanding. She has the grace and fruits of the Holy Spirit to be my consistent and ever- present friend.

As I think about my special friend, I am reminded that Jesus is our closest friend and the one who knows us best. May we lean on Him.

The Lord would speak to Moses face to face, as one speaks to a friend. Exodus 33 v 11

Jesus- "the friend of tax collectors and sinners".

A friend loves at all times. Proverbs 17 v7

One who has unreliable friends soon comes to ruin, but there is a friend who sticks closer than a brother. Proverbs 18 24

What a Friend we have in Jesus, All our sins and griefs to bear!
What a privilege to carry Everything to God in prayer!
O what peace we often forfeit, O what needless pain we bear,
All because we do not carry Everything to God in prayer

Have we trials and temptations? Is there trouble anywhere?
We should never be discouraged. Take it to the Lord in prayer.
Can we find a friend so faithful, Who will all our sorrows share?
Jesus knows our every weakness. Take it to the Lord in prayer.

Joseph Medlicott Scriven

Pray

May we show kindness in a practical way to someone who really needs it this week. We cannot be a best friend, but may we be the one who is on the lookout for those who are needing that crucial connection. Help us to connect with someone who is needing a phone call, text message, card, or magazine. Contact from a friend or supporter can lift the spirits and the day.

Walking and Talking

Jesus and his disciples now left Galilee and went out to the villages of Caesarea Philippi. As they were walking along, he asked them, "Who do the people think I am? What are they saying about me?" Mark 8 v 27

Now they were on the way to Jerusalem, and Jesus was walking along ahead; and as the disciples were following, they were filled with terror and dread. Taking them aside, Jesus once more began describing all that was going to happen to him when they arrived at Jerusalem. Mark 10

As they were walking along someone said to Jesus, "I will always follow you no matter where you go." Luke 9 v 57

That same day, Sunday, two of Jesus' followers were walking to the village of Emmaus, seven miles out of Jerusalem. As they walked along, they were talking of Jesus' death, when suddenly Jesus himself came along and joined them and began walking beside them. But they didn't recognize him, for God kept them from it. "You seem to be in a deep discussion about something," he said. "What are you so concerned about?" Luke 24 v 13-17

Connection, conversation, and communication are vital and build trust. All aspects of talk are needed- from simple greetings, casual conversation to exchanging ideas, sharing personal information and concerns and in-depth conversations. There are some lovely examples of times when Jesus was walking and talking with His disciples and with others on His journeys. Jesus turned these essential road trips and walks into wonderful times of sharing and the exploration of questions, opinions, heart-searching moments, and times of decision.

Walking and talking is good. When you are walking with a partner, friend, colleague, or someone needing support, in the countryside or park, it is easier to be open about concerns. Face to face conversation and eye contact can be difficult and a little too intense for some people, and so walking and talking in this way may be easier and allow the person to relax a little more. The natural rhythm of a walking pace can be helpful and there is generally a more casual and calming atmosphere as you walk. If someone is feeling 'stuck' or' boxed in.' with a particular issue or problem, then the open spaces can somehow help that person to process experiences and thoughts and achieve some clarification. I really recommend 'walk and talk.' Equally good is sitting on a bench!

Careful listening is one of the most important gifts that we can give to someone else. That person will feel accepted, valued, encouraged, and supported. We need to look for the opportunities to form new links, re-establish old ones, find sustainable ways of being and doing, and help everyone to flourish. And may we be good listeners as we journey-whether walking or sitting.

Pray

You have called us to connection and family. Help us to give space and time to those who need it. May we speak with love and kindness to those we meet this week. You have promised to give wisdom to those who ask.

Give us wisdom and understanding in every decision that we make. Guide our thoughts and direct our steps. When there is uncertainty and confusion, may we know your limitless wisdom. Help us to think clearly and calmly, and to act with confidence, grace, and wisdom.

Loving without getting tired

"Do not think that love, in order to be genuine, has to be extraordinary. What we need is to love without getting tired." Mother Teresa

During the challenging Covid-19 Pandemic of 2020-2021, many groups and individuals were attempting to support those who were isolated, anxious and in need of practical support. We were doing small things. We were making phone calls, writing letters, sending cards, doing shopping, giving practical signs of encouragement etc. These were small things and not extraordinary things. But they were extraordinarily important. May we always have a heart for the lonely and for those who are in pain emotionally. May we offer support and love 'without getting tired'.

But the wisdom that comes from heaven is first of all pure. It is also peace loving, gentle at all times and willing to yield to others. It is full of mercy and good deeds. It shows no partiality and is always sincere. And those who are peacemakers will plant seeds of peace and reap a harvest of goodness. James 3 17-18

This love of which I speak is slow to lose patience—it looks for a way of being constructive. It is not possessive: it is neither anxious to impress nor does it cherish inflated ideas of its own importance. Love has good manners and does not pursue selfish advantage. It is not touchy. It does

not keep account of evil or gloat over the wickedness of other people. On the contrary, it is glad, with all good men, when truth prevails. Love knows no limit to its endurance, no end to its trust, no fading of its hope; it can outlast anything. It is, in fact, the one thing that still stands when all else has fallen. All gifts except love will be superseded one day. 1 Corinthians 13 v 4-7 JBP

Love endures with patience and serenity, love is kind and thoughtful, and is not jealous or envious; love does not brag and is not proud or arrogant. It is not rude; it is not self-seeking; it is not provoked [nor overly sensitive and easily angered]; it does not take into account a wrong endured. It does not rejoice at injustice but rejoices with the truth when right and truth prevail. Love bears all things regardless of what comes, believes all things looking for the best in each one, hopes all things remaining steadfast during difficult times, endures all things without weakening. Love never fails it never fades nor ends. 1 Corinthians 13 v 4-7 AMP

Be like children

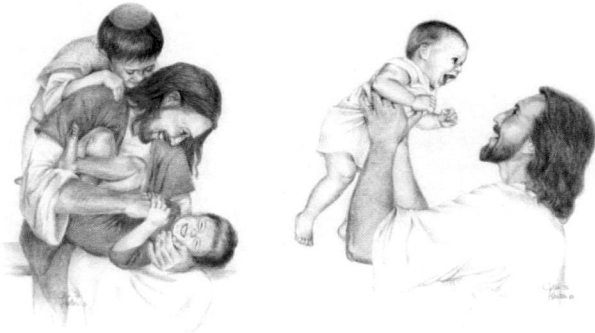

Some years ago, I saw an amazing drawing of Jesus with a small group of very little children climbing over Him, with Jesus happily carrying a little one on His shoulders piggyback style. Jesus was laughing and it was such a delightful, natural scene of joy, fun, and connection. I cannot remember the name of the artist, it could have been Jean Keaton or another artist, but it made a deep impression on me. I believe that Jesus would have had little children around Him in the extended family and in the village. He would have met them on His travels and would have welcomed them.

Once when some mothers were bringing their children to Jesus to bless them, the disciples shooed them away, telling them not to bother Him. But when Jesus saw what was happening, He was very much displeased with his disciples and said to them, "Let the children come to me, for the Kingdom of God belongs to such as they. Don't send them away! I tell you as seriously as I know how that anyone who refuses to come to God as a little child will never be allowed into his Kingdom." Then He took the children into his arms and placed His hands on their heads, and He blessed them. Mark 10 v 13-16

Throughout my career, I have worked with children and families. I have especially enjoyed teaching six- and seven-year-old children. These young children have enthusiasm, energy, openness and are just beginning to have a tiny bit of independence and a little bit of self-control. They happily absorb information, have a wonderful creativity, an eagerness to learn new things and the ability to take on board new challenges. They play happily together, most of the time, and though aware of different languages, cultures, and skin tones, these are not significant. Small children are trusting and need to have a level of dependence on the adults around them.

In the following thoughts by Michel Quoist, he wishes that we were all children on the inside, bearing the likeness of Jesus. So, whatever age we are, may we be a child on the inside, reflecting His face, His character, and His love. May we always listen carefully, have openness, creativity, trust in others, and the ability to face new challenges. May we get rid of hardness, pride, fixed ideas and behaviour patterns, prejudice, and closed ways of thinking. May we be willing to go down new paths.

Even children show what they are like by the things they do. You can see if their actions are pure and right. Proverbs 20 v 11

God says: I like youngsters I want people to be like them.
I don't like old people unless they are still children.
I want only children in my Kingdom; this has been decreed from the beginning of time.
Youngsters- twisted, humped, wrinkled, white bearded- all kinds of youngsters but youngsters.
There is no changing it. It has been decided.
There is room for no one else.
I like little children because my likeness has not yet been dulled in them.
They have not botched my likeness, they are new, pure, without a blot, without a smear.
So, when I gently lean over them, I recognise myself in them.

I like them because they're still growing, they are still improving.
They are on the road; they are on their way.
But with grown-ups there is nothing to expect anymore.
They will no longer grow, no longer improve.
They have come to a full stop.
It is disastrous- grown-ups think they have arrived.
Alleluia! Alleluia! Open all of you little old men!
It is I your God, the Eternal, risen from the dead, coming to bring back
to life the child in you.
Hurry! Now is the time. I am ready to give you again the beautiful face of
a child, the beautiful eyes of a child.
For I love youngsters and I want everyone to be like them.

I like youngsters, Michel Quoist (Prayers of Life)

A very popular Bible verse

"So do not fear, for I am with you; do not be dismayed, for I am your God.
I will strengthen you and help you; I will uphold you with my righteous
right hand." Isaiah 41 verse 10

Each year YouVersion has a tradition of announcing its most popular verse of the year among the users of its Bible App. The Bible App has more than 545 million installs worldwide and has seen an increase in engagement in almost every country since launching in 2008. Statistics for 2022 include the app being opened 5.5 billion times, and 2.3 billion highlights, bookmarks, and notes were created. Meanwhile, 550 million Bible verses were shared, and 303 million in-app searches were made. The scripture that people shared, bookmarked, and highlighted most was Isaiah 41:10:

Bobby Gruenewald, founder and CEO of YouVersion said: "The popularity of this verse speaks to our desire to be reminded that even when we feel like we're alone in our struggles, we're not. As this verse says, God is our strength and He's always with us."

YouVersion also pointed out how the war in Ukraine in 2022 impacted engagement in the Bible App. It said as Ukrainians began to flee to neighbouring countries, the app's Ukrainian-language Bible engagement spiked in many of the countries by triple digits. Poland saw a 241 per cent increase, while Germany saw 733 per cent. "These families are going through something most of us can't imagine. In the middle of what's likely the most difficult time of their lives, they're turning to the Bible for comfort, peace, and hope. It's an honour that we get to be a part of making God's Word available to His people in their greatest moments of need." Gruenewald said. Overall engagement rose by 55 per cent in Ukraine, with trending search terms in the language at the beginning of the war including "war", "fear" and "anxiety." Now, many months on from the start of the war, the top search term in the Ukrainian language is "love".

Compassion - Meghan and Harry

"Everyone you meet is fighting a battle you know nothing about."

When he saw the crowds, He had compassion on them, because they were harassed and helpless, like sheep without a shepherd. Matthew 9 v 36

I love the word compassion. Compassion is more than coming alongside another person, being concerned for them, and empathy. It is the tangible expression of love and a response to the person who is in pain, any kind of pain. Jesus showed compassion to those He met on His journey- the woman with the issue of blood, the Samaritan woman, Rabbis and Teachers, Matthew Levi, the demoniac in a graveyard, Nicodemus, the Centurion, lepers, and beggars, Jairus, the rich young ruler, the dying thief on the cross- the rich and poor, those from racial groups, religious groups and those from none. The nature of their need was different and unique to each, but Jesus offered the same care, grace, and compassion to all. He identified the need and responded with compassion.

Jesus offers that same compassion to us. We are individually known and understood, the need is responded to, and we are changed by that meeting with Him.

I have not watched the Oprah Winfrey interview with Harry and Meghan. I have caught some selected, pre-digested highlights of the interview on TV only. I have tried not to make judgements about either the couple themselves and "their truths" or the statement from the Queen and the 'Royal Institution'. It is painful to be on the receiving end of a report, with judgements made based on a version of the truth that has been given, with negligible information or context provided, and without the opportunity to determine true facts from all parties or the context in which something may have been written or said. So, my reaction is sadness, concern and empathy for all parties involved. I do not know any of the facts, but I can see the turmoil, pain, and emotional distress that a young woman and her husband have experienced and are experiencing.

Therefore, my response is to offer compassion and grace in my thinking about these matters, and to keep a suitably dignified silence, whatever the rights and wrongs, the truths or the untruths, the accusations, and the falsehoods. These disclosures are deeply personal family matters.

Many people that we may meet and speak with are perhaps hiding hurts and distress that they have been unable to share with others. They may have put on a brave face, concealed the truth, felt trapped and conflicted, unable to share their inner thoughts and pain, and been inwardly preoccupied, troubled, and isolated, without external help for a very long time. We never know what is truly behind the fixed smile and outward, calm appearance. Our role is to give that person the confidence to share their account without rushing to judgement or early unfounded conclusions. Our role is to be the careful, active listener and the person who offers compassion.

The Lord is compassionate and gracious, slow to anger, abounding in love. Psalm 103 v 8

Praise be to the God and Father of our Lord Jesus Christ, the Father of compassion and the God of all comfort, who comforts us in all our troubles, so that we can comfort those in any trouble with the comfort we ourselves receive from God. For just as we share abundantly in the sufferings of Christ, so also our comfort abounds through Christ. If we are distressed, it is for your comfort and salvation; if we are comforted, it is for your comfort, which produces in you patient endurance of the same sufferings we suffer. And our hope for you is firm because we know that just as you share in our sufferings, so also you share in our comfort. 2 Corinthians 1 v 3-7

The one who states his case first seems right, until the other comes and examines him. Proverbs 18 v 17

PRAY

We thank you that your love is constant and overwhelming. You are with us in the best of times and in the worst of times. You are with us when we feel ok and when we feel wretched. You see our heart and our need. May we not hide from you. Help us to see the needs of those around us. May we listen and hear the need behind the façade, the pretence, and the exterior. May we be slow to judge and to form an opinion. May we also have the desire to give the support and help that is needed.

The Ministry of Presence and Listening

During the Pandemic of 2020-2022, the many restrictions on contact with others hit people very hard. We are made for connection and communication. I have been made more aware now that we need to give people our love, time, and presence-as much as they need. This can be costly to us when there are other demands on our time and perhaps more challenging now, bearing in mind the strict limits on contact that we had to experience. There is a wonderful phrase that I read a short while ago which struck me forcibly and which I keep turning over in my thoughts. "This is called the ministry of presence".

I was recently struck very powerfully by a daily reading by Rick Warren. Rick Warren commenting on Job, and the three friends who had come to sit with him, when Job had lost everything. The friends had travelled from their homes, sat, and stayed with Job for seven days, yet said nothing during the whole of that time.

" For they saw that his suffering was too great for words." Job 2 v 11,13

He goes on to say these very wise words.

"When you are ministering to someone in pain, you must remember this: the deeper the pain, the fewer words you use. If you're always in a hurry, then you're never going to be a great listener. To have great conversations, you start by looking with love at the other person, but then you must invest as much time as needed. Why? Because you can't listen well in a hurry. Great listening takes time."

What a wonderful phrase. The ministry of presence. I keep repeating it to myself. I want to have this gift of 'presence', of being with someone in an unhurried way and giving them time and the space to be and to share if they need to- and if they do not want to speak or share, then to give them the comfort and security of knowing that I am 'just there' to be with them.

Let us pray for God's gift of grace and presence in all our communications this week.

Make me a channel of Your peace
Where there is hatred, let me bring Your love
Where there is injury, Your pardon Lord
And where there's doubt, true faith in You.
Make me a channel of Your peace
Where there's despair in life, let me bring hope
Where there is darkness, only light
And where there's sadness, ever joy.
Oh Master, grant that I may never seek.
So much to be consoled as to console
To be understood as to understand
To be loved as to love with all my soul.
Make me a channel of Your peace
It is pardoning that we are pardoned
In giving to all men that we receive
And in dying that we're born to eternal life.
Francis of Assisi

Unfailing love

Let the morning bring me word of your unfailing love, for I have put my trust in you. Show me the way I should go, for to you I entrust my life. Psalm 143 v 8

I have always been mindful of your unfailing love and have lived in reliance on your faithfulness. Psalm 26 v3

His compassions never fail. Lamentations 3 v 22

Things are constantly in a change of flux. The weather is unreliable. Things change. That is for sure. Things are unreliable. We are unreliable.

Inconsistency and failure seem to be a familiar feature of our lives. In life, we may occasionally have the experience of 'being let down' and disappointed. So, the word 'unfailing' is quite a difficult concept for our minds to grasp and fully understand. But the message is that our God is an unfailing God. His love for us is constant, never changing, ceaseless, sure, and never failing. His love is 'boundless' and sure. That means to me that there is no limit or boundary. His love is not dependent on what I do or do not do. It does not change if I make mistakes or fail Him. It is not performance related. In our modern society it is easy to slip into a performance driven framework sometimes even when considering our own Christian walk. Having a strong work ethic, it is easy for me to be performance driven in my goals and aspirations and even in my Christian life at times. But I need to keep reminding myself that I do not have to be a 'Do-er'. I cannot earn His favour.

Jesus is about relationship. The relationship with Him is non quantifiable. I am loved immeasurably, and I am fully accepted. In this relationship, Jesus keeps calling to us to come closer and to settle into His love. I just must keep telling myself this- over and over and over again.

O Love that will not let me go
I rest my weary soul in Thee.
I give thee back the life I owe.
That in Thine ocean's depth its flow may richer, fuller be.

Hymn by George Matheson:

Jesus, thou art all compassion
Pure unbounded love thou art

From Love divine all loves excelling by Charles Wesley

ENCOUNTERS

Strengthened to serve: Simon Peter's Mother-in-Law

Simon's mother-in-law was bedridden, sick with a high fever, so the first thing they did was to tell Jesus about her. He walked up to her bedside, gently took her hand, and raised her up! Her fever disappeared and she began to serve them. Later in the day, just after the Sabbath ended at sunset, the people kept bringing to Jesus all who were sick and tormented by demons, until the whole village was crowded around the house. Jesus healed many who were sick with various diseases and cast out many demons. Mark 1 v 29-32 TPT

No sooner had the fever left than she was up fixing dinner for them. MSG

I live in Capernaum and love and support my daughter and her husband, a Galilean fisherman. Times are hard and their income is uncertain. He is a good man, he works hard, and endures impossible hardships to make a living, selling the fish in the market that he and his brother catch. Fishing on the Sea of Galilee is a treacherous and demanding business and there are the boats and nets to manage. The dramatic changes in the weather on the water make the fisherman's life and work even harder. Their life together is challenging. For all his faults- which in my opinion are many, Simon is strong, hardworking, and a good and faithful man. He may not be the most stable of characters as he can be strong willed, impulsive, and doesn't always think through his plans. He is full of ideas, schemes, and crazy notions, tends to speak before thinking, and often fails to consider the impact of his words on others. But I love him dearly and I do what I can to help them both.

Recently, his time has been taken up with other things. The two brothers have met with a local itinerant teacher who visits the towns and villages. By report, this man has been doing some amazing things. I hear accounts of Him healing ailments and diseases. But more than that, He brings a message of love and transformation which is certainly different to what you might hear in our local synagogue. I am intrigued by this man and have heard Andrew and Simon give Him high praise. They are keen to follow Him. But what of my daughter? If they go off to the countryside, leaving boat, net, and livelihood behind, what will become of her?

One day, I began to feel very unwell, and my sickness turned to a high fever. I was unable to carry on with any daily chores, and unable to help my daughter. I became so ill that I had to take to my bed. I could take no food and my condition was growing worse. Barely opening my eyes, I felt a gentle touch on my hand. It was the teacher who had been calling the men to leave their nets and to follow. His touch and His voice were gentle. The strangest of things happened next. I immediately felt the fever go from my body and my energy return. How could this be? From being so sick and laid up in my bed, I was restored, energized, renewed. I got up out of the bed, washed and dressed and immediately thought that food should be prepared for our guests. Then, later in the day, after Sabbath, our little house was surrounded by other visitors- many visitors, dozens of visitors! It seemed as if the whole village was descending on our little home. They came with various illnesses and Jesus began to heal them, one by one. They were healed, restored, and freed.

I was restored and renewed, and I had a place to serve the One who had touched my life.

Thoughts

We have trusted in Christ and received His free grace and salvation. But we are also saved to serve- not in our strength but with His strength and power. We are strengthened to serve.

As you live this new life, we pray that you will be strengthened from God's boundless resources, so that you will find yourselves able to pass through any experience and endure it with courage. Colossians 1v 11

I pray that out of his glorious riches he may strengthen you with power through his Spirit in your inner being, so that Christ may dwell in your hearts through faith. And I pray that you, being rooted and established in love, may have power, together with all the Lord's holy people, to grasp how wide and long and high and deep is the love of Christ, and to know this love that surpasses knowledge—that you may be filled to the measure of all the fullness of God. Ephesians 3 v 16-19

A Roadblock Situation: The Rich Young Ruler
Matthew 19 v 16-30

I am from a privileged family. I have always known security, received a sound, quality education and a good religious upbringing. I have been taught to be morally upright, to do the right thing, to follow the teachings of the scriptures and the Pharisees. I have followed the commandments to the letter and the instructions of the Teachers and the Rabbis at the synagogue. I have learned well, so that now I am one of the youngest leaders, joining those of senior years, who are teaching others in the ways of God. I have conformed to the rules, maintained high standards of behaviour, and earned the respect of all in the community. I am set for high things, but I am not at peace. Why do I feel so dissatisfied? There is a discontent in my soul, a void that I cannot fill and for all my superior moral behaviour and high standards there is something lacking. I have learned and followed the Pharisaic rules from early childhood. I am a conformer of the first order so why do I feel so empty?

I heard of this young, untrained itinerant Teacher whom many are following and was eager to find out the secret to His ministry, success and following. I sought Him out in good faith, coming before Him respectfully, open minded, with a genuine need to learn, being aware of the void in my life. I needed to ask Him- what particular thing do I need to do in order to have eternal life? I have followed all of the rules and commandments and so what one, good thing do I need to do now? Have I done enough for a reward in heaven? Is there a guarantee of my place in the eternal? I will do whatever is required.

His answer was straightforward and shocking. I was to sell all I had and follow Him. He had discerned that my strongest, my hearts attachment, was to my wealth, status, position, and privilege. He was asking me to relinquish the control of my life to Him and to simply follow. He had read my heart. I now saw that eternal life is not by 'doing' but by 'being'.

I was cut to the core. His words had penetrated deep and caused immense conflict. To say that I was troubled was an understatement. This was too much to ask. How could it be that my high moral life would count for nothing in the new kingdom? My heart was heavy and with great sorrow I quietly turned away from Him, returning to the privilege of my wealth and the security of all that was familiar.

Thoughts

This rich young ruler had hit a roadblock, a crossroads and he could go no further until he had relinquished the control of his life to the One who was calling him to follow. There was a hindrance, an obstacle that prevented him from moving forwards. He had stalled and could not move forward to his desired path of knowing his place in the kingdom of God. So, he was immobilized, stifled, and frustrated. A breakthrough would not come easily now.

There is one significant and perhaps life changing sentence in this account of the rich young ruler.

And Jesus looking upon him loved him, and said to him Mark 10 v 21

Perhaps if he had continued in conversation with Jesus, he may have begun to see things from a new perspective. He may have realized that he could not begin do this by himself and that Jesus would not ask Him to do it on his own. When the disciples asked Jesus to explain the challenge of riches to them, Jesus gave a simple, clarification- trust God to help you.

The disciples were staggered. "Then who has any chance at all?" Jesus looked hard at them and said, "No chance at all if you think you can pull it off yourself. Every chance in the world if you trust God to do it." MSG

We may each face some turning point, a blockage on our journey of faith, something that we are holding onto, or some unexpected challenge. He does not expect us to do this on our own. His grace and power to change us, is sufficient. We can't pull it off by ourselves. We need to keep reminding ourselves of this.

This wonderful hymn was written by Frederick William Faber. (1814-1863):

There's a wideness in God's mercy, like the wideness of the sea;
there's a kindness in His justice which is more than liberty.

There is no place where earth's sorrows
are more keenly felt than heaven:
there is no place where earth's failings
have such gracious judgement given.

For the love of God is broader than the measure of man's mind;
and the heart of the Eternal is most wonderfully kind.

But we make His love too narrow, By false limits of our own.
And we magnify His strictness, With a zeal He will not own.

If our love were but more simple, we should take Him at his word;
And our lives be filled with gladness from the presence of the Lord.

Crumbs under the table: Matthew 15 v 22-28

My daughter is ill. My emotions are raw, I am empty, drained of energy, physically exhausted with no help and no place to turn to. It has been this way for years. There is no respite and no hope. I have prayed to the God of Heaven, and the God of the Jews, but He is deaf to my cries. My neighbours now avoid me as they too feel helpless, without comfort or kind words, overwhelmed by my needs. They will do no more.

I hear rumours of one Jewish Teacher who is gentle, merciful and who heals. There are rumours that He has travelled to Tyre and Sidon, into our Gentile area, but that He is lying low. Why would He come if He does not want to be seen? Why is He here at all? We are Canaanites, with ancient hostilities between us and the Jewish nation. We are Gentiles, outsiders, of mixed nationalities and so why would He come here?

My heart is racing. I must find this teacher healer. If the reports are true, then He is my only hope. I am Greek, born in Syrian Phoenicia and so what am I to Him? I have no position or claim on Him, no status or privilege that He should even speak to me. I am no insider. I am a foreigner, an outsider. Yet I will go.

I came down from the hills and found Him out in His place of rest and retreat as He sat with His followers. I dared to approach. The words startled even me as they came out of my mouth. "Lord, Son of David, have mercy on me and heal my daughter." There was only silence and the strange looks of those who were with him. Silence. A painful silence. I told my story, shared my pain and pleaded but there was only silence. I was turned away by the followers, but I continued to plead my case, my daughter's needs, her need for healing, my hope. They grew frustrated, angry with me, forceful, unkind even. "Send her away, or take care of the woman, she's driving us crazy, she won't go, she's calling after us, following us" they called to the Master.

I came back to the healer and dropped to my knees at his feet. My words were simple. "Master, help me". His gaze touched my heart and my soul, but His words were few. "I was sent to the lost sheep of Israel. It is not right to take the bread out of the children's mouths and throw it to the dogs." I sensed what He was saying – what He meant. He was the Jewish Jesus, the Messiah. My reply came quickly. "But the little dogs eat the scraps from the children's hands and that fall from the master's table." There was a change, a smile, and a gentle response. "Woman, you have great faith. Your request is granted."

My faith, my confidence in Him and His power was the turning point. He had put hurdles in my way to prove and test my heart. My daughter was healed at that very moment. I knew it. Few words needed to be spoken. I returned home and everything was different.

But here is the strange thing. He left our region and went back to Galilee. I heard that there was a miracle involving bread and fish among thousands. What a strange affair. He gave bread to the hungry by their thousands. But I had been given a crumb, a morsel of bread and that was enough. I was changed.

But she came and bowed down before him and said, "Lord, help me!"

She knew that she had no rightful claim to His grace, but she asked and kept asking.

"Ask and it will be given to you; seek and you will find; knock and the door will be opened to you". Matthew 7 v 7

Pray

Jesus, you seek out those in need. Your grace reaches out beyond borders, boundaries, and groups.

Help us to see others-all others- as you see them. To see them as those who need of your love and care irrespective of nationality, status, or cultural group.

Broaden our vision.

Bent Double: Luke 13 v 10-17

I see feet and not faces. It has been this way for as long as I can remember. I look down at the dirt, the stone path, the mud, the dirty feet, and sandals of those who pass me by. I do not look up to the trees, the birds, the sky, the window, the doorway, or the eyes of those who pass me by. I am unseen though a familiar presence, a non-person, nameless, insignificant and of no value. My world is small. Every simple task poses new challenges of pain and inconvenience. I cannot lift, I cannot carry, I cannot reach up high and I cannot contribute. I am invisible yet a target of children's jokes and laughter. I am humiliated, sorrowful, ashamed, a burden to others and the burden of my shame and weakness has been with me for most of my life-for eighteen whole years. I shuffle silently into the synagogue each

Sabbath and hide with the women at the back. I do not want to be seen. My hiding is almost complete as I stand among the flowing robes and scarves.

But I am seen. There was One whose grace and compassion saw me in my hiding place though I could not hope to see His face. I was called forward. It was an invitation that I could not avoid. There was a stunned silence as I was guided to the front to where the gentle voice had called me. I had no expectation, no understanding of what might happen, or desire to meet this new teacher. I was in the familiar place, the safe place- hidden in plain sight. His words came as a shock. "Woman you are set free." There was no pre-amble, exchange of introductions, announcement to the gathered or the synagogue leader. Those simple words only and a gentle touch. And I was released. How it happened I cannot say. I only know that my back grew stronger, my weakened and limp muscles were renewed and for the first time I could stand tall. I was straight and I could see faces. Those faces changed and there was a surge of joy, praise to God, gasps of wonder and for the first time in many years I opened my mouth and I publicly praised and glorified God for my release.

The synagogue leader was not pleased. I could see his scowl of disapproval and dismay. For the first time I could read the faces of others. And for the first time I saw His face, the face of Jesus. I was no longer the nameless one, the ignored, the cripple but I was now 'the daughter of Abraham'. I was significant, valued, part of a community with a contribution to offer. I was changed. But I was not the only one who was changed. The whole synagogue erupted with praise and thanks. I was released, set free, rescued, and redeemed. I can never forget that day. But there were others there that day who were also released.

Pray

Jesus you are all compassion.
I want to fall into your grace, compassion, and mercy all over again.
You see me. You call me. You set me free. How can I not praise you?

The alabaster jar: Luke 7 v 36-50

The alabaster jar has been sitting on the shelf for as long as I can remember. Just sitting there, unopened, gathering the dust of years. I can barely look at it. The jar is meant to be so full of promise- a gift from a parent to a child to be given to the new husband and broken at his feet as an act of commitment, honour, and devotion. But I have no need of such a gift or promise. There is no one who would consider me as a bride. My hopes are unfulfilled, wasted, as the jar sits there accusing me, as I have given myself to so many different men. I have lost count of the number of men who have used and abused me. I do not know their names and I am now nameless and ashamed, my entitlement to marriage gone. But the jar of precious perfume, the oil that should be poured out as an act of extravagant love, sits there still.

I heard that a new teacher had arrived in town. It was said that He was a friend of tax collectors and sinners, that He loved the un-loveable, that He touched the untouchable, that He could heal, and that He could forgive sin. My sin lays heavily upon me and burdens my soul and my very being. The weight of it is crushing me. Could this teacher lift the weight of my guilt and sin and set me free? I was no longer afraid of those who judged, accused, tormented, hurt, and spat at me in the street. I would walk past them and their taunts and find this Jesus. I would pass their doors and windows and seek the mercy of the One who says that He can forgive and redeem.

But how can I enter the house of the Pharisee? I have met with so much rejection that it is an old friend to me. so, I will not knock at the door to be turned away. I have decided. I will take my precious jar, the one thing that I have, and enter secretly, quietly, unnoticed. My one thing I will give to Him, pouring out the precious oil from the jar, as my act of love. I am nothing. So, I entered the room secretly, hiding my face and settled at the feet of the prophet, the One on whom all my hopes were laid as He reclined at table. My heart was bursting with emotion- my overwhelming need, my longing for forgiveness and relief, my love and devotion for the one who could turn my life around. And so, my scarf falls away and as my tears fall freely, I wash His feet, dry them with my hair and pour out the precious perfume on His feet. The room is filled with the perfume but also the angry silence of the onlookers and the Pharisee. He says nothing. He does nothing. They are all stunned by the sight before them.

The horrified silence is broken by the gentle words of the teacher Himself. He spoke to the Pharisee. "Simon, I have something to say to you". A story of forgiveness followed, a story of two debtors, one who owed little and one who owed a great deal. Both were relieved of their debt and released. Then a gentle rebuke to the Pharisee. "You gave me no warm greeting, water for my feet, or oil for my head and yet this woman has not failed to wash and kiss my feet and anoint them with oil." He knew me. He had seen my need and my love, my silent pleading and repentance, and gave His forgiveness and His peace. I will remember His words until my dying day. "Your sins are forgiven." "Your faith has saved you, go in peace." Those words are written on my heart.

My precious alabaster jar with its perfume is gone- but so is my sin.

The Pharisee had seen my lifestyle, my notoriety and my many sins. He had not seen me. The teacher had seen my heart, my sorrow, my desperate need for change, and my longing for a new way of love. He had found me. I left that place in peace.

Pray

Lord, I am in that place again. Thank you that on the cross you cried out, "It is finished." I ask for your forgiveness again. I can live in your grace.

A frantic search: Luke 2 v 41-45

I cannot forget that dreadful time. How can you lose a child? My mind still reels from the memory of those days, and I feel again that dreadful mix of emotions- guilt, horror, despair, anger, frustration, desperate anxiety, trauma, and the nagging question-how could he do that to me, to us. How could I do that to him? How do you lose a child? But that time was a turning point for me.

We had been making the journey for as long as I can remember. It was our twelfth year of journeying to Jerusalem for Passover. I am an old hand at the preparation, packing and organising for the trip. The preparation starts well before we even get to Festival. It is getting easier now as the children are a little older. It was so hard when I had a baby to manage. Can you imagine being away from home for a two-week trip? We travel twenty miles each day before stopping to camp overnight and as Jerusalem is sixty miles from Nazareth, the journey alone takes three or four days before we reach the city. The last part of the journey is the hardest as we climb the hills towards Jerusalem. Then the festival celebrations follow, before the arduous journey back again. We are weary and longing for home by the time we have finished. Every year I worry about the cost of such a journey and whether we need to do this every year. But we are faithful and loyal to the Jewish requirements.

But that year's Passover journey will be etched in my mind forever! We had had made our journey and had celebrated Passover, enjoying time with family, friends, and the acquaintances with whom we had travelled over so many years. Jesus and the other children had played happily along the route there and new friends had been made. On our return journey we were preoccupied with the packing and moving and as we travelled from the city, had not noticed that the boy was not with us. We imagined that he was with one of our other family groups or with friends travelling in our large caravan as we made our way back to Nazareth. But by the end of that first day of travel I could not find my child. How does a mother do that? How do you overlook your child in the busyness and activity of a journey? Our frantic search was futile and so we returned to Jerusalem. Another desperate day of travel and painful worry. By now two days had gone. I could not sleep or eat. By the third day we were in Jerusalem and searching all the places that were familiar to us and where a child may go. Then at last we found him- and it was not where we expected him to be.

He was sitting in the Temple with the scholars and teachers, asking questions and joining their discussions. I was joyful, relieved, and angry all at the same time. "Why have you done this to us? Your father and I have been out of our minds looking for you" were my first words. I was frantic with worry. His reply was short and simple. "Didn't you know that I must be in My Father's house?" Then I began to see more clearly. Through my tears of relief, I began to see the Man and not the child. I reached back into the secret stores of my mind for the words of promise for the child- my child, but not just my child. I held these things dearly, deep within myself. These thoughts were my secret treasure store of truths that I had sadly overlooked in the ordinariness and routine of life. We returned quietly, occasionally silently, to Nazareth. I watched my child mature, grow strong in body and spirit, being blessed by God, and admired by those who knew Him.

In the child I now had seen the man, the Son of Man, the promised teacher, and saviour, the one that we were hoping for.

Thoughts

In the routine, the busyness, the ordinary, the stuff of daily life, and the demands we can lose sight of Jesus. We lose Him. He was there and then He was not. Maybe we have been walking this way for years and we have failed to turn and look for Him while we keep on walking.

A costly Compassion: The Good Samaritan
Luke 10

Perhaps I was foolish for being a solitary traveller on that mountain road, but my journey was urgent. The attack, when it happened was brutal, shocking and I lost everything that I had including my clothing. I was left for dead with no means of identification, little chance of discovery or help. Although barely conscious I was aware of two people who had passed on the road without stopping. I was frightened for my life, fearing that it would end here, battered, abandoned and alone. But then my rescue came and from someone who would be regarded as my enemy, the 'other', the outcast, the infidel, the foreigner and the despised one. It was life-saving compassion. He had no regard for my 'otherness', my tribe, status, religious connection, or observance. He dealt with my wounds and made plans for my care. The Injured

When I saw the tangled mess of flesh and blood how could I turn away and not stop to help? Here was a desperate man struggling with injuries that could cause his death. His identity, status, racial group became irrelevant. At that point, he became my neighbour, my family, my brother- a relationship not defined by any normal boundaries - but by his sheer need. I had the means to help him. The risk to my own life on that road was hopefully small. I knew the road, the Inn, and I had the means to help. The Inn keeper knew that I am a man of my word and that I would be good for the money when I next returned. My heart stirred and action followed. The Rescuer

Thoughts

The Samaritan offered a costly compassion. He could have acted out of fear and so taken no action but to move along, considering his own safety. But he did not act out of fear. He acted out of compassion for 'the other'. It was scary, involved physical effort and energy, was financially costly, took initiative, planning, promises and assurances.

"Who is my neighbour?" My neighbour may be one to whom I would least expect to be a neighbour. Jesus changed the question round completely to "what does a neighbour do?" Jesus showed a very clear picture of what a neighbour does. His final words are "Go and do likewise" further reinforcing the message "Do this and you will live". May we never act out of fear but always out of love.

When Jesus saw the crowds, he had compassion for them, because they were harassed and helpless, like sheep without a shepherd. Matthew 9 v 36

Martha and Lazarus: I am the resurrection

I cannot begin to describe the range of conditions and emotions that I experienced- exhaustion, despair, grief, loss, confusion, anger, shock, joy, and elation. Our brother had died and been restored to us. How can I explain such an event?

We had nursed our brother for many days and had sent word to Jesus asking Him to come to us quickly. Every day that had passed we had hoped that Jesus would come. When death finally came to our home, we were overwhelmed with grief. It was with very heavy hearts that the burial went ahead without our dear friend Jesus and his followers. Then I received word that Jesus was on His way to Bethany and so leaving my sister with the gathered mourners at home, I hurriedly went out to the edge of the village to meet with Jesus. In my distress, words burst from my mouth- "My Lord, if only you had come sooner, my brother would not have died." The words sounded accusatory, hostile almost with an element of blame. The weariness of the whole period of mourning had taken its toll on me and so my words were perhaps harsh. Checking the tone of my words I added "but I know that if you ask God for anything, he will do it for you." What was I saying? What was I hoping for?

His gentle reply followed. "Your brother will rise and live." My hope was only of resurrection on the final resurrection day, an event that was sometime in the future and yet the impact of His words seemed to point to something different. "Martha", Jesus said, "You don't have to wait until then. I am the Resurrection, and I am Life Eternal. Anyone who clings to me in faith, even though he dies, will live forever. And the one who lives by believing in me will never die. Do you believe this?" My words flowed quickly and easily. "Yes, Lord," I replied, "I believe that you are the Messiah, the Son of God, who is to come into the world." In that moment I knew that all would be well.

I hurriedly returned to Bethany, to our house of grief, mourning and loss, but with a new sense of expectation and hope. I quietly and discretely called for my sister to follow me, as the Teacher had arrived at the edge of the village and was calling for her. In her haste and eagerness, she aroused the interest and concern of the gathered mourners and comforters, who immediately followed us, thinking that we were heading for the tomb. On reaching Jesus, our common grief touched our friend deeply as we wept at our shared loss. Together we journeyed to the tomb, a simple cave with a stone laid across the entrance. There were those in the group who followed who muttered and questioned the Teacher's care and commitment to our family. "Could not He who opened the eyes of the blind man have kept this man from dying?"

Then His words stunned and shocked. "Take away the stone from the tomb". I hoped to intervene, quietly stating the obvious to our loving friend, saying that any odour from the tom would be distressing. But He was in control, His words powerful, announcing that we would see the glory of God in this moment, His manner firm yet gentle. He prayed to His Father in heaven and then called out to our brother, "Lazarus, come out!" All eyes were on that cave entrance as Lazarus stumbled and shuffled out of his cold tomb. Then in gentle tones Jesus instructed the men to remove the strips of linen cloth and grave clothes and to set him free. And now Lazarus was truly free. We had seen it with our own eyes.

I cannot tell you of the emotions that I went through in those moments. Tears flowed freely- tears of confusion, release, joy- a range of feelings for which there are no words. Many of our friends and fellow mourners now came to believe in Jesus, the healer, the Teacher, the Messiah.

I am Martha- a single woman from an insignificant village on the outskirts of Jerusalem and yet it was to me that Jesus declared those profound words that I can never forget. "I am the resurrection and the life." I am Martha, the village girl, the practical, the organized, the hard worker, the girl at home, and yet from me Jesus had drawn from deep within my soul, words of faith and trust, and an understanding of true resurrection.

Resurrection is not an event in some future time, but resurrection is a Person.

Jesus said to her, "I am the resurrection and the life. Those who believe in me will live, even though they die; and those who live and believe in me will never die."

Pray

When you are at your lowest point, Jesus is not absent. He sees, He knows, and He will come. When you need His presence the most, He will come, with perfect timing, bringing His peace and words of grace. When all seems to be lost, and without life, He will bring His life.

I can see clearly: Bartimaeus

Bartimaeus of Jericho

I live in Jericho. I spend my days sitting by the roadside, unable to work or provide for myself. It is lonely by the roadside, but I have learned to listen carefully, to read the mood of passers-by and to know if they will help or ignore the blind man begging at their feet. I have learned to listen to the crowds, to the children with their games, to the mothers scolding or singing to their children. I have also heard tales of the Teacher Jesus, the Jesus of Nazareth who people called the son of David and who they hope will be the One to save Israel.

I will never forget the day it happened. On that day there would be a breakthrough in my life that I could never have thought possible. Let me tell you how it happened. I was begging by the roadside as usual when I heard the noise of a very large crowd. Someone shouted across to me that it was Jesus of Nazareth and His followers on their way out of the city. So, I started to shout out for help. "Son of David, have mercy on me!" I got louder and louder. "Son of David, have mercy on me!" The crowd tried to shut me up. They told me to stop, to leave the roadside. They would have kicked me into silence if they could have. But I shouted even more and called out even more loudly. I would not be silenced. I would not be rebuked or held back.

He had such a gentle voice. I heard Him say "Call him." He had heard my cries and called for me. I was helped up to my feet and throwing off my cloak I was directed into the presence of Jesus. "What do you want me to do for you?" He asked. My words were brief. "Rabbi, I want to see." He simply said, "Go, your faith has saved you."

It was instant, dramatic, life changing. I saw the crowd. I saw the face of Jesus, the Teacher, the One who had healed me and at that moment I made the decision to leave everything and to follow Him.

The man of Bethsaida

I live in Bethsaida. One thing that you should know about me is that I am blind and so I depend on others to lead and to help. One day, news spread in the town, with great excitement, that Jesus, the healer was travelling through with His disciples. He had been this way before and so His reputation had gone before Him. The news was now out there and could not be silenced. My friends had heard of this Jesus and were determined to get me to Him. "Surely He will heal you" they said, "as He has healed others". So, they almost dragged me out of my home, leading me hurriedly to the Healer. They brought me before Him and pleaded with Him, begged Him, urging Him to consider my situation and to show mercy and to heal. What happened next was strange beyond words.

The Healer gently took hold of my arm and carefully led me out of the town to a quiet place, away from prying eyes. I am used to this kind of help, but His hand, His touch was different- gentle, sensitive, loving. What happened next was even stranger, almost bizarre and totally unexpected- a shock really. I was aware of Him spitting on my eyes and gently touching them. Then He asked me "do you see anything?" Things at first seemed to be blurred, unclear, hazy and indistinct. Once again, He touched my eyes and as I looked intently into the far distance I could see clearly, perfectly and the realization of what had just happened began to dawn on me. I could see men. I could see clearly. And I could see Jesus. But the strangeness continued as He told me not to go straight back to town. "Do not enter the village," He said. I believe that He did not want me to immediately broadcast what had just happened to me. But surely within days the news would spread? How could I keep this quiet?

Thoughts

It was after this event that Jesus took His disciples to one side and asked them some very significant and searching questions. "Who do people say I am?" and then "Who do you say I am?" Jesus. I believe that He was asking them to deeply consider what kind of Christ they thought Him to be. What was their understanding of Jesus as Saviour or Messiah, and could they understand the nature of the suffering that He would encounter?

Often, I lose sight of Jesus. I don't have my eyes fixed on Him. Quite often my vision is blurred, out of focus or just short sighted. Like the man of Bethsaida, I need to look intently, carefully and to keep looking. I need to see Jesus for who He is and to keep Him in my sights. The Message version puts it this way. "The man looked hard and realized that he had recovered perfect sight, saw everything in bright, twenty-twenty focus". v 26

May we have Jesus in twenty-twenty focus and follow Him.

The Faith of the Centurion: Luke 7 v 1-10

There are things about me that you need to know. I am a Gentile, but a God fearer, and sympathetic to the Jewish faith and nation. I have many friends who are Jews and being of significant wealth, I helped to finance the building of the synagogue here in Capernaum. I am a centurion at the Capernaum Roman garrison being responsible for about a hundred Roman troops stationed here. I realize that to many, I represent enemy occupation, but I have tried to be humane and sensitive to a horrendous situation. I believe that I have secured the favour of the local people. I am a person in authority, but I am also a person under the authority and rule of others. I understand authority, leadership, and the chain of command. I understand the power of commands and orders and I can recognize such authority in others.

I have a loyal squad and value those who work for me and under me. Sadly, one of my special servants, someone I value highly, became seriously ill, to the point of death. I heard that a Jesus of Nazareth, a Jew, and His followers had just entered Capernaum. I had heard many things about this teacher and recognized His growing power and authority, even to heal. He seemed to be a person with the power of words, and authority over sickness. By reputation He was a godly man under the authority of God Himself. I was anxious that He should not feel concerned about a request from a Gentile Officer at an army garrison and so, I sent some Jewish elders, to speak on my behalf, with the request that He might come to heal my servant.

But as I considered our different positions in society- Gentile and Jew, Army Captain and charismatic teacher and healer, yet both with authority to issue a clear command and the word would be done, I then sent a few faithful friends to the Teacher with the following message. "Lord, I do not consider myself worthy to come to you myself, or for you to enter my house, so I simply ask that you just say the word, and my servant will be healed. Do not trouble yourself to come-just say the word."

A short while later, as I checked on my servant, to my delight and amazement, I discovered that he was well and was anxious to go about his duties once again. As my friends and the Jewish elders returned to my home, they reported their conversations with Jesus, the Teacher. Jesus had commended me, a gentile, a centurion, an enemy of the Jewish nation, for my faith in Him and because of my faith in Him, my servant was healed.

His friends had said to Jesus, "He is worthy." The centurion himself said, "I am not worthy." "I am-not worthy to come to you or for you to come to my house" but he recognized One who was worthy.

Then I looked, and I heard around the throne and the living creatures and the elders the voice of many angels, numbering myriads of myriads and thousands of thousands, saying with a loud voice, "Worthy is the Lamb who was slain, to receive power and wealth and wisdom and might and honour and glory and blessing!" Revelation 5 v 12

Jairus: Jesus is never too late

I am one of the rulers in the Capernaum synagogue, well known, a person of status, and position with responsibilities and power, but I am also a father, in anguish, consumed by grief, misery, distress and worry. My only child, my little girl of only twelve years, so desperately ill, is now seemingly at the point of death. I have heard that this Jesus, the Nazarene, the One that the Pharisees and religious groups say that we should shun, has been doing amazing things and has even healed some. So, what am I to do? I am desperate, my heart is breaking, I have exhausted all other means of help and I will do anything to save my child. It was, in the end, an easy thing to do. The Jesus Teacher was surrounded by the crowd. People were crushing in from all sides, pressing in, this mass of human need surrounding, encircling, enclosing Him and almost swallowing Him up. It was so clear as to who He was. There was no mistake. I pushed a path through the crowd, some moving to let me pass, recognizing me, others had no such manners and pressed in more closely, some even blocking my way, but I had to reach my only source of hope.

My colleagues would be shocked to know and hear of what I did next. But I had no concern now for my reputation or standing at the synagogue, my pride or position in the community. I approached and fell at His feet, pleading with Him to come with me to my house and to lay His hands on my little daughter. The situation was urgent, critical, time was of the essence, there could be no delay or attempt to find a new solution. As soon as His gaze turned to me, and He saw my need, my longing, I could sense His gentle strength and knew that He would respond. But now the crowd grew even larger, curious, moving in still closer to hear my words. Then, the unexpected interruption happened. He stopped abruptly, aware of another individual need in the crowd. A woman had reached out to Him for healing- another desperate, anguished soul. But please, oh please do not delay further, how long will this take, I cannot bear this delay, this setback that will hold up any chance of us getting to my daughter. But the Teacher was unhurried, calm, firmly but gently in control of all that was happening. He called the woman, 'daughter', commended her faith and trust in Him, confirmed her healing and invited her to go home in peace. He called her 'daughter'. It should have given me hope and reassurance, but I was more distressed and agitated. And then something traumatic happened. Some people from my house arrived with the crushing and devastating news. "Your daughter is dead. Do not trouble the teacher anymore." It was abrupt, stark, shocking. I nearly fell to my knees again. This was too much to bear. Had the Teacher come straight away could she have been saved?

My mind was reeling. I felt physical pain and grief. I had reached the end. But the Teacher spoke gently, lovingly and with no sense of hurry or urgency, simply said, "Do not be afraid, only believe and she will be healed." Three short phrases. I will remember those words for the rest of my life. As I think back to those words now, I think, for what or who or how was I supposed to believe? But I was asked to believe. His words meant that there is nothing to be afraid of. Be calm. Hold on to me for this. Count on me. Be assured. I had no energy to do anything else. From leading Him, I was now following Him to the door of my home.

We were met by such a commotion and din. People were wailing and crying. The sound of their lamenting was a dreadful painful sound to the ears and the heart. The wailing soon turned to derision and scorn as Jesus stated that the girl was only sleeping. But with calm authority he disbanded the family mourners and crowd and a small group of us entered the room to be faced with the bed on which my daughter was laid.

Jesus took her hand in His and with a word of gentleness and love, with life giving power and authority, He just said, "little girl, get up." And she did. It was as if she had just been asleep and was now woken by a loving voice. We were floored- quite literally! How can you go from desperate grief and loss to sudden elation and joy in a matter of seconds?

Her life was restored. My life was restored. How can I explain what has just happened? But Jesus told us to say nothing. I do not have the words to explain. Where would I begin?

Jesus was not delayed. He was not late. The time element did not matter to Him. He had plenty of time. It would all be done in His good time.

Thoughts

There are times when we are in distress, confused, struggling with a problem and we have prayed and yet our prayers have hit the ceiling. We long for God to intervene and yet there is delay, protracted delay and waiting. Nothing changes. But our time scale is not the same as His. In His wisdom, He will act when the time is right. Can we trust His timing? Can we be patient while we wait? In the Gospel accounts there were other individuals who felt that Jesus had come too late. But Jesus had a loving purpose.

Wait and see what He will do.

Then Martha said to Jesus, "Lord, if You had been here, my brother would not have died.

When Mary came [to the place] where Jesus was and saw Him, she fell at His feet, saying to Him, "Lord, if You had been here, my brother would not have died.

I waited patiently for the Lord; he inclined to me and heard my cry.
He drew me up from the desolate pit, out of the miry bog,
and set my feet upon a rock, making my steps secure.
He put a new song in my mouth, a song of praise to our God.
Many will see and fear, and put their trust in the Lord. Psalm 27

Let us then fearlessly and confidently and boldly draw near to the throne of grace (the throne of God's unmerited favour to us sinners), that we may receive mercy [for our failures] and find grace to help in good time for every need [appropriate help and well-timed help, coming just when we need it]. Hebrews 4 v 16

Wait for the Lord; be strong, and let your heart take courage; yea, wait for the Lord! Psalm 40

The Samaritan woman

Some years ago, I spent a short time in Herat, Afghanistan, teaching at an International School and I had to adopt certain important cultural sensitivities. As a woman, I had to dress with my head, hair, neck, wrist, and ankles always covered and in modest Afghan dress. I had to avert my eyes if men approached, I would never speak to a man in public and always I sat with and joined a group of women. Women would always sit with the women in a different room to the men. I had to walk in front of or behind the house security guard by a suitable distance when we were walking on the road. He did not wish to be seen with a westerner. This was how things were done.

The encounter between Jesus and the Samaritan woman is one that never should have taken place if normal protocols had been followed. The woman was avoiding any contact with others by collecting water at noon and Jewish men would have avoided any association with this foreign woman. She would have turned away and returned later avoiding even eye contact with the stranger. However, Jesus goes against all the rules and not only remains seated at the well but speaks to her and goes further by making a request of her.

Jesus created an opening, recognizing her deep needs. He opens a safe space for her. As Jesus asks His probing questions, He creates the potential for a new perspective. His approach is gentle. His questioning sensitive and insightful. He challenges her about her life choices, but He does not condemn or damage her self-esteem, so that later she can say "He told me everything that I've ever done." He sees that she is searching for a spiritual understanding and begins to help her focus. She knows that someone called Messiah is coming. Catching the depth of her understanding, searching, and longing, Jesus leads her forward and openly declares to her who He is.

Jesus is a model of empathy, insight, and compassion. His understanding and perception of her, deep and focussed. His own needs for food, rest and resourcing are laid aside. He is available to help to meet her needs. The conversation with Jesus gave the woman a testimony to share with others and leading from that, many people in the town came to believe in Him. "Many of the Samaritans from that town believed in him because of the woman's testimony."

In our conversations, we may be listening to someone who is sharing their story. We do not know the experience, trials, circumstances, and personal situations behind their mask. We need this same sensitivity and compassion.

But the Lord said to Samuel, The Lord does not look at the things people look at. People look at the outward appearance, but the Lord looks at the heart. 1 Samuel 16 v 7 NIV

Pray

For girls and women, in predominantly Muslim countries, where they are vulnerable, unable to play a role in their societies, and may often abused and persecuted. For places and circumstances where there is persecution of Christians and their communities. For those in our society who feel that they have no voice. As we speak with each other, may we hear the unspoken words and needs. May our testimony and words attract others and share your good news.

The voice of a bystander: John 8 v 1-11

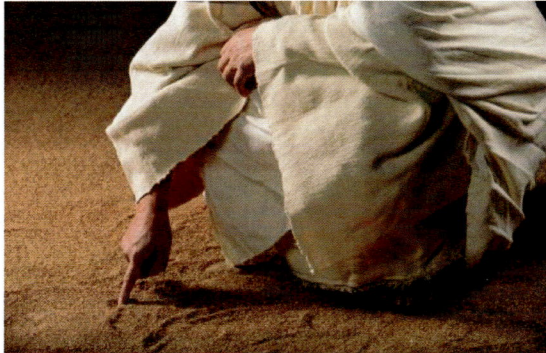

It was Tabernacles, and such a fun time to be at the temple- a celebration of harvest and joy, thankfulness, promises, a time of remembering, sharing and family togetherness. Today was so special as there was a new young teacher and such a large crowd to hear Him. His ideas were so fresh, so gentle, so different and the claims that He was making-well, they would get Him into trouble! I could already see some harsh and angry faces among the temple leaders. But for most of us, the common people, we were curious. We were all whispering about Him, though we dared not speak out or be overheard. I heard some people say that He was a prophet or even the Messiah. Some whispered that they had seen Him perform a miracle. But we kept quiet out of fear of the Pharisees.

Then something alarming, horrifying, happened. Some teachers of the Law of Moses and a group of Pharisees brought in a woman and made her stand before everyone in the very centre of the Temple Court, right in front of the Teacher. The poor creature was dishevelled, frightened, humiliated and exposed to everyone's judgement and public display. They announced her crime to all present and demanded a judgement from the Teacher. Then the strangest of things happened. The angry mood quietened, the crowd became silent and expectant, and the Teacher, ignoring their questions, simply bent down to the ground and began to draw or write with his finger in the sand beneath His feet. I tried to push forward to see what the words might be. I tried to see what He was writing. How strange was this! The loaded questions from the Leaders kept coming, forcefully, angrily. But He was unperturbed, calm, with an air of quiet authority as He stood up and looking directly at them, invited those without sin to be the first to stone her. Then the strangeness continued as He bent down to the ground again and started to write. I hardly dare tell you what happened next. Without a word, the leaders and Pharisees began to skulk away and walk into the crowd. One by one they went. Not a word was said. That was some retreat! They had failed to get Jesus to fall into their trap. Everyone was in a stunned silence.

The poor woman was left alone, with her shame and condemnation, in front of the Teacher. Then the Teacher straightened up and looked at her - deep into her eyes. A simple question followed." Has no one condemned you?" In her trembling voice, she answered "no one, Sir." "Then neither do I condemn you but go and sin no more." She no longer had to fear those who were threatening her life. The Teacher was gentle, respectful. His words were words of grace as He gave her a new direction-, a turning point.

I'd give a month's wages to know what He wrote on the ground. Was He just gathering His thoughts? Was He silently speaking to His God? Was He writing the names of God - *The Lord our righteousness, the Lord who sanctifies, the Lord who heals?* We will never know.

The woman gathered her few tattered garments closely to her and walked out of the temple court. I never saw or heard of her again.

There is therefore now no condemnation for those who are in Christ Jesus. For the law of the Spirit of life in Christ Jesus has set me free from the law of sin and death. Romans 8 v 1-2

The Pharisees were using this woman as a tool, a non-person, an object lesson as they attempted to trap Jesus. Jesus saw her through eyes of love, and offered her grace, mercy and a turning point for her life.

Jesus, thou art all compassion, pure unbounded love thou art.
Visit us with thy salvation, enter every trembling heart.
Come, almighty to deliver, let us all thy grace receive.
Suddenly return, and never, never more thy temples leave.
Charles Wesley

A single touch

In Mark 5 v 24-34 we read the account of a woman who had suffered from a chronic illness for 12 years and who was hopeful of meeting Jesus secretly, but in plain sight.

She had endured years of misery, shame, isolation, and financial loss. The nature of her illness meant that she was treated as an outcast and unclean. She was fearful of any social interaction and so would have no independence or ability to move out of her home freely She was truly in a state of permanent lockdown. Her medical appointments and treatments meant that both her energy and money ebbed away, yet there was no relief or improvement- in fact her condition became worse. She was despairing, defeated and despondent. She was a prisoner to her illness with little prospect of hope or healing. And then she heard of Jesus. She may have heard Jairus's request to heal his twelve-year-old, daughter. If Jesus was willing to go with this desperate father, then surely there was hope for his child and now also for her. She dared to believe. "If I just touch His clothing, I will be healed". She was determined to go to Jesus for healing. But she could not do this openly. By this time, a huge crowd had gathered around Jesus pressing in from every side. She came in fear and trembling, hiding her identity. She could not risk being seen and so she came behind him secretly, slipping in under the cover of the jostling crowd and reached out to touch his outer robe. She dared to believe that this one single touch would bring her the healing that she was so desperate for.

As soon as she touched the cloth, she knew that she had been healed. There was no doubt in her mind and in her body. How could she control the emotions and thoughts suddenly flooding through her mind? And now she hoped to steal away quietly. She had come secretly but she could not leave secretly. His voice rang out asking "Who touched me?" His searching gaze swept across the crowds looking at the faces of those around him to see who had done this. Would she dare to identify herself? In great fear, perhaps more of the crowd than her Healer, she raised her head and returned to fall at his feet, once again in fear and trembling and recounted her story-the whole crowd listening to her account.

Jesus desired her to go in peace, not with fear, secrecy, and uncertainty. His purpose was one of love for her. The whole crowd would see and hear her. They would hear Jesus call her "daughter". They would hear Jesus commend her faith "your faith has healed you". and His blessing to "go in peace". No longer would she need to hide away like the leper that she once felt that she was. She was free of shame and sickness and free to hold her head up in the crowd. "Be freed from your suffering". She would now be free in so many ways.

Praise the Lord for it is good to sing praise to our God.
For He is gracious, and a song of praise is seemly.
The Lord builds up Jerusalem, He gathers the outcasts of Israel.
He heals the broken hearted and binds up their wounds.
Psalm 147 v 2

PRAY

I bind unto myself today the power of God to hold and lead.
His eye to watch, His might to stay. His ear to hearken to my need.
The wisdom of my God to teach. His hand to guide, His shield to ward.
The word of God to give me speech, His heavenly host to be my guard.
From the Hymn of St Patrick

LESSONS IN THE DESERT

Lessons in the desert:
Abram, A travelogue - Into the unknown

It was by faith that Abraham obeyed the summons to go out to a place which he would eventually possess, and he set out in complete ignorance of his destination. It was faith that kept him journeying like a foreigner through the land of promise, with no more home than the tents which he shared with Isaac and Jacob, co-heirs with him of the promise. Hebrews 11

Images from the Atacama Desert, Chile

Abram, at the age of 75, was called by God to leave Haran, a place of security and stability, and to step out into an uncharted, unknown land, but a promised land, even though that land was already occupied. God had promised Abram a land, a blessing and a nation that would come from Abram and Sarai. Believing God's promises, Abram became a tent dweller travelling south, with no permanent base or land of his own, and so the chapters in Genesis read a little bit like his travelogue. Abram travelled to Sychar, then on to Bethel and his journey with family and flocks would take him hundreds of miles from his first home in Ur of the Chaldeans, now Iraq.

While trusting God and His promises, with the occurrence of a devastating famine in this parched, inhospitable land, Abram feared that he would not be able to provide for his family and livestock, and so travelled to the safety of Egypt. This decision to go south into Egypt was a very human, rational, understandable, and life-saving decision, to escape famine. But God had called Abram to a promised land and not to Egypt. In alarming, and worrying circumstances, God's promise still held true. Even though Egypt would prove to be a place of trouble, trauma and setback for Abram and Sarai, and there would be challenging consequences in connection with Hagar, the Egyptian handmaid that they took with them, God continued to bless and protect them, bringing them out to a better place, with lessons learned about faith and trust. God's long-term plan for Abram, Sarai and their descendants, no human error or weakness could ultimately disrupt.

Leaving Egypt, Abram travelled across the Negev Desert, the largest area of desert in Israel, returning to Bethel. It was here that Abram and Lot parted company. This was a difficult separation. Abram gave first choice of the land to Lot, Lot choosing the fertile plains of the River Jordan, leaving Abram with the area around Hebron. From a human perspective, Abram's land would seem to be second best and far from ideal. But God here renewed His promises to Abram and Abram built his altar of thankfulness. God again promised that all the land that Abram could see would be his, and that his descendants would be like the dust of the desert, so vast a number that they could not be counted. Abram's descendants would be as numerous as the stars-that were so clearly visible in the desert night sky.

Abram and his descendants would not take ownership of the land for more than 400 years and only after the Israelites had escaped captivity in Egypt. Abram himself would only ever own a small piece of land near Hebron that he purchased for a burial ground. Yet Abraham, the 'Father of Nations', would be known as one of the great heroes of faith. Abram had no road map for where he was going and the timing of it, but he stepped out in faith- one step at a time.

Pray

Father God, you see me. You have seen me from the beginning. You have a roadmap for me. Help me to trust you- but with one step at a time. When I feel that I have no idea where I am going or what I am doing, you will be with me. Help me to see the next little step and not worry about the big journey. Your desire to bless me will always win out even when I mess up or take a wrong turn. You can handle my mistakes and the consequences of them. What I might think of as second best, you can turn into a crowning glory. You are the God of reversals. Help me to be patient in waiting for your goodness and not to think that I can solve things by myself. Your purpose and timing are better than mine.

I will instruct you and teach you in the way you should go; I will counsel you with my eye upon you. Psalm 32 v 8

Lessons in the desert: Moses

When the going gets tough, the tough get….. We all go through tough times. We often find ourselves in situations that are uncomfortable, uncertain, and insecure, but God wants to teach us important lessons as He leads us through a shaping process. Process is key. Lessons of trust and faith are not learned instantly. We learn lessons of faith and trust over time and often through unsettling experiences. It is a long process. God takes His time, to bring us from the tough place into something better. This was the case for the Israelites and Moses.

The area of Goshen, a huge region of ancient Egypt, east of the Nile delta, had been granted to Joseph, Jacob, and their descendants by the Pharoah, and inhabited by the Israelites until the Exodus and their escape. It was a place of separation from Egyptian culture, and a place of comfort and plenty, a land suitable for crops and livestock, granted to them by the favour of Pharoah. It was in Goshen, that the people had settled for over 400 years but had also endured years of slavery.

But when the children of Israel were dramatically delivered from Egypt, God was going to take them across the Sinai Peninsula, a desert area of vast size, into the wilderness and there His lessons in trust would begin.

When Pharoah saw that the escaping Israelites were heading into the wilderness he surely felt confident that he could stop them in their tracks. Pharoah believed "they are entangled in the land - the wilderness has shut them in". In his mind, the desert and the wilderness would be the end of the escaping Israelites and they would be recaptured and brought back to Egypt. But at the Red Sea, God delivered them in a dramatic way and continued to guide them by the cloud by day and the pillar of fire by night.

The Israelites were then taken to the wilderness, to Shur, a journey of three days and thirty-three miles. As they found no water there, at this point, the murmuring and complaining began. They continued to Marah where again their need for water was now urgent, but the water there was bitter and undrinkable. By this time, the people were complaining about Moses himself and pleading, "what shall we drink?" When Moses cried to the Lord, the Lord showed him how to turn the water sweet and it was here at Marah, that the Lord "proved them".

Travelling on to Elim, the hungry people again complained and murmured. God again intervened and provided quail in the evening and manna in the morning-enough food for each day's needs- no more and no less.

At Rephidim, the trouble and disquiet started again, as again, there was no water to be found.

Therefore, the people quarrelled with Moses and said, "Give us water to drink." And Moses said to them, "Why do you quarrel with me? Why do you test the Lord?" But the people thirsted there for water, and the people grumbled against Moses and said, "Why did you bring us up out of Egypt, to kill us and our children and our livestock with thirst?" Exodus 17

It was at Mount Horeb that Moses struck the rock and the waters flowed to satisfy the thirst of the people and their livestock. At each point in the journey to the Promised land, this new beginning, new challenges appeared for the Israelites, their hearts failed them, and they looked back to what they once had, but God always made new provision. God was faithful to his promises. God is always faithful.

"Remember not the former things, nor consider the things of old.
Behold, I am doing a new thing; now it springs forth, do you not
perceive it? I will make a way in the wilderness and rivers in the desert.
The wild beasts will honour me, the jackals and the ostriches,
for I give water in the wilderness, rivers in the desert,
to give drink to my chosen people,
the people whom I formed for myself

that they might declare my praise.   Isaiah 43 v 18-21

The desert is beautiful. What makes the desert beautiful is that somewhere it hides a well.

Then, on the last day, the climax of the festival, Jesus stood up and cried out, "If any man is thirsty, he can come to me and drink! The man who believes in me, as the scripture says, will have rivers of living water flowing from his inmost heart." (Here he was speaking about the Spirit which those who believe in him would receive. John 7 v 37

Pray

Father God, I like my comfortable place, the familiar, the safe, the secure. I don't like the unknown, the shifting sand, the stepping out into a strange and uncertain future. When things are hard, I complain and murmur and doubt and accuse and find fault. I want to go back to the safe space.

Help me to trust you and your plan for my life. The route that you have planned is a good one, a perfect one with precious lessons for me to learn. But I am impatient. I want to arrive quickly. Help me to stick with the journey and not look back.

I am parched and dry. Those around me in family, community, church, and world are thirsty for something real, for living water. You have promised water in the dry and wilderness places. You are faithful.

Lessons in the Desert: Elijah

Some years ago, my husband and I went to the Atacama Desert in Chile. Not your usual holiday destination of course, but this was a working trip for Phil to Santiago, Chile, and I had the opportunity to travel with him. We spent several days in the desert, walking the mountains, (2,250 meters above sea level), Rainbow Valley and the Valle de La Luna, where the moon landings were trialled, enjoying the hot springs in the desert, observing the night sky, the sunsets, the extinct volcanoes, and enduring the vast differences in temperatures between night and day. It was a very memorable trip. Now, if you tell someone that you were to holiday in the desert, they might think that you were slightly crazy. But the desert is beautiful and magical. The colours of the rocks, earth and sand dunes are breath taking. It can be a place of stillness.

Many individuals in the Bible accounts had key times when they experienced life in the desert. I think of Abraham, Moses, Elijah and of course Jesus himself. Times when they were isolated or wandering in these arid, bare, wilderness places- times which dramatically shaped and transformed their lives.

In 1 Kings we read that Elijah spent several periods in the desert or wilderness. He had challenged the evil King Ahab and his Queen Jezebel about their Baal worship. Consequently, God sent drought and famine for a period of years. God instructed Elijah to go to the Brook Cherith in the wilderness where he would be fed by the ravens. His desert stay was a place of rescue, hiding, safety, protection, and stillness. A place of quiet and hiddenness.

God then sent Elijah to Zarephath where he, the woman and her son would be cared for and miraculously provided for, as protection from the intense three-year drought and famine. The desert was his place of refuge, rest, and recovery and provision. God had pressed the pause button for Elijah.

After Elijah returned to challenge King Ahab and Elijah's victory over the prophets of Baal, Elijah once again ran to the desert in fear for his life. Elijah had been hounded, hunted, and was in a place of exhaustion, isolation, and depression. Sitting under his broom bush, the desert was a place of despair. But it became the place of grace, re-setting, reassurance, and recommissioning. Elijah was not left in solitary isolation. After declaring to God, "only I am left!" he is reassured that there are 7,000 men who have not worshipped Baal. He is not alone. And then the rains come. The drought is over.

The desert or wilderness can be beautiful, providing lessons that perhaps cannot be learned elsewhere. We should not be afraid of the desert. There is water in the desert.

"Forget the former things; do not dwell on the past. See, I am doing a new thing! Now it springs up; do you not perceive it?
I am making a way in the wilderness and streams in the wasteland. The wild animals honour me, the jackals and the owls, because I provide water in the wilderness and streams in the wasteland, to give drink to my people, my chosen, the people I formed for myself that they may proclaim my praise. Isaiah 43 v 18-21

Pray

I want to stop and be still. The world is a noisy and distracting place. Help me not to be alarmed by the lonely place, the dark place, the wilderness, and the desert. You are there with me. You will never leave me. What may feel like a wasteland, can be turned into a place of plenty. You will hide me and shelter me. You make a way in the desert places.

Lessons in the Desert:
David - Praise and Purpose in a dark Place

We all have highs and lows. When we have 'highs' we might feel ecstatic, joyful, even victorious. Then there will be those 'lows' when we are in danger of feeling 'down' or defeated. Over the many years that I have been a follower of Jesus I have aimed for emotional stability- being 'fixed', steady and calm, no matter what life has tried to throw at me, whether highs or lows. As I have been following David's journey, I can see that he was a person who was 'fixed' and 'centred' even though he had dramatic highs and lows. David knew that he could sing and praise his God even when things were dire and dangerous.

After David's victory over Goliath and the favour shown to him by the people and the royal household of Saul, it was clear that the Lord was with David, a young man who was held in high regard by all and greatly favoured. "David acted wisely in all his ways and succeeded, and the Lord was with him. When Saul saw how capable and successful David was, he stood in awe of him." 1 Samuel 18 v 14-15

However, things were to change dramatically as Saul grew fearful of David's growing popularity and in Saul's fits of jealousy, rage, and anger, he sought to end the young man's life. Saul became David's constant enemy. "Saul was afraid of David because the Lord was with him but had departed from Saul."

David fled for his life, escaping from Saul's hatred, repeated threats and attempts to end his life. Saul's continued hatred of David persisted so that David was forced to become a fugitive in hiding and resorted to desert, wilderness strongholds, caves, and isolated rocky hideouts to escape.

David fled to Naioth, then to the cave of Adullum in the hills of Judah, Mizpah in Moab, the wilderness of Ziph, the rock in the wilderness of Maon, later called 'the rock of escape', and to the 'rocks of the wild goats' in the wilderness of Engedi. David was constantly on the move as each time he camped and remained, Saul would discover his hiding place and send a murder squad to find him and end his life. The wilderness places became safe hiding places and places of refuge for David.

At the cave of Adullum David was joined by a motley collection of men who went out to him there. Now these men were not high-ranking soldiers or officials, men of good reputation and standing, but they were a rabble of discontents. "And everyone in distress or in debt or discontented gathered to him, and he became a commander over them. And there were with him about 400 men." David would turn this disaffected group into a powerful force to be reckoned with, under his leadership and the grace of his God.

Adullum means 'refuge' and this place, this safe hiding place, retreat, and temporary fortress would be the place where David and his supporters would be transformed into a mighty group of warriors under David, a wise, anointed leader- learning lessons in the desert. They were remote from power, wealth and other influence but were under the grace and mercy of their God. We learn that God strengthened David in that cave. Psalm 57 and Psalm 142

Saul continued to hunt down David, but David trusted in God's protection. On two occasions David had the opportunity to harm Saul and even to end Saul's life, but he refused to do so, remaining faithful and loyal to his king, who was still the Lord's anointed one. David knew that he had been selected and anointed by God and by Samuel as future king and leader of the kingdom, but for now, he would wait with patience for God's timing.

The words of Psalm 57 were written while David was still in the cave. It was while he was in the very centre of torment and distress, being hunted down, that he could write words of confidence, gratefulness, praise, and trust. God was his place of safety, his refuge, and his strength, at the very time of his trouble and distress.

O God, have pity, for I am trusting you! I will hide beneath the shadow of your wings until this storm is past. I will cry to the God of heaven who does such wonders for me. He will send down help from heaven to save me because of his love and his faithfulness. O God, my heart is quiet and confident. No wonder I can sing your praises! Rouse yourself, my soul! Arise, O harp and lyre! Let us greet the dawn with song! I will thank you publicly throughout the land. I will sing your praises among the nations. Your kindness and love are as vast as the heavens. Your faithfulness is higher than the skies. Psalm 57 v 7-10 TLB

O God my Strength! I will sing your praises, for you are my place of safety. My God is changeless in his love for me, and he will come and help me. But as for me, I will sing each morning about your power and mercy. For you have been my high tower of refuge, a place of safety in the day of my distress. O my Strength, to you I sing my praises; for you are my high tower of safety, my God of mercy. Psalm 59 v 9-10, v 16-17 This was written when Saul's men were sent to kill him.

O God, listen to me! Hear my prayer! For wherever I am, though far away at the ends of the earth, I will cry to you for help. When my heart is faint and overwhelmed, lead me to the mighty, towering Rock of safety. For you are my refuge, a high tower where my enemies can never reach me. I shall live forever in your tabernacle; oh, to be safe beneath the shelter of your wings! For you have heard my vows, O God, to praise you every day, and you have given me the blessings you reserve for those who reverence your name. Psalm 61 v 1-5

O God, my God! How I search for you! How I thirst for you in this parched and weary land where there is no water. How I long to find you! How I wish I could go into your sanctuary to see your strength and glory, for your love and kindness are better to me than life itself. How I praise you! Psalm 63 v 1-3

Pray

When I feel overwhelmed, burdened, or in a dark place, help me to look up. When I feel desperate, and feel that there is no-one at my side, help me to get close to you. When I feel powerless, weakened, reduced, immobilized, in a corner- help me to feel safe in you. When I am in the scary place and the walls are closing in, help me to stretch out a hand to you. I will trust you. I will sing. I will praise you.

Lessons in the desert:
Jonah - God is gracious and forgiving

I recently read the report and testimony of Michael Packard, aged 56, a commercial lobster diver, who was swallowed by a Humpback whale while diving off Cape Cod. He was about 45 feet (14 meters) deep in the waters off Provincetown when "all of a sudden I felt this huge bump, and everything went dark". He initially thought he had been attacked by a shark. He estimates that he was in the whale's mouth for about thirty seconds but was able to breathe as he was still connected to his breathing apparatus. Then the whale surfaced, shook its head, and spat him out. He was rescued by his crewmate in the surface boat. A whale scientist has commented that Humpbacks are not aggressive and that this would have been an accidental encounter while the whale was feeding on fish. Thankfully, these things are extremely rare!

So, my thoughts have turned to the familiar account of Jonah and his attempts to run from God and His call. How can this be a lesson in the desert I hear you ask? Please read on. Jonah had run away to Tarshish, a very remote place, in the direct opposite direction to Ninevah. Jonah was running from the 'presence of the Lord' and ended up first, in the inner part, the bottom of the ship, then in the belly of the fish at the bottom of the sea and then spewed up on the shoreline until he finally got the message that he should do as God had asked him to do. While in the belly of the fish, with his head wrapped in seaweed, Jonah was in a horrible, stinking 'abyss,' for a period of three days and nights. This was truly a desert experience for Jonah, the sand being replaced by water-too much water. Jonah's places of hiding and isolation were desolate, forgotten, miserable places where he feared for life itself. But 'then Jonah prayed to the Lord his God from inside the fish.'

After realising that he could not run and hide, being given a second chance to fulfil God's call to be obedient, Jonah finally reached Ninevah. But somehow, Jonah was still unhappy and angry with God and His mission of grace and mercy. Now Jonah sits sulking, cross and out of sorts, overheating in the scorching sun.

So, Jonah went out and sat sulking on the east side of the city, and he made a leafy shelter to shade him as he waited there to see if anything would happen to the city When the leaves of the shelter withered in the heat, the Lord arranged for a vine to grow up quickly and spread its broad leaves over Jonah's head to shade him. Then when the sun was hot, God ordered a scorching east wind to blow on Jonah, and the sun beat down upon his head until he grew faint and wished to die. For he said, "Death is better than this!" Then the Lord said, "You feel sorry for yourself when your shelter is destroyed, though you did no work to put it there, and it is, at best, short-lived Why shouldn't I feel sorry for a great city like Nineveh with its 120,000 people in utter spiritual darkness?

So, what are the lessons that Jonah had to learn in the boat, the storm, the belly of the fish, and the scorching desert heat and wind? Jonah was learning that God is a forgiving and merciful God and that no nation or people group is favoured by Him. God wants all to come to Him and know His gracious care- even those people such as the Ninevites who had a reputation for evil and wrongdoing, and who Jonah regarded as being beyond forgiveness.

Jonah learned that you cannot run and hide- not for long anyway. Jonah learned that if God had a role and a mission for him, then he had better attend to it straightaway- no delay, no messing, no hiding, no running away. Jonah learned that God is a God of second chances. You can begin again even when you have messed up and gone in the wrong direction.

Jonah learned that even in the most desperate of circumstances, God will hear the feeblest and most desperate of cries and will respond.

Pray

Father God, forgive me when I am in a bad mood, when I sulk and when I am unhappy with things as they are. I kick against your plan and your purpose and for no good reason. Keep reminding me that you are a loving God who longs for all to come to you. Help me to look out and not to look in. Remind me that your plan for me is good even if it seems hard. When I see something that needs to be done help me to do it straight away with a gracious, willing spirit- and without complaining. I can begin again, and again, and again.

Lessons in the Desert-Transformation

Isaiah chapter 35 is a wonderful and rich chapter in the Bible, and I can barely do it justice in a brief comment. This poem contains words to encourage and reassure the despairing and sorrowful Judah exiles who had lost everything. It talks of transformation, in a physical sense, from burning desert sands to lands with pools and springs of water, from wilderness and barrenness to a place of abundant growth like that of Carmel, Lebanon and the rich, fertile coastal plains. There would be streams in the desert, water in the wilderness and waste places, pools in place of burning sand, and springs of water bubbling up. But with God's hand there would be transformation in other ways too. There would be a returning, songs of joy instead of sorrow and sighing, strength instead of weakness, hope instead of fear, courage instead of anxiety, stability, and steadiness instead of fear and uncertainty, renewal and growth instead of lack, and safety instead of danger. This is a chapter of hope.

Judah had experienced exile for too long. They had 'drooping hands and tottering knees.' They were discouraged. This may echo our feelings. We have no energy to go forwards. Maybe we need to be challenged to get up and get going! This same image of weak knees and hands is used by Paul when he tells the early church to be strong and go forward.

So be made strong even in your weakness by lifting up your tired hands in prayer and worship. And strengthen your weak knees, for as you keep walking forward on God's paths, all your stumbling ways will be divinely healed! Hebrew 12 v 12-13

How can we get from a place of discouragement to a place of delight and dancing? The answer is here. *"Look, here comes your God! He is breaking through to give you victory!* Jesus has made a highway.

Jesus Himself used verses from Isaiah 35 in answer to questions sent by John the Baptist.

When John, who was in prison, heard about the deeds of the Messiah, he sent his disciples to ask him, "Are you the one who is to come, or should we expect someone else?" Jesus replied, "Go back and report to John what you hear and see: The blind receive sight, the lame walk, those who have leprosy are cleansed, the deaf hear, the dead are raised, and the good news is proclaimed to the poor. Matthew 11v 2-5

May we take encouragement from these wonderful words and get up and get going. Let's get on that highway with songs of joy.

The wilderness and dry land will be joyously glad!
The desert will blossom like a rose and rejoice!
Every dry and barren place will burst forth with abundant blossoms,
dancing and spinning with delight!
Lebanon's lush splendour covers it, the magnificent beauty of
Carmel and Sharon.
My people will see the awesome glory of Yahweh,
the beautiful grandeur of our God.
Strengthen those who are discouraged.
Energize those who feel defeated.
Say to the anxious and fearful,
"Be strong and never afraid.
Look, here comes your God!
He is breaking through to give you victory!
He comes to avenge your enemies.
With divine retribution he comes to save you!"
Then blind eyes will open, and deaf ears will hear.
Then the lame will leap like playful deer
and the tongue-tied will sing songs of triumph.
Gushing water will spring up in the wilderness
and streams will flow through the desert.
The burning sand will become a refreshing oasis,

the parched ground bubbling springs,
and the jackal's lair a meadow
with grass, reeds, and papyrus.
There will be a highway of holiness called the Sacred Way.
The impure will not be permitted on this road,
but it will be accessible to God's people.
And not even fools will lose their way.
The lion will not be found there;
no wild beast will travel on it—
they will not be found there.
But the redeemed will find a pathway on it.
Yahweh's ransomed ones will return with glee to Zion.
They will enter with a song of rejoicing
and be crowned with everlasting joy.
Ecstatic joy will overwhelm them;
weariness and grief will disappear!

Isaiah 35 v 1-10

Lessons in the Desert: John the Baptist

The child grew up, healthy and spirited. He lived out in the desert until the day he made his prophetic debut in Israel. Luke 1 v 80

John the Baptizer appeared in the wild, preaching a baptism of life-change that leads to forgiveness of sins. People thronged to him from Judea and Jerusalem and, as they confessed their sins, were baptized by him in the Jordan River into a changed life. John wore a camel-hair habit, tied at the waist with a leather belt. He ate locusts and wild field honey.

As he preached, he said, "The real action comes next: The star in this drama, to whom I'm a mere stagehand, will change your life. I'm baptizing you here in the river, turning your old life in for a kingdom life. His baptism—a holy baptism by the Holy Spirit—will change you from the inside out." Mark 1 v 7-8

John was born in exceptional circumstances and with pinpoint accuracy in terms of the timing of his birth and appearance in the desert. For four hundred years there had been no other prophet in Israel. John had lived in the obscurity of the desert until the time was right for a dramatic entrance on the scene. With the isolation of the desert wilderness and away from the pressures of life in town and city, he was focussed and prepared for his unique mission. His voice was to be the voice crying out in the wilderness, pointing only to Jesus. At this exact point in time John knew what he had to do. He was meant to be different, outlandish, challenging hypocrisy and injustice and calling people to repentance and to transformed values. In a nutshell, it was to have a changed life from the inside. In the desert he gathered around him followers, disciples and the curious, as people flocked there to see and hear him. But he did not seek success, popularity, fame, or position. His message was one of repentance and his sole purpose was to herald in the Saviour. He knew clearly that he was not the Messiah but that he was to prepare the way like the 'best man' at a wedding, for Jesus, the coming bridegroom. The best man's role was to wait for and listen for the voice of the bridegroom coming and then to step back into the wings and let the bridegroom take centre stage and take his bride.

You yourselves can testify that I said, "I am not the Messiah but am sent ahead of him. The bride belongs to the bridegroom. The friend who attends the bridegroom waits and listens for him and is full of joy when he hears the bridegroom's voice. That joy is mine, and it is now complete. He must become greater; I must become less. John 3 v 28-30

I baptize you with water to show that you have repented, but the one who will come after me baptize you with the Holy Spirit and fire. He is much greater than I am; and I am not good enough even to carry his sandals. Matthew 3 v 11

John's water baptism would signify a changed life, with Kingdom values from the inside. But John knew that when Messiah came that His transformation would be by the power of the Holy Spirit. John was merely paving the way for His arrival. When John's own disciples left him to join Jesus, John had no jealousy, ill will or regret. John knew that they were joining the bridegroom's party. He knew that the Messiah was greater than he and that His time had now come.

Pray

Forgive me for the many times that I mess up in the way that I act, speak and relate to others. I ask for your forgiveness. Forgive me when I so often want to take centre stage and be noticed. Help me to point others to you and not to seek attention, praise, and recognition. Would you change me from the inside out so that I may go in a new direction with your grace and help. When things are tough help me to keep going and to trust you and your perfect timing.

Lessons in the Desert:
Jesus - the Testing of the Desert

At this time, Jesus came from Nazareth in Galilee and was baptized by John in the Jordan. The moment he came out of the water, he saw the sky split open and God's Spirit, looking like a dove, come down on him. Along with the Spirit, a voice: "You are my Son, chosen and marked by my love, pride of my life. At once, this same Spirit pushed Jesus out into the wild. For forty wilderness days and nights he was tested by Satan. Wild animals were his companions, and angels took care of him. Mark 1 v 9-13

After Jesus's baptism, we learn that Jesus was seemingly pushed out into the desert by the Spirit, for this time of isolation, testing, conflict, and struggle with the enemy. It is widely believed that the desert that Jesus was taken to by the Spirit, was the Judaean Desert- an inhospitable, forlorn, and desolate place with sand, shingle, jagged rocks, ridges, crags, and cliff edges. Mark's Gospel also refers to the wild animals there as if to heighten the dangerous nature of the place. Jesus was now truly alone with the human resources that He would normally be able to rely on, stripped away. It is in this place that we see and feel the humanity of Jesus- the Christ who has truly stepped out of heaven, through birth and baptism, and into our own lives and frailty. But it is out of this experience in the desert that Jesus comes with a clear vision, a new perspective and in total dependence on God His Father. His ministry was now clear and focussed and after these days in the desert Jesus immediately goes public and declares that 'the time is fulfilled, the kingdom of God is at hand, repent and believe the gospel.' The teaching, preaching and the ministry of Jesus now begins.

Jesus continued to seek solitude and isolation during His ministry. We often discover Jesus going off to a quiet place by Himself, or with a small group of his disciples. It was clear that Jesus needed to have these times of retreat, solitude and prayer. It was also clear that the crowds were able to seek Him out even to these isolated places. These times of isolation and withdrawal were also times when He could speak privately and personally with His disciples.

When Jesus heard what had happened, (the death of John) He withdrew by boat privately to a solitary place. Hearing of this, the crowds followed him on foot from the towns. When Jesus landed and saw a large crowd, he had compassion on them and healed those who were ill. Matthew 14 v 13-14

Once when Jesus was praying in private and his disciples were with him, He asked them, 'Who do the crowds say I am?' They replied, 'Some say John the Baptist; others say Elijah; and still others, that one of the prophets of long ago has come back to life.' But what about you?' he asked. 'Who do you say I am?' Peter answered, 'God's Messiah. About eight days after Jesus said this, He took Peter, John and James with him and went up onto a mountain to pray.   It was on this occasion that Jesus was transfigured before them. Luke 9

One of the most significant times of withdrawal and prayer was perhaps to the Garden of Gethsemane. 'Then Jesus went with his disciples to a place called Gethsemane, and he said to them, 'Sit here while I go over there and pray.' Matthew 26 v 36

So many sermons will have been written about each of the three challenges that Jesus faced in the wilderness, and it is not my place to do so here. But as Christians we all face times of challenge that feel like this wilderness experience. We know that Jesus understands our struggles perfectly as He was tested in all points as we are, and we know that He is present with us.

We all experience times of testing, which is normal for every human being. But God will be faithful to you. He will screen and filter the severity, nature, and timing of every test or trial you face so that you can bear it. And each test is an opportunity to trust him more, for along with every trial God has provided for you a way of escape that will bring you out of it victoriously. 1 Corinthians 10:13 TPT

I became a Christian at one of the Billy Graham Crusades that had been relayed to the Queens Hall in Leeds, from London. As I was at the front of the hall being counselled by a Billy Graham volunteer, I was given a pack of information for new Christians and a set of memory verses, I think about 20 to 30 verses that I dutifully put to memory. This verse was one of the memory verses, but in the KJV of course. There hath no temptation taken you, but such as is common to man: but God is faithful, who will not suffer you to be tempted above that ye are able; but will with the temptation also make a way to escape, that ye may be able to bear it. I am so glad this verse is in my memory bank.

Pray

Alone with none but thee, my God,

I journey on my way.

What need I fear, when thou art near O king of night and day?

More safe am I within thy hand

Than if a host did round me stand.

Columba, c.521 - 597

Lessons in the Desert:
The Untouchables and the Rejected

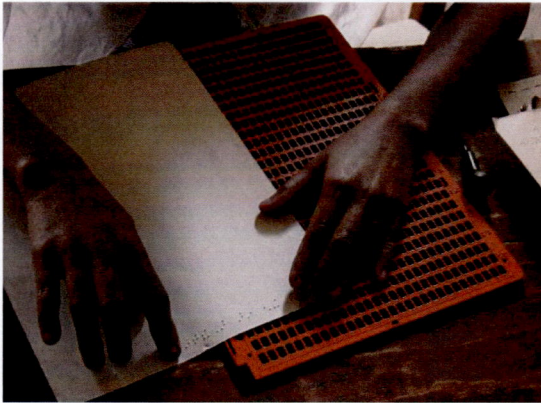

Some years ago, I joined a small team of people for two weeks at Chandraghona Hospital, Bangladesh and the nearby village of Jhum Para, where most of the families had been leprosy patients over many years, and had been sponsored by a small charity which provided water supplies, basic amenities, better roofing for their simple houses, food, school fees and clothing. In addition to spending time at the hospital, I also had the chance to visit local primary and secondary schools, the Treatment Centre for leprosy patients and the local Blind School. It was quite a life changing experience for me. This lovely gentleman in Jhum Para, whose body had been damaged by leprosy, possessed nothing but his simple hut, a few cooking pots, and a Bible. Yet he was filled with the love of Christ. I was very much affected by this lovely individual. There are many people in our society and world today who are on the very margin of life. Jesus wants to reach these people.

In Matthew 8 we read that Jesus came down from the mountain with the cheers of the crowd still ringing in his ears. Then a leper appeared and dropped to his knees before Jesus, praying, "Master, if you want to, you can heal my body." Jesus reached out and touched him, saying, "I want to. Be clean." Then and there, all signs of the leprosy were gone. Jesus said, "Don't talk about this all over town. Just quietly present your healed body to the priest, along with the appropriate expressions of thanks to God. Your cleansed and grateful life, not your words, will bear witness to what I have done." Then, in the country of the Gadarenes Jesus and his disciples were met by two madmen coming out of the cemetery, victims of demons. The men had terrorized the region for so long that no one considered it safe to walk down that stretch of road anymore. Seeing Jesus, the men screamed out, "What business do you have giving us a hard time? You're the Son of God! You weren't supposed to show up here yet!" Once again, Jesus dealt with the situation and the men were freed from their horrible bondage.

Mental ill health, leprosy and other skin diseases came with terrible consequences. Each of these men were regarded as unclean, defiled, and were shunned and isolated from any community. They met with isolation, rejection, prejudice, and stigma and they were treated as if they were dead. They would experience great need and desperation. A person with leprosy had to keep 2 meters away from any other person-this was social distancing in Bible times. It would be a desert existence for them. The men among the tombs in the graveyard, were forced to live quite literally among the dead.

We read that this leper came and worshipped Jesus. His need was impossible and yet he came with a simple request. "If you are willing" you can heal me. He was not doubting that Jesus could heal him, "I know you can do it", he was questioning whether Jesus was willing to do this thing. With an overwhelming act of love and compassion, Jesus touches him. The first human touch that this man had felt in a very long time, and he is healed. His changed and thankful life would witness to the power of Christ in his life.

There are many people in our society who may feel marginalised or ostracised, and left out in a 'desert', and yet the compassion of Jesus needs to reach them through us. We are the ones who can bring the touch of Jesus to them. As we begin to come out of the harshest of restrictions may we not simply be glad to meet up with our friends, those 'who are like me', my social group, but may we look out for those who are on the edge of things and bring them in from the desert.

An ancient prayer Clement c. 96 AD

We ask you, Master, be our helper and defender. Rescue those of our number in distress; raise up the fallen; assist the needy; heal the sick; turn back those of your people who stray; feed the hungry; release our captives; revive the weak; encourage those who lose heart. Let all the nations realize that you are the only God, that Jesus Christ is your Child, and that we are your people and the sheep of your pasture.

LESSONS FROM LIFE

Lessons from a leather cushion

Jesus Calms the Storm

That day when evening came, he said to his disciples, "Let us go over to the other side." Leaving the crowd behind, they took him along, just as he was, in the boat. There were also other boats with him. A furious squall came up, and the waves broke over the boat, so that it was nearly swamped. Jesus was in the stern, sleeping on a cushion. The disciples woke him and said to him, "Teacher, don't you care if we drown?" He got up, rebuked the wind and said to the waves, "Quiet! Be still!" Then the wind died down and it was completely calm. He said to his disciples, "Why are you so afraid? Do you still have no faith?" They were terrified and asked each other, "Who is this? Even the wind and the waves obey him!"
Mark 4 v35-41

I love this account in Mark's gospel as it clearly shows the human side of Jesus. The crowds had been with Him all day and Jesus had delivered a full teaching programme to His disciples and the crowds who were thronging around Him. Jesus had taught the lessons of the new kingdom and His parables and by late afternoon He would have been drained and exhausted. Had He gone on to the shore from the borrowed boat the crowd would have followed Him and so at His request they launched the boat out on to the lake. But even then, a little flotilla of small boats attempted to follow. There was to be no respite for the weary Jesus. He needed time to be away from the crowd, to find a little solitude, peace, and rest. Mark tells us that Jesus was asleep on a cushion in the stern of the boat. The stern of the boat had a wooden bench with perhaps a leather cushion placed on it where a boatman could take a rest or even sleep for a while. It was here that Jesus was fast asleep.

I love the reality and the personal touch of the details that Mark adds to the account. Jesus is weary and sleeps. Sometimes for us too, being with the crowd, no matter how wonderful, can be draining and it is not wrong to want to be in a quiet, solitary place. We all need rest, recovery, and recuperation at times.

The boats were heading towards the Gentile lands of the Gadarenes on the other side of the lake. A sudden and violent storm appeared which threatened to overwhelm and endanger the boat. Storms were common on the lake and the experienced sailors would be used to handling their boats in the many different weather conditions, squalls, and storms. But this storm was different- fierce and frightening and the waves threatened to capsize the boat. They had never seen anything like this before. The wind was a tempest and the raging waves large enough to overwhelm and sink the boat. The sailors feared for their lives. And yet in the storm, Jesus remained asleep on a cushion in the stern of the tossing boat.

The sailors had done all that they could to stabilize the boat and feared shipwreck and loss of life, and so finally, in desperation, they woke up the sleeping saviour and called out, "save us Lord, we are dying."

There was panic, alarm, fear, distress, and manic activity to deal with the emergency but Jesus calmly took control of the situation. In His calm voice and with quiet authority, He ordered peace to the wind and stillness to the waves and the storm immediately disappeared and all was calm. Jesus then challenged His disciples. Surely you should realize that because I am with you then no harm will come to you. The boat could not be lost while ever Jesus was with them. His followers only then began to realize the nature and the power of this Jesus. "Who then is this that the wind and the waves obey Him?" The sudden calmness and stillness were perhaps just as alarming as the storm had been.

He stilled the storm to a whisper;
the waves of the sea were hushed.
They were glad when it grew calm,
and he guided them to their desired haven.
Let them give thanks to the Lord for his unfailing love
and his wonderful deeds for mankind.   Psalm 107 v 23-29

Sometimes we may wonder where Jesus is when we are going through the mill and dealing with tough situations or when we hear of frightening things happening in our world. It may seem as if Jesus is not aware of our distress and inactive, or that He is even sleeping. But He is there. He is always there. Call out to Him. The simplest of prayers will do-Help!

Wake up, Lord! Why are you asleep?
Rouse yourself Don't reject us forever!
Why are you hiding from us?

Don't forget our suffering and trouble!
We fall crushed to the ground;
we lie defeated in the dust.
Come to our aid!
Because of your constant love save us!
Psalm 44 v 23-24 GNT

When I lie down, I go to sleep in peace;
you alone,   Lord, keep me perfectly safe. Psalm 4 v 8

Pray

Lord I am weary. I am overwhelmed and my energy is low. I need your rest. I need your resources.

This world is sometimes a disturbing and a frightening place. The world news is distressing. Yet I know that you are there. We need your voice to bring peace and stillness to a troubled world. We pray for your peace.

Lessons from a Dry-Stone Wall

In Him and in fellowship with one another, you also are being built together into a dwelling place of God in the Spirit. Ephesians 2 v 22

Brick walls are made using identical shaped blocks glued together with mortar, but dry-stone walls are just a stack of stones- stones of different sizes and shapes, laid together, one on top of another. The stones are placed slowly and carefully, tightly packed together, locked under their own weight, by the skilled and experienced eye of an expert builder. There are no gaps between the stones so that the stones in each layer look like interconnected jigsaw pieces. Dry-stone walls really have two walls or sides, built very close together and 'in-filled' with smaller stones. As the twin outer sides are built, they form an 'A' shape, with the wall at the base being a little wider than the wall at the top for stability. Each layer of wall has large stones (tie-stones or through stones) at key places, holding the two sides together, with the essential smaller stones packed in between them.

As I have thought about these beautiful walls, perhaps there are lessons about 'being church' that we can learn from them and their construction.

Specialist builders use the stones that they have or that can be found in the fields nearby. It would be lovely to have perfectly formed and shaped stones, but very unlikely that such perfectly flat, squared off stones would be available and just where they need them. So, the builders must use what they have-stones with bulges and bumps, and a vast array of odd shapes too. The wall is only held together by the sheer weight of stone, and so it is the skill of the builder that is crucial when he selects and fits the stones together. Each stone is used to its maximum benefit by a master builder. Many different stones are needed- face stones for the front, filling stones, through stones (for strength), cover stones, capping stones (the protective stones at the top) and so on. Every kind, shape and size of stone is essential and needed. The large, flatter 'through' stones are essential for the wall's strength and must be placed at regular intervals to hold the sides of the wall together. Without these stones the wall would bow and might collapse. As a guiding principle each stone rests on two others and each stone supports the stones on top of it.

The brilliance of the dry stone-wall is that it can flex and move- it is flexible! As the ground settles or moves a well-built dry stone-wall will simply move with the ground. So, good construction is vital. The dry stone-wall is fundamentally held up by friction and gravity. The friction between the stones keeps them from sliding apart and the sheer weight of the stones means that it will stand firm.

The good builder steps back at regular intervals to look at his work. Is the wall pleasing to the eye, is it standing true and is it following his marked-out guidelines?

He's (God) using us all—irrespective of how we got here—in what he is building. He used the apostles and prophets for the foundation. Now he's using you, fitting you in brick by brick, stone by stone, with Christ Jesus as the cornerstone that holds all the parts together. We see it taking shape day after day—a holy temple built by God, all of us built into it, a temple in which God is quite at home. Ephesians 2 v 22 MSG

So, you are no longer outsiders or aliens, but fellow-citizens with every other Christian—you belong now to the household of God. Firmly beneath you in the foundation, God's messengers and prophets, the actual foundation-stone being Jesus Christ himself. In him each separate piece of building, properly fitting into its neighbour, grows together into a temple consecrated to God. You are all part of this building in which God himself lives by his spirit. Ephesians 2 v 22 JBP

And now you have become living building-stones for God's use in building his house. What's more, you are his holy priests; so, come to him—you who are acceptable to him because of Jesus Christ—and offer to God those things that please him. 1 Peter 2 v 5 Living Bible

Welcome to the living Stone, the source of life. The workmen took one look and threw it out; God set it in the place of honour. Present yourselves as building stones for the construction of a sanctuary vibrant with life, in which you'll serve as holy priests offering Christ-approved lives up to God. 1 Peter 2 v 5 MSG

Pray

Father God, you are the master builder and you have set Jesus, your Son as the chief cornerstone. You are building your church with living stones, people of different identities, cultures, backgrounds, shapes, and sizes. We are imperfect, with rough edges, and we sometimes rub against each other, but each one is needed. I am needed. I may be concealed in the centre, I may attract attention on the outer edges, I may be a significant 'tie stone' or a cap stone but I am needed. You have placed each one carefully and deliberately. May we support each other as we stand in the place of your choice.

Lessons from a lump of clay

The Lord said to me, "Go down to the potter's house, where I will give you, my message." So, I went there and saw the potter working at his wheel. Whenever a piece of pottery turned out imperfect, he would take the clay and make it into something else. Jeremiah 18 v1-4 GNT

O Lord, you are our Father. We are the clay, and you are the Potter. We are all formed by your hand. Isaiah 64 v 8

I have been fascinated by the television programme The Great Pottery Throwdown and the expertise and flair of the potters as they create beautiful pots formed out of the most basic of materials- clay. Clay is used to make functional things such as bricks, wall and floor tiles and clay is also used to make decorative and beautiful things such as vases, bowls, and dishes. There are clays of different qualities which can make earthenware, stoneware and even the finest of porcelains. As I have watched the potters preparing the clay and then as they turn it on the wheel, occasionally the emerging shape is not pleasing to them, and they remould the clay again to produce what they hope will be a prize-winning pot. This reminds me of those verses in Jeremiah where God is giving Jeremiah a very practical and visual lesson of His right to mould and remould His people according to His design- to refine them so that they are pleasing in His sight.

The process of preparing the clay looks to be quite brutal as the potter throws it down onto a hard surface, squeezing, compressing it, rolling, and shaping it. But preparation is key. I am fascinated by the process of attaching and fixing a delicate handle to a vase or a cup using only a thin liquid clay called slip. It is wonderful to watch. If the pot should prove to be unsatisfactory then the potter remoulds it. This is the lesson that Jeremiah was given.

God may often use this shaping and moulding process, either individually or as a church perhaps, shaping and moulding us according to His good purpose and pleasure. It might be an uncomfortable process but often a very necessary one. Paul reminded us that we are like common clay pots so that all the praise and recognition is given to God. We cannot claim the credit for any success ourselves.

For it is not ourselves that we preach; we preach Jesus Christ as Lord, and ourselves as your servants for Jesus' sake. The God who said, "Out of darkness the light shall shine!" is the same God who made his light shine in our hearts, to bring us the knowledge of God's glory shining in the face of Christ. Yet we who have this spiritual treasure are like common clay pots, to show that the supreme power belongs to God, not to us. 2 Corinthians 4 v 5-7

When I was in India, many years ago, I would buy tea in the street markets and the drink would be given to you in a common, tiny clay pot. The finished pot would then be thrown on the ground and broken under foot by the stall holder. This was done for specific cultural reasons, but it seemed that the cups were treated then as our common plastic or paper cups are now. I managed to keep hold of a few of the cups to bring home.

Father, I want to place myself in your expert hands. You are the skilled craftsman. But it is hard to let go and to leave the shaping to you. You have created me with a purpose in mind. May I find that purpose and not desire to be something different. If I am earthenware, then may I not seek to be fine porcelain. We are all clay and we each have your treasure within us.

Lessons from a set of oars

Directly after this, Jesus made his disciples get aboard the boat and go on ahead to Bethsaida on the other side of the lake, while he himself sent the crowds home. And when he had sent them all on their way, he went off to the hillside to pray. When it grew late, the boat was in the middle of the lake, and he was by himself on land. He saw them straining at the oars, for the wind was dead against them. And in the small hours he went towards them, walking on the waters of the lake, intending to come alongside them. But when they saw him walking on the water, they thought he was a ghost, and screamed out. For they all saw him, and they were absolutely terrified. But Jesus at once spoke quietly to them, "It's all right, it is I myself; don't be afraid!" And he climbed aboard the boat with them, and the wind dropped. But they were scared out of their wits. They had not had the sense to learn the lesson of the loaves. Even that miracle had not opened their eyes to see who he was. Mark 6 v 45-52

After the miracle of the feeding of the five thousand, Jesus instructed the disciples to make the return journey of about six miles, back by boat, from Bethsaida to Capernaum. But the weather turned against them. These hardy sailors were struggling against fierce wind and storm, were now in the middle of the lake, were in serious trouble, and making no progress. They were straining at the oars, fighting against a direct head wind, but making no advance. It would be a terrifying situation, rowing like crazy in the pitch black, making no headway or progress. Their muscles would strain and ache with the monumental effort of pulling on the oars.

From high up on the hillside, Jesus saw their struggles. He saw and came down to them, walking on the water. Jesus spoke peace to them." I Am "is here. Do not fear. Jesus climbed on to the boat with them and the wind dropped.

We are often in situations where we feel that we are not making any headway. We are working impossibly hard, 'straining at the oars' and getting no further forward. We are up against it! We are fighting against the current and the tide. It may be that we need to lay down our oars. But as Jesus did with the disciples, Jesus sees our struggle, Jesus comes alongside, Jesus speaks quietly to us with words of peace and encouragement, and Jesus gets on board. Jesus may not come straight away, and He may turn up in surprising and unexpected ways- but He will come. It would be lovely if there were calm waters all the time, but this is not our reality. Be prepared for the storms, for they will surely come.

God's wisdom is so deep, God's power so immense,
who could take him on and come out in one piece?
He moves mountains before they know what's happened,
flips them on their heads on a whim.
He gives the earth a good shaking up,
rocks it down to its very foundations.
He tells the sun, 'Don't shine,' and it doesn't;
he pulls the blinds on the stars.
All by himself he stretches out the heavens
and strides on the waves of the sea.
He designed the Big Dipper and Orion,
the Pleiades and Alpha Centauri.
We'll never comprehend all the great things he does;
his miracle-surprises can't be counted.
Somehow, though he moves right in front of me, I don't see him;
quietly but surely, he's active, and I miss it.   *Job 9 MSG*

Pray

In our world, we are often straining against the world's ways, culture, and trends. Many things are against us. Jesus, come alongside and come on board. We need your peace and presence.

There are things that we cannot understand, and which are too painful to watch- the war in Ukraine, the suffering in your world. But You see and we ask you to come near.

Sometimes our struggles and hardships may be of our own making. We need to put down our oars.

Sometimes our projects and missions are not the ones that you intend for us. We need to put down our oars.

Sometimes life is just a struggle, we are 'up against' it all the time and we are straining at the oars. Help us to let go of the controls.

Open our eyes to who you are.

Lessons from a walking stick
and a pair of sandals

Jesus called the Twelve to him and sent them out in pairs. He gave them authority and power to deal with the evil opposition. He sent them off with these instructions: "Don't think you need a lot of extra equipment for this. You are the equipment. No special appeals for funds. Keep it simple. "And no luxury inns. Get a modest place and be content there until you leave. "If you're not welcomed, not listened to quietly withdraw. Don't make a scene. Shrug your shoulders and be on your way." Then they were on the road. They preached with joyful urgency that life can be radically different; right and left they sent the demons packing; they brought wellness to the sick, anointing their bodies, healing their spirits. Mark 6 v 7-13

Jesus always calls.

Jesus always sends.

Jesus promises to equip and empower.

Jesus was sending off His twelve disciples on their first ever local outreach trip to the nearby villages, to preach the Jesus message, and to challenge people to live changed lives. Jesus called them, then sent them, gave them His authority and power, and assured them of the resources that would be theirs. The disciples were instructed to take nothing for their journey except a walking stick and sandals – no food, no traveller's bag, no money, and without a change of clothes. They were to travel 'light' without worrying about the resources that they might need as they would go in dependence on Him and the generous hospitality of those who would welcome them. They may not have felt ready for this responsibility, but Jesus was trusting them to go, and to live and share the good news of the kingdom. They would be learning 'on the job' so to speak. They were to go in two's so that they would have each other for support, encouragement, and protection and they were to both speak out and live out the Jesus message. They had to let go of their normal securities as they were assured that they would have all that they needed, and they were to be ready to engage with those that they would meet. Jesus was trusting His disciples to go and just try it His way. Their missions would not always be this way but in this instance, there were important lessons for them to learn about trust.

Perhaps there are lessons for us here too. It may be something about hanging on to what provides our security or by contrast letting go and trusting Jesus more. We live in a very self-reliant society where we depend on house, car, education, security, reputation, and so on to give us the 'safe' position that we are happy with. There are many things that are 'mine' that I have come to depend on and that I feel that I am entitled to, and many ways that we have always done things that we are reluctant to let go of, and yet sometimes it is good to let go, travel light and to trust that Jesus will provide the resources that we need.

We are Christ's ambassadors. God is using us to speak to you: we beg you, as though Christ himself were here pleading with you, receive the love he offers you—be reconciled to God. 2 Corinthians 5 v 19 TLB

Lessons from the Watchtower

I will climb my watchtower now and wait to see what answer God will give to my complaint. Habakkuk 2 v 1

Watchtowers have been built since the earliest of times and were frequently built as part of a defending wall and occasionally as a single structure on high ground as an important lookout station. We have had the privilege of walking on a part of the Great Wall of China and discovering its beautiful watchtowers. In its original design and form The Great Wall is thought to have had 25,000 watchtowers built along its length.

The watchtower had several very important functions. As I was thinking about this, for me, the most important aspect was the watchtower as a place of resource and supply. It was where all supplies were kept and so was the place of supply. It was also the place of safety, security, and refuge. The watchtower was the place of communication, to give and receive signals and give an early warning. The watchtower was a beacon, a significant landmark, and could even be thought of as a lighthouse as it was always built with a clear view of the landscape. Often signalling fires would be lit at the watchtowers.

There are a few times that the word watchtower occurs in the bible. The prophet Habakkuk spoke of retiring to his watchtower while he waited for God to respond to his struggles and questions. Habakkuk had foreseen God's judgement on His people and the downfall of Judah at the hands of the Babylonians, and he was struggling with some very tough questions. "God why are you doing this and why are you doing it this way?" He took his frustration, struggles, questions, and confusion to God, and in his waiting at the watchtower, he was giving God time to respond in His own good time. He knew that God would answer him. The watchtower would be his quiet place of retreat while he prayed and waited. He would watch and wait, confident and expectant that God would speak and answer.

Unless the Lord builds the house,
They labour in vain who build it.
Unless the Lord guards the city,
The watchman keeps awake in vain.
It is vain for you to rise early,
To retire late,
To eat the bread of anxious labours—
For He gives blessings to His beloved even in his sleep. Psalm 127 v 1-2

If God doesn't build the house,
the builders only build shacks.
If God doesn't guard the city,
the night watchman might as well nap.
It's useless to rise early and go to bed late,
and work your worried fingers to the bone.
Don't you know he enjoys
giving rest to those he loves? MSG

The Lord is a refuge for the oppressed, a stronghold in times of trouble. Psalm 9 v 9

You have been a refuge for me, a strong tower in the face of the enemy. Psalm 61 v 3

Pray

Lord, we watch and wait in your watchtower. This is our place of supply and where your resources for us are to be found. When we are confused, troubled, dismayed and don't know the way ahead, we come to you in the watchtower and wait to hear your voice. Give us patience as we wait. Don't let us run ahead with our own building plans. We are in a place of resource and supply. You long to bless. May we trust you.

Lessons from cups, jugs, basins and pans

The Pharisees, along with some religion scholars who had come from Jerusalem, gathered around him. They noticed that some of his disciples weren't being careful with ritual washings before meals. The Pharisees— Jews in general, in fact—would never eat a meal without going through the motions of a ritual handwashing, with an especially vigorous scrubbing if they had just come from the market, to say nothing of the scourings they'd give jugs and pots and pans. Jesus answered,

"Isaiah was right about frauds like you, hit the bull's-eye in fact: These people make a big show of saying the right thing, but their heart isn't in it. They act like they are worshiping me, but they don't mean it. They just use me as a cover for teaching whatever suits their fancy, Ditching God's command and taking up the latest fads." Mark 7 MSG

Jesus had just come from the marketplace where He had healed many, when He was met by an official delegation from Jerusalem, some ninety miles away, people who were there to judge His credentials and His possible threat to the status quo. The Pharisees and officials had instantly noticed that the disciples did not follow the required traditions before preparing to eat. These oral traditions were complex, requiring more than simple hand washing for purposes of cleaning the hands, but elaborate ceremonies and rigid rituals, requiring special prayers during the hand washing process, with a final rinsing of the hands and elbows using water that had been preserved in a stone basin for this sole use. There were complex rules for the preparation of the utensils also. Jesus correctly concluded that these men were more concerned with image, appearance, ritual, and their man-made traditions than with a heart searching for God and His law. Jesus tells them that they have skilfully sidestepped God's law to hold on to their own traditions and concludes that 'their heart is far from me'. Jesus then explains that it is from within, and not from without, from the heart, that evil intentions and thoughts come.

For the Pharisees and law makers, contact with the marketplace and the people who gathered there, spoke of contamination, from which they had to be cleansed. For Jesus, the marketplace was where the needy and sick were to be found and where He could bring His grace, healing, and kingdom values. What a contrast!

Jesus makes it clear that in His kingdom He is looking for a heart and life transformation and not a 'going through the motions' way of living. The phrase 'going through the motions' is a powerful one. Jesus is looking for authentic being and living. For those of us who have been Christians for a very long time, then perhaps it is helpful to occasionally ask the question 'what is the state of my heart?' Why do I do or don't do certain things? Have I fallen into patterns of behaviour and being that may need a major review and overhaul? And am I going to the marketplace to bring the light and love of Jesus? Or do I remain at home in the safe place where I do not need to be troubled?

Pray

Jesus, I don't want to be a 'going through the motions' follower.

I ask for your Holy Spirit to stir me up and transform my life.

I ask for your forgiveness when I settle for anything less than a true commitment to you.

Change me from the inside out.

Lessons from three shelters

Six days later, Jesus took Peter and James and John with him and led them high up on a hillside where they were entirely alone. His whole appearance changed before their eyes, while his clothes became white, dazzling white—whiter than any earthly bleaching could make them. Elijah and Moses appeared to the disciples and stood there in conversation with Jesus. Peter burst out to Jesus, "Master, it is wonderful for us to be here! Shall we put up three shelters—one for you, one for Moses and one for Elijah?"

He really did not know what to say, for they were very frightened. Then came a cloud which overshadowed them, and a voice spoke out of the cloud, "This is my dearly loved Son. Listen to him!"

Then, quite suddenly they looked all round them and saw nobody at all with them but Jesus. And as they came down the hillside, he warned them not to tell anybody what they had seen till "the Son of Man should have risen again from the dead". They treasured this remark and tried to puzzle out among themselves what "Rising from the dead" could mean. Mark 9 v 2-11 JBP

Don't you just love Peter and his honesty and openness? He had quite recently announced that Jesus was the Christ, the Messiah, speaking clearly and confidently in front of the other disciples. And now here Peter is again, opening his mouth and just blurting out some words because he was clueless as to what else he could say in this unique moment. Peter just had to fill the space with some words, no matter how foolish or inappropriate they might be. My sympathies are with him because he and the two others, James, and John, were terrified. He was babbling and did not know what he was saying because they were terrified by what they were witnessing. Peter's attempt to process what they had just seen and heard, and to do something practical, was to make three shelters or booths for Jesus, Elijah and Moses as memorials for the event that they have witnessed on that solitary hillside. "Let's make three shelters as memorials" Peter announces.

Peter had misunderstood the significance of what he had just seen. His error was in seeing Jesus, Elijah and Moses as three equals, each of equal significance. His error was to try to box in the moment in time. His error was to try to put Jesus and His Kingdom teaching into a memorial shelter when He is a living saviour outside of time and space. The significance of this moment was way beyond what any one person could have comprehended.

The voice of the Father breaks through just as it did at Jesus's baptism. "This is my beloved Son. Listen to Him- and continue listening to Him." Peter, listen! Peter, keep listening to Jesus, my Son. Peter was now stunned into silence and without discussing this momentous event further with Peter, Jesus instructs Peter and the others to remain silent, to hold their peace and to tell no one of what they have just witnessed until Jesus has risen from the dead. Peter had to stay silent- 'to bite his tongue'- to keep these things to himself. How hard would this be for someone with Peter's outspoken nature? The disciples considered what the 'raising from the dead' might mean, but what had happened in that solitary place on a hillside was a secret to be concealed for the time being.

We often have a problem with our mouths. We often tend to blurt things out prematurely. We frequently try to put Jesus in a box- to contain Him. But Jesus cannot be contained. We think that we know what should be done- we have a good solution. We need to lift our eyes again and again and again to who Jesus is. "This is my beloved Son, in whom I am well pleased- listen to Him and keep listening to Him." May we never try to make a box for Him. He is a living Saviour, constantly active.

Pray

"For we live by faith not by sight." 2 Corinthians 5:7

Open my eyes, not to see the world more clearly, but to see You. Open my eyes to see you working around me and in me and through me.

Nothing happens by accident. You orchestrate every day of my life. Allow me to see your hand in the mundane and the fantastic. Help me to trust in what I cannot see and believe in Your invisible presence.

Forgive me when I try to box you in or when I fail to acknowledge that you are in control. Your ways are so much better than my ways. Help me to place into your hands the things that I cannot do or understand.

BIBLE ACCOUNTS

Building the walls again - Nehemiah

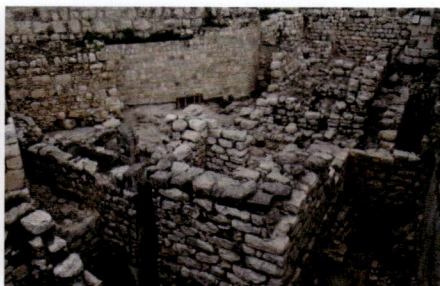

The walls of Jerusalem were broken. Families had been living next to the broken walls for years, seeing the decay, which had become familiar and normal. Personal preoccupations, busy lives, family circumstances and jobs must have taken over and the broken walls had become less relevant and for some insignificant. Over time they had barely noticed those walls anymore. The stones were fallen, scattered, hidden under rubbish and some burned. But then Nehemiah comes on to the scene with his leadership, example, and vision.

Then I said to them, "You see the trouble we are in, how Jerusalem lies in ruins with its gates burned. Come, let us rebuild the wall of Jerusalem, so that we may no longer suffer disgrace. Then I replied to them, "The God of heaven is the one who will give us success, and we his servants are going to start building. Then they said, "Let us start building!" So, they committed themselves to the common good. Nehemiah 2.17-18

He created a taskforce- people from different walks of life, priests, Levites, rulers, common people, merchants, women, guards, farmers, goldsmiths, perfumers working together. Everyone was involved in the rebuilding - Every person was needed, everyone was involved and worked on the wall at the place where they belonged or lived. The repeated phrases in the text are 'made repairs'   and 'next to him'. Families made repairs to the broken walls that were next to, beside or opposite their homes. They were invested in the work and had a clear purpose to see it through. They even had a building Fund for the work. Nehemiah had to cope with attempts to undermine and weaken him, attempts to trick, distract, and threaten his reputation. However, the building work was coordinated and shared.

Nehemiah communicated with and supported the teams of workers. He accepted that some people could only build and contribute a little and others could do much more. But all were valued and encouraged for what they could do. Nehemiah kept going and the wall was rebuilt in 52 days.

Perhaps there is an analogy here. In many groups and churches, it is easy for members to sleepwalk into brokenness almost without realising it. It is easy to become complacent, disengaged, drift, without each person rightfully taking their place in the life and decisions of the church. The broken walls have barely been noticed. But a time may come when the state of the walls becomes clear for all to see. A decision needs to be made to go forward and build. The re building will need everyone to play their part. There must be no apathy, disengagement and leaving of the work to the few. All are needed, all must re-build, all must be invested in the work.

So then let us pursue what makes for peace and for mutual upbuilding. Romans 14 v 9

Pray

Jesus, build us, strengthen us, grow our faith. We are your church. We are Yours. Use our church as you will, not as we will. Do what only You can do. We stand in faith, with You as our source of life and strength. We find security and victory in the all-powerful, supreme King of Kings and Lord of Lords, our Saviour Jesus Christ. In your name we pray, Amen.

Nehemiah- Rebuilding the walls

After more than three months of social restrictions we are now entering a period when things are starting to be relaxed - churches, restaurants, bars, theatres, cinemas and clubs are beginning to open again and we are possibly entering a rebuilding stage. We are trying to get things back to normal. This very much reminds me of the account of Nehemiah and his re-building programme.

I love the book of Nehemiah. It is largely an autobiographical book with Nehemiah telling his own story. Nehemiah was a gifted leader, a strategist, analytical, practical and a man of prayer and dependence on God. He was a man of influence, character and ability, who by God's timing was in the right place at the right time. He was an action hero with a responsive heart. When he was aware of the scale of the rebuilding project in Jerusalem, he did not jump in feet first- he waited, prayed, and considered for 4 months, asking God for guidance. Then, when the time was right, Nehemiah had his requests ready for the king, was able to put practical plans in place, re assess and then go into action to start the re-building programme. Nehemiah came into the problem with a new perspective and a new vision.

The work began well but then they came to the toughest time in any project - the halfway point. At this halfway point Nehemiah kept going. There was hostility from enemies, discouragement, pessimism, ridicule, insults, personal attacks, temptations to compromise and limited resources. But he kept going and encouraged his workers. He knew how to motivate and encourage the workers. He knew that it had to be a shared effort and so he spoke of 'we' and' us' and not of 'you' and 'them'. Nehemiah's default position was to always go back to the One who had called him. Seven times Nehemiah went back to God needing to see things from God's perspective again and to know God's purpose, timing, and power. In a record time of 52 days the wall was rebuilt.

The Covid-19 Pandemic of 2020 and beyond, was devastating on many levels and even today it feels as if we are still not even half -way in getting to a measure of normality again. Some people are still very nervous and anxious, with energy levels perhaps drained by isolation and practical concerns at home. It is perhaps hard to sustain work and energy levels and to see the light at the end of the tunnel. The halfway point is sometimes the hardest place to be. May we encourage each other to keep going. We are the living stones that are being built together.

Come to Christ, who is the living Foundation of Rock upon which God builds; though men have spurned him, he is very precious to God who has chosen him above all others. And now you have become living building-stones for God's use in building his house. 1 Peter 2 v5

Pray

There may be many 'broken wall 'situations that are troubling us, within our families, our friends, and colleagues. We may seek to understand, but we cannot fix them alone. We need God's help and guidance in resolving the challenges.

Lord, be with us this day,
Within us to purify us
Above us to draw us up.
Beneath us to sustain us
Before us to lead us
Behind us to restrain us
Around us to protect us.
Patrick c 389-461

His banner over me is love: Song of Solomon 2 v 4

You have given a banner to those who fear you, that it may be displayed because of the truth. Psalm 60 v 4

There are many families and individuals who are carrying burdens, worries and family concerns that are not their own and that this can cause great personal distress and tension. Following the death of George Floyd in Minneapolis, many of individuals and families, some much more than others, as they belong to the BAME community, have shared the outrage and deep sadness that his death and the deep-seated racial injustice, has caused. George Floyd's death was emotionally exhausting for many in the BAME community and raised deep rooted issues. For some, these problems and family worries have been too hard to bear and even to share. They have been unable to verbalize their distress.

I am very much a visual learner needing the support of images and illustrations. One image that immediately came to my mind, concerns the Old Testament story of Moses, Aaron and Hur. Moses in his weariness, needed the help of others- he needed Aaron and Hur, to hold up his arms, as he prayed. Sometimes our personal or family issues are so all consuming that we need others to pray-we have run out of resources ourselves. This is where our Christian supporters are needed- to hold up our hands.

In Exodus 17 we read that the Amalekites fought with the Israelites at Rephidim. Moses told Joshua, "Choose some men for us and go out to fight against the Amalekites. Tomorrow I'll stand on top of the hill with the staff of God in my hand." So, Joshua did as Moses told him and fought against the Amalekites, while Moses, Aaron, and Hur went up to the top of the hill. Whenever Moses raised his hand, the Israelites prevailed, but when his hand remained at his side, then the Amalekites prevailed. When Moses' hands became heavy, they took a stone and put it under him, and he sat on it. Aaron and Hur supported his hands, one on one side and one on the other, and so his hands were steady until the sun went down.

After the victory Moses built an altar and named it "The Lord is My Banner" -Jehovah-Nissi.

Moses' rod was the symbol of God's personal and powerful involvement and his outstretched arms, his prayers and appeal for God to intervene. May we know that we are under that banner of love and may we have good friends who will hold us up in prayer.

In terms of racial inequality and injustice there is a battle and there is a need for all hands to work together and to give support.

And in that day there shall be a root of Jesse which shall stand as a banner to the people, for the gentiles shall seek Him, and his resting place shall be glorious. Isaiah 11 v 10

Jesus is our banner.

A Peaceful Night's Sleep

In Mark 4 v 35-41 we read the account of Jesus stilling the fiercest of storms.

Then came a violent squall of wind which drove the waves aboard the boat until it was almost swamped. Jesus was in the stern asleep on the cushion. They awoke him with the words, "Master, don't you care that we're drowning?" And he woke up, rebuked the wind, and said to the waves, "Hush now! Be still!" The wind dropped and everything was very still. "Why are you so frightened? What has happened to your faith?! he asked them. But sheer awe swept over them, and they kept saying to each other, "Whoever can he be? —even the wind and the waves do what he tells them!"

Have you ever thought that it was strange that Jesus could sleep peacefully in the middle of a violent storm? His disciples and followers certainly thought that it was strange. They might correctly assume that Jesus would be extremely tired after teaching and being with the crowds all day. But here was Jesus- sleeping on a cushion, a sailor's leather cushion, in the stern of the boat. Around Him there was a violent squall of wind, a fierce windstorm which drove the waves over and into the boat, until the boat was in danger of being swamped and overwhelmed. The seasoned sailors were terrified thinking that they would lose their boat and their lives. The other small vessels with them were equally tossed around and there was the fear of an even greater loss of life. Jesus, still sleeping, had to be woken by the crew. "Master, do you not care that we are drowning?" Jesus addressed the wind and the raging sea and immediately there was a great calm (a perfect peacefulness.) AMP

When we are in the middle of a perfect storm where can we find a cushion, a pillow on which to rest our head and to sleep peacefully? In life, we must face turbulence of all kinds, the unexpected news or unwelcome report or letter, the family crisis, the financial bills that rock the boat, the relationship breakdown, the chronic stresses and tensions at work or church. Our little boat is about to be swamped and submerged. We are anxious, disturbed, and fearful of the future. We are tossed like driftwood on the ocean and have no peace. How can we sleep?

We can sleep knowing that Jesus is with us in the boat. While ever He is with us then no lasting harm or distress can sink us. We can lie down and sleep in peace at night knowing that Jesus is still ultimately in control. "Who then is this, that even the wind and the sea obey Him?" This same

Jesus now never slumbers or sleeps. He keeps watch over us day and night. Jesus can rebuke our circumstances and fears just as He did the wind. So, whatever storm you are facing, even if it feels like a cyclone, a tidal wave, a downpour, or a squall, please know that Jesus can handle it and that He is with you. The cushion on which I lay my head is the knowledge that He is faithful and that He has been in so many turbulent times in the past and I am confident that He will do so again. I just need to put my head on the cushion.

I will both lie down and sleep in peace; for you alone, O Lord, make me lie down in safety. Psalm 4 v 8 A Psalm of David

It is in vain that you rise up early and go late to rest, eating the bread of anxious toil; for he gives sleep to his beloved. Psalm 127 v 2 A Song of Ascents Solomon

He who keeps Israel will neither slumber nor sleep. Psalm 121 v 4 Assurance of God's protection. A Song of Ascents

Calm me, Lord, as you calmed the storm;
Still me, Lord, keep me from harm.
Let all the tumult within me cease,
Lord, enfold me in your peace.

Calm me, Lord, as you calmed the storm;
Calm me, Lord, as you calmed the storm;
Still me, Lord, keep me from harm.
Let all the tumult within me cease,
Enfold me, Lord, in your peace.

Calm me, Lord   Margaret Rizz, David Adam

Do it for one:
Jesus Heals a Demon-Possessed Man

So, they arrived in the region of the Gerasenes, across the lake from Galilee. As Jesus was climbing out of the boat, a man who was possessed by demons came out to meet him. For a long time, he had been homeless and naked, living in the tombs outside the town. As soon as he saw Jesus, he shrieked and fell down in front of him. Then he screamed, "Why are you interfering with me, Jesus, Son of the Most High God? Please, I beg you, don't torture me!" For Jesus had already commanded the evil spirit to come out of him. This spirit had often taken control of the man. Even when he was placed under guard and put in chains and shackles, he simply broke them and rushed out into the wilderness, completely under the demon's power. Luke 8 v 26-28 NLT

This is a very unusual story in any ways. Jesus and the disciples had crossed the Lake from Galilee, heading for the land of the Gerasenes. On their journey across the lake, they had experienced a most dreadful storm with wind, raging waves that had almost swamped their boat. The disciples had been terrified and fearful both for their own lives and for their little boat, until Jesus had miraculously calmed the storm. In this Bible account of the healing of this man, it almost seems as if Jesus had headed to the Gerasenes just to meet this one individual-He 'did it for one'.

This individual was naked, uncared for, and been living in the tombs outside of the town. He was a danger to others and to himself and was possessed by a demon. Whenever he was placed under guard, put in chains and shackles, he simply broke them and rushed out into the wilderness, completely under the demon's power. The whole community were frightened of him and isolated him to the town's graveyard, where he lived his sad, solitary life among the tomb stones. But Jesus came for him. After healing the man, the group who had gathered from a distance, to witness the incident, found him sitting at Jesus' feet, fully clothed and perfectly sane- and they were all afraid. In fact, a great wave of fear fell over them. The man, now restored and in his right mind, begged to go with Jesus and His followers, but Jesus insisted that he stay with his community, in the land of the Gerasenes. "So, he went all through the town proclaiming the great things Jesus had done for him".

After Jesus had healed the man, He and His disciples then returned across the lake to Galilee.

As individuals, we write a letter, make a phone call, knock on a neighbour's door, bake a cake, send a gift pack of goodies, collect some items of shopping, make representations on behalf of someone, collect someone's child from school for them, visit the Care Home or hospital, listen to a need- and when we do each of these things, we are doing it for one person. We are 'doing it for one.' No one else may see or ever know what we do. The act will be unseen and unknown, and we will never want recognition for what has been done. May we continue to 'do it for one'. We do not have to think big, reach a big audience, be visible, or have public recognition. We can do the small thing. But the effect and the consequences are powerful. We 'do it for one'.

The Hole in the Roof

One day Jesus was teaching, and Pharisees and teachers of the law were sitting there. They had come from every village of Galilee and from Judea and Jerusalem. And the power of the Lord was with Jesus to heal those who were ill. Some men came carrying a paralysed man on a mat and tried to take him into the house to lay him before Jesus. When they could not find a way to do this because of the crowd, they went up on the roof and lowered him on his mat through the tiles into the middle of the crowd, right in front of Jesus. When Jesus saw their faith, he said, 'Friend, your sins are forgiven.' Luke 5v 17-20

When I read this account of the paralyzed man, my mind naturally focusses on the group of four and the desperate man on his pallet bed. These men took every possible step to get their friend to Jesus and were determined and coordinated. There was no room here for a lone ranger. The task could not be done alone. They had to agree how to proceed, with great courage, innovation, and determination, balancing the risks and consequences. The obstacle to overcome was the crowd in the doorway.

But step into the story and place yourself at the scene and you will see that there are significant others in the account - the Pharisees, the Doctors of Law, the religious professionals who had come from every part of Galilee, Judea, Jerusalem and surrounding areas. They had come to scrutinize this local upstart teacher who was gaining quite a reputation for Himself. Because of their position and authority, they were seated. They were people of importance and rank. They perhaps had no sense of need for themselves or for others around them. They were cool, cynical, were there perhaps to find evidence against this young teacher.

In addition, there was a great crowd of people gathered outside, standing, pressing in, hoping to catch every word that was said inside this simple home. Perhaps some were mere observers.

But now Jesus steps into the middle of the frame. Jesus, seeing the faith of the four and the desperate man-- the outward, tangible, physical effort of their faith, forgives and heals. Wow! This will cause a storm. Jesus 'perceived their thoughts.' He knew exactly what they were thinking. But His words and act of healing demonstrated clearly that the Son of Man has power and position to forgive and heal. The crowd are ecstatic, praising, and glorifying God, witnesses to wonderful and incredible things. Jesus has challenged the system! He has bypassed the Temple, the priests, the sacrifices, and the rituals. They would go home rejoicing and telling others of the amazing things that they had just witnessed.

Sometimes we need to do something differently, to find the alternative way, to take a risk. We need to understand the situation, take stock and move forward. I cannot be a bystander, an observer, one in the crowd. Faith needs to be real and active. I cannot take up a seat without engagement or block the doorway for others. Jesus knows my innermost thoughts and motives. He can read my heart.

Lydia at Philippi

Numbers seem to count. The numbers of subscribers on YouTube, the number of followers on Facebook, Instagram, Snapchat, and TikTok and the number of likes or dislikes on things like Twitter. Our grandson, Sam follows a YouTuber called Sam Taber who has 1.14 million subscribers to his skateboarding and Gaming YouTube channels. Audience ratings for TV programmes count and of course we have just had significant elections where the number of votes counted are crucial. We like big numbers, large congregations, large followings but God, I am sure, works in a different way. He does not count numbers as we do. God works to a very clear purpose. As I continue to read through Acts, I have discovered Lydia.

From there we travelled to Philippi, a Roman colony, and the leading city of that district of Macedonia. And we stayed there several days. On the Sabbath we went outside the city gate to the river, where we expected to find a place of prayer. We sat down and began to speak to the women who had gathered there. One of those listening was a woman from the city of Thyatira named Lydia, a dealer in purple cloth. She was a worshiper of God. The Lord opened her heart to respond to Paul's message. When she and the members of her household were baptized, she invited us to her home. "If you consider me a believer in the Lord," she said, "come and stay at my house." And she persuaded us. Acts 16 v 12-15

After Paul and Silas came out of the prison, they went to Lydia's house, where they met with the brothers and sisters and encouraged them. Acts 16 v 40

Paul believed that he had been called, in a vision, to a new mission field in Macedonia, now Northern Greece. This would be the first time that the gospel had reached modern day Europe. Paul, Silas, Timothy, and Luke aimed to visit Philippi, a Roman colony, and a leading city in Macedonia. In Paul's vision, a man from Macedonia had called to Paul to 'come over and help us. There was no synagogue in Philippi, as there were insufficient numbers of men there to permit the formation of a synagogue, the group went to the river where they thought that there might be a place where people gathered for prayer, and soon found a group of women meeting there. If you were in Paul's shoes at this point, you might be checking your understanding of the vision and calling, or feeling disappointed, confused, thinking where are the believing men of this town?

But Paul began to speak to the group and to share the good news of Jesus with them. Lydia, one of those meeting at the riverbank, was a woman of significant standing and who, although not Jewish, was a believer in the one God. She was receptive to what Paul was saying and "The Lord opened her heart" to the message of Jesus. Lydia was to become very significant new Christian as she not only gave her heart to Christ but also opened her home to become the base for the new Christian community that would be established there. As a trader in luxury purple dyes, cloths and garments from Thyatira, her hometown, she would have been a woman of some means and influence with significant connections. The new community of Christians grew rapidly, so that by the time Paul and Silas left Philippi, there was a significant group of men and women meeting there.

Lydia's home had also become a place of refuge and restoration for Paul and Silas, after their brutal imprisonment, dramatic release from prison, and before the continuation of their mission and church planting ministry. Lydia offered what she could- her home, her skills, her support, her connections, her good standing and position and no doubt her financial support to the new church and her new Lord. She was one. She was perhaps the first Christian in Europe and would soon be followed by many more. The Philippian church was born and would soon grow.

Pray

The Lord opened her heart to pay attention and to respond.

Your word says I will seek you and find you when I seek you with all my heart. I want to hear your voice, Lord. Help me to desire your presence more than anything else. More than answers, more than direction, more than blessings. Your presence is a gift. Help me to respond to your love and to offer what I can.

Barnabas, The Encourager

Therefore encourage one another and build each other up, just as in fact you are doing. 1 Thessalonians 5 v 11

While reading through the Book of Acts, I have discovered the lovely character of Barnabas, who was delightfully given the name 'son of encouragement' by those who knew him well and worked with him. Barnabas was his given name, not his birth name, and so this was a wonderful, descriptive name. The word 'encourage' comes from an old French word apparently, meaning 'to make strong'. We all need people who can 'make us strong' and we need to encourage others to 'be strong'. We need folk in our circle who can give us support, confidence, who inspire and spur us on, and who say 'you can do it'. Barnabas had an eye for the potential in people, he looked for the positives, he was willing to be their champion and to stick with them. I am liking Barnabas and I would like to have some of the qualities that he demonstrated.

He had a generous, giving heart. We first hear of him in Acts when he sold perhaps a field or property in Cyprus, his home, donating the money to the early Christian community in Jerusalem.

Barnabas encouraged the early Christians, during the intense opposition that he faced personally.

When the Jerusalem Christians were doubtful of Paul's conversion claims, it was Barnabas who vouched for him, giving him a character reference and which lead to Paul being welcomed into the Christian community. Paul would go on to become the amazing preacher and evangelist. Barnabas saw beyond the fear and scepticism of others, accepted, and encouraged Paul, and drew him in.

Upon arrival in Jerusalem Paul tried to meet with the believers, but they were all afraid of him. They thought he was faking! Then Barnabas brought him to the apostles and told them how Paul had seen the Lord on the way to Damascus, what the Lord had said to him, and all about his powerful preaching in the name of Jesus. Then they accepted him, and after that he was constantly with the believers. Acts 9 v 26-28

Barnabas identified and mentored the young John Mark, possibly his cousin or nephew, defending him, even when Paul felt let down by the young man's desertion, at a crucial time in the ministry. John Mark had been put in 'the doghouse'. But Barnabas saw the potential of the young man and did not right him off. With Barnabas's mentoring, John Mark was supported and later gifted us with the Gospel of Mark. Barnabas dealt wisely with his sharp disagreement with Paul, over John Mark, Paul later acknowledging that Barnabas had done the right thing.

Like Paul, Barnabas had funded missionary journeys by undertaking paid work to raise the needed finance. When Paul emerged as the stronger teacher and evangelist, Barnabas was content to take second place. Position in the pecking order was not important to him.

Barnabas defended the place of the Gentile Christians and facilitated the inclusion of Gentile Christians into the early church without enduring the burdens of Jewish tradition and laws. Barnabas had a 'mission of encouragement' returning to the groups of new Gentile Christians, to strengthen them, sharing wise teaching and ministry.

Paul and Barnabas also appointed elders in every church and prayed for them with fasting, turning them over to the care of the Lord in whom they trusted. Acts 14 v 23

Barnabas was a kindly person, full of the Holy Spirit and strong in faith. As a result, large numbers of people were added to the Lord. Acts 11v 24

May we be people who give encouragement to others. May we be those who look out for others to try to draw them in. Let us be quick to see the potential in others.

Pray

Father God, help us to be positive people. Show us those people that we can come alongside to support and draw in. Help us to include others. Help us to look beyond the flaws and weaknesses in others to the potential hidden within. Jesus, you are our model of grace in word and deed. May we fix our eyes upon you.

WORDS OF LIFE

Flourish

I have realised that I am not good with house plants. My plants do not thrive, stay fresh and green. Even the common house plants that are supposed to be indestructible struggle under my care and the hardy succulents do not flourish as guaranteed. My plants are most likely in the wrong place, the wrong medium, and are either starved or overwatered. In the November magazine of House Beautiful was a timely article entitled How not to kill your houseplants by the gardening expert Joe Swift. Then as I looked at Psalm 92, a song for the Sabbath day, I was really encouraged that God's hope for us is to flourish, to be fresh and green even into our senior years and to continually bear fruit for Him, because of His faithful care for us. God knows what He is doing. He is the ace gardener and creator.

The righteous will flourish like a palm tree,
they will grow like a cedar of Lebanon;
planted in the house of the Lord,
they will flourish in the courts of our God.
They will still bear fruit in old age,
they will stay fresh and green,
proclaiming, "The Lord is upright;
he is my Rock, and there is no wickedness in him".
Psalm 92 v 12-15 NIV

The Amplified Version of the Psalm has a clearer description of God's longing for us to flourish, thrive and bear fruit. As the cedar, we are to be majestic and stable. As the date palm, we are to be long lived, upright and useful. Where He has planted us, we are to grow in grace, be vital, thrive, be fresh and be living memorials for Him. So, when I am struggling, feeling exhausted, shrivelled, and feeling my age, I am reminded that I can still thrive, flourish, and prosper into my old age and be a living memorial to a faithful, promise keeping God, who has care of me.

All the trees of the forest will know that I the Lord bring down the tall tree and make the low tree grow tall. I dry up the green tree and make the dry tree flourish. "I the Lord have spoken, and I will do it.'" Ezekiel 17 v 24 NIV

Pray

I confess that I do not feel fresh and green. I feel worn, shrivelled, and dried out. I am struggling for nourishment and water. In my season of drought and lack of visible growth and expansion, please encourage me with your presence and nurture. You are always there. May I set aside my feelings and trust in your word and promises. Autumn may be here now but Spring will surely come.

Fruit

My next-door neighbour and our local garden centre have had such bumper crops of apples that they have been thankful for people going to collect a share of their super abundance of fruit – fruit that they are not able to use. So, I have benefitted from both cooking apples and eating apples for free. Apparently, fruit trees can do this kind of thing -alternate years of a poor crop followed by a bumper crop. Sometimes a wet autumn, then a cold or icy spring and finally a very hot summer can make for the best growing season and a super yield of fruit. But whatever the cause for the extravagant crop, I have been glad for the abundant fruit. But what can you do with all that fruit? The fruit can be used in so many ways and turned into so many things- apple puree, compote, apple sauce, crumbles, pies, tarts, cereal bars, dried apple, baked apples, toffee apples, cakes, muffins, chutney, cider, added to porridge, donated, or just stored away. The list is almost endless.

Fruit shared in this way becomes versatile, a gift, to be used and developed imaginatively, creatively, and freely by others. There is no constraint or rule as to how they should use the fruit. There is a freedom to take it and to use it as they choose. The fruit can be added to, to make new, perhaps more inspiring dishes. The blessing of the fruit grows and spreads.

Jesus wants us to bear fruit that will last- just like the bumper harvest of the summer. Jesus is looking for lasting fruit-fruit that just keeps on giving.

You didn't choose me. I chose you. I appointed you to go and produce lasting fruit, so that the Father will give you whatever you ask for, using my name. John 15 v 16

Godly men are growing a tree that bears life-giving fruit, and all who win souls are wise. Proverbs 11 v 30 TLB

In Ezekiel and Revelation there are references to fruit trees growing and bearing lasting fruit. In Ezekiel's vision, the water that supplies the fruit trees flows from the sanctuary. It is God who provides the nourishment and water.

Fruit trees of all kinds will grow on both banks of the river. Their leaves will not wither, nor will their fruit fail. Every month they will bear fruit because the water from the sanctuary flows to them. Their fruit will serve for food and their leaves for healing. Ezekiel 47 NIV

Pray

We pray for our church, that there may be good, lasting fruit-fruit that can be shared with others. We pray that all may benefit from the fruit. Will you supply all that is needed for a large and generous crop.

Heirs

On the death of our daughter Charlotte, Sam, our grandson, at six years of age, became the legal heir of all the property, money and possessions that had belonged to his parents before their deaths. Phil and I act as the legal guardians of Sam's estate, until the time comes when he can act independently and manage his own financial affairs, although Sam is able to access and benefit from his inheritance is some circumstances. But Sam, as heir, beneficiary, and inheritor, is entitled to his inheritance. His inheritance is there for him now, held in trust and cannot be taken from him. He has not had to work for his inheritance, but it comes to him by right, by birth and by legal contract.

Sam's circumstances present a very clear picture of our status as children of the Father, as heirs with Jesus and as beneficiaries of all that is to come, both now and in the future-our inheritance. When we accepted Christ as our Saviour, we were adopted into God's family as His children. We are His rightful heirs, we are joint heirs with Christ, and we have an inheritance that we share with all of God's children. We do not have to work for it. It is a gift of grace and not of works. This is a mind-blowing privilege. I am a daughter of the heavenly Father, and you also are a daughter or a son.

I don't have to 'work' to prove myself as worthy of this gift and this inheritance. There are things of the inheritance that I can access now but there is even more waiting for me in the future.

For those who are led by the Spirit of God are the children of God. The Spirit you received does not make you slaves, so that you live in fear again; rather, the Spirit you received brought about your adoption to sonship. And by him we cry, 'Abba, Father.' The Spirit himself testifies with our spirit that we are God's children. Now if we are children, then we are heirs – heirs of God and co-heirs with Christ, if indeed we share in his sufferings in order that we may also share in his glory. Romans 8 v 14-17

When you believed, you were marked in him with a seal, the promised Holy Spirit, who is a deposit guaranteeing our inheritance until the redemption of those who are God's possession – to the praise of his glory. Ephesians 1 v 14 NIV

So, in Christ Jesus you are all children of God through faith, for all of you who were baptised into Christ have clothed yourselves with Christ. There is neither Jew nor Gentile, neither slave nor free, nor is there male and female, for you are all one in Christ Jesus. If you belong to Christ, then you are Abraham's seed, and heirs according to the promise. Galatians 3 v 26-29 NIV

He saved us through the washing of rebirth and renewal by the Holy Spirit, whom he poured out on us generously through Jesus Christ our Saviour, so that, having been justified by his grace, we might become heirs having the hope of eternal life. Titus 3 v 7 NIV

We are heirs of God Almighty,
Apple of the Father's eye;
Free, forgiven, loved, accepted,
Clothed in righteousness divine.
Chosen to be pure and blameless
From before the world began;
Grace for every situation,
Sheltered in the Father's hand.
Stuart Townsend

Available

God wants each of us to be 'available', to be willing to be used. He desires each person to be a part of His work. Each person has something of themselves to bring. We may feel that we do not have much or even anything to offer, but this could not be further from the truth. We are to bring and to contribute whatever we can- big or small. God has uniquely designed each person with their personality and gifts, to do unique works, that He prepared in advance for each one of us to do. No exceptions. Our role is to discover those talents and gifts and then to step forward and to be available.

"God seems to look past the obvious and the qualified to choose the hidden and the unqualified to do his greatest work. He doesn't want to use a few super gifted people. He wants to use all of us. He wants His whole body to come alive and thrive. He uses ordinary people to do amazing things, so the glory goes to Him and not to us." Mining for Gold by Tom Camacho

"Now remember what you were, my friends, when God called you. From the human point of view few of you were wise or powerful or of high social standing. God purposely chose what the world considers nonsense to shame the wise, and he chose what the world considers weak in order to shame the powerful. He chose what the world looks down on and despises and thinks is nothing, to destroy what the world thinks is important. This means that no one can boast in God's presence. 1 Corinthians 1 v 26-29

When Moses was setting before the people the instructions that he had received from God for the construction of the Tabernacle, the tent of meeting and the ark of the covenant and everything that went with it, he needed everyone to step forward with their gifts, skills, and talents. All who were willing, men and women alike. It even mentions the women who spin the goat hair as well as the expensive silk. Each person did what they could and brought to the table what they could.

Then the whole Israelite community withdrew from Moses' presence, and everyone who was willing and whose heart moved them came and brought an offering to the Lord for the work on the tent of meeting, for all its service, and for the sacred garments. All who were willing, men and women alike. Exodus 35 v 20-22

When David outlined the instructions for the building of a permanent Temple, which Solomon his son would oversee, once again it would be a case of every person being needed and being involved. They were willing, they were available, and they stepped forward.

"I have seen with joy how willingly your people who are here have given to you. Lord the God of our fathers Abraham, Isaac, and Israel, keep these desires and thoughts in the hearts of your people forever, and keep their hearts loyal to you."

We don't have to be great, super clever, rich, successful, or influential. We just need to be willing. We just need to be available.

Restore to me the joy of your salvation and grant me a willing spirit, to sustain me. Psalm 51 v 12 David NIV

Jesus reached out his hand and touched the man. "I am willing," he said. "Be clean!" Immediately he was cleansed of his leprosy. Matthew 8 v 3

Dwell Remain Abide

Lord, who can dwell in your tent? Who can live on your holy mountain? David Psalm 15 v 1

I long to dwell in your tent forever and take refuge in the shelter of your wings. Psalm 61 v 4

When I was teaching with Amity, a Chinese Christian Organisation, I had the privilege of being the guest for a day in a traditional Inner Mongolian Yurt. These structures can be assembled and disassembled in about one hour and so are ideal dwellings for the nomadic Mongolian herders and farmers. I am sure that David would have known quite a lot about nomadic tent dwelling. But I for one prefer my dwelling to be of a more permanent and fixed abode. We have had the privilege of owning several houses during our marriage- most of them with fixed foundations.

David longed to 'dwell' with God and to be in a continuous relationship with Him within His shelter- His tent. He wanted to 'settle,' to be at home with,' 'to make himself feel at home with,' 'to be fixed with' his loving God. In this dwelling, David knew that he would be safe- he would dwell in safety.

One thing I have desired of the Lord, that will I seek: That I may dwell in the house of the Lord all the days of my life, to behold the beauty of the Lord, and to inquire in His temple. Psalm 27 v 4 KJV

I'm asking God for one thing, only one thing: To live with him in his house my whole life long. I'll contemplate his beauty; I'll study at his feet. Psalm 27 v 4 MSG

Surely goodness and mercy shall follow me all the days of my life, and I shall dwell in the house of the Lord forever. Psalm 23 v 6

In peace I will both lie down and sleep; for you alone, Lord, make me dwell in safety. Psalm 4 v 8

He who lives in the safe place of the Most High will be in the shadow of the All-powerful. Psalm 91 v 1

To dwell or to take up residence somewhere is more than just to 'occupy' the space. It means to live there, to make yourself comfortable and at home in that place, to be established there. We talk about 'putting down roots.' John, speaking of future times, says that God will live with us in His home among men.

I heard a loud shout from the throne saying, "Look, the home of God is now among men, and he will live with them, and they will be his people; yes, God himself will be among them. Revelation 21 v 3

In Christ alone my hope is found
He is my light, my strength, my song
This cornerstone, this solid ground
Firm through the fiercest drought and storm
What heights of love, what depths of peace

When fears are stilled, when strivings cease
My comforter, my all in all
Here in the love of Christ I stand.
Keith Getty / Stuart Townend

Purpose

I was not brought up in a Christian household, although I did attend the local C of E Sunday School and occasional Parish Church service as a child, and even though Christian contact was limited, I was certain of three things. I never doubted that God existed, I knew that God loved me, and perhaps more significant, I knew that He had a plan and a purpose for my life. So, the word 'purpose' is a key one for me. As a young person, what I did not understand was the death of Jesus by crucifixion. When I entered a church of any denomination, there would be a simple empty cross or a cross on which was placed the body of Christ, prominently displayed. So, it was not until the days of the preaching tours of Billy Graham, that I began to realize what Jesus's death was truly about, about redemption and salvation, and what this could mean for me personally. I heard the gospel explained clearly and simply for the first time. I became a Christian at the age of sixteen at a Billy Graham Crusade meeting. So, for many years since that time, I have walked with Jesus, and I have tried to find His purpose for my life.

One of the books that has perhaps had the biggest influence on me, is the book The Purpose Driven Life by Rick Warren. The author emphasizes that we are called on purpose for a purpose. God has always had a plan, a design, and a purpose for each of us. Rick Warren, in this journal style book, identifies several key purposes for life. He encourages the reader to discover what they were 'made to do', designed for, and to perform those as acts as a form of worship. How we serve Him, and others depends of course on our natural gifts, spiritual gifts, talents, experiences, personalities, and opportunities. The book helps the reader to discover their role in God's plan and His mission. His purpose for their life.

As a child I was aware that God had a plan for my life and as a very senior person now, I am still discovering new aspects of his plan. There have been many new discoveries of His purpose along the way.

And we know that in all things God works for the good of those who love him, who have been called according to his purpose. Romans 8 v 28

For it is God who is at work in you, enabling you both to desire and to act for his chosen purpose.

Philippians 2 v 13

Many are the plans in a person's heart, but it is the Lord's purpose that prevails. Proverbs 19 v 21 NIV

We humans keep brainstorming options and plans, but God's purpose prevails. Proverbs 19 v 21 MSG

Plans

We may make our plans, but God has the last word. Proverbs 16 v 1 GNT

People make plans in their hearts. But only the Lord can make those plans come true. Proverbs 16 v 1 NCV

I am a planner. My key strengths are planning and organisation. Twenty-seven years of Primary School teaching further developed those skills. As a teacher, you are constantly planning, organising, and watching the clock. Working full time, in addition to family duties and family life with four growing children was a test of organisation and planning. Our kitchen calendar required a separate line for each member of the family for each day of the week. Swimming lessons, music lessons, play dates, Cubs, Brownies, Guides, Scouts, parties, family get togethers, holidays, staff meetings, Parents Evenings, appointments, school trips and the list goes on! Then build in church activities and fellowship, family contacts and holidays and you can appreciate the need for planning- and the diary!

The danger is that I am such 'a planner and forward organiser' that I can run ahead and believe that I know exactly what to do and when. I know how it should be done and when. I know what the next step should be. I am objective, rational, and make decisions quickly and then may attempt to convince those around me that this is the right course of action or plan to follow. The temptation is to bring any plans, thoughts for next steps, a direction, a new path or even a change of career or role before God for rubber stamping.

Instead, it is important to be reflective, and to try to seek God first and lay any options before Him. When you are busy, stressed and over committed then this can be a challenge to say the least. I have learned to rationally look at all options and write down a pros and cons list about any major decisions. I try to be guided by peace and a word from scripture. It is good to talk with others to gain their reflections, comments, advice, and the benefit of their experience. The Holy Spirit is a good prompter, reading our hearts, thoughts, hopes, ambitions, and longings. As a good rule of thumb, if you are a little unsettled about any course of action then it is wise to put a decision on hold.

The Book of Proverbs has a lot to say about plans and planning. We need to commit our plans, our work, our activities to God and seek the support and wise counsel of others.

Commit to the Lord whatever you do, and he will establish your plans. Proverbs 16 v 3 NIV

Put God in charge of your work, then what you've planned will take place. Proverbs 16 v 3 MSG

"Refuse good advice and watch your plans fail; take good counsel and watch them succeed." Proverbs 15 v 22 MSG

Pray

Forgive me when I rush in and rush on. Forgive me when I plan my days, my week, my year without any reference to you. Forgive me when I act as if I always know best. I know that you have a perfect plan for my life and that my times and my future are in your safe hands. May your Holy Spirit and your peace be my guide.

For I know the plans I have for you, declares the Lord, plans to prosper you and not to harm you, plans to give you hope and a future. Jeremiah 29 v 11 NIV

Roots

"Deep roots are not reached by the frost."
JRR Tolkien

"When the roots are deep, there is no reason to fear the wind." – African Proverb

"A tree's beauty lies in its branches, but its strength lies in its roots." Matshona Dhliwayo

As I sit at my window now, and as we are heading into Autumn, I am watching the leaves gradually fall from the trees and the bare branches appear once again. This is a wonderful process which ensures future growth for the trees. Deciduous trees lose their leaves in Autumn and the leaf litter falling to the floor provides a growth medium for new plants, and so this is a beautiful system of ensuring future fruitfulness and growth both for the tree itself and other plants. The roots hold the tree firmly in place and help it to withstand even the fiercest storm.

There are some wonderful idioms about roots. 'Getting to the root of the problem', 'being rooted to the spot', 'at grass roots level', and 'finding the root cause of something'. Being 'rooted' means being established, dwelling securely, or 'putting down roots. The Bible also has some wonderful things to say about 'being rooted'.

So then, just as you received Christ Jesus as Lord, continue to live your lives in him, rooted and built up in him, strengthened in the faith as you were taught, and overflowing with thankfulness. Colossians 2 v 7

I pray that you may have your roots and foundation in love, so that you, together with all God's people, may have the power to understand how broad and long, how high, and deep, is Christ's love. Ephesians 3 v 17-19 GNT

The book Green Leaf in Drought by Isobel Kuhn describes the experiences of two China Inland Missionaries, who endured starvation, isolation, persecution, and unknown hardships during their time in China. Despite their harsh and sometimes horrific circumstances, they remained strong and rooted in their faith. Their experiences, resilience and 'rootedness' challenged many in China and beyond. Isobel Kuhn wrote the biography to encourage Christians to remain strong and faithful in all circumstances-however bad. The following verse from Jeremiah became a strong image for her book.

They will be like a tree planted by the water that sends out its roots by the stream. It does not fear when heat comes; its leaves are always green. It has no worries in a year of drought and never fails to bear fruit. Jeremiah 17 v 8

May we be rooted and grounded in the love of Jesus. May we be able to withstand the fiercest storm and frost that any 'winter' or 'drought' may throw at us.

Pray

Lord In life, we can experience knocks, setbacks, uncertainties, fierce storms and times of drought.

We may waver and shake but help us to be rooted in your love for us and within us, so that we can stay strong. May we have the confidence to say, 'I can do all things through Christ who strengthens me'.

Hope: Pandora's box

As a young child I remember listening to the story of Pandora's box. It captured my imagination. It is a story about hope. In this story, Zeus created a box that contained all manner of evils without the owner of the box realising. Unfortunately, Pandora opened the box after being warned not to and unleashed a multitude of harmful spirits that inflicted all sorts of unhappiness into the world- greed, envy, hatred, mistrust, anger, sorrow, revenge and more. Inside the box however there was also an unreleased healing spirit named Hope. From ancient times people have realized that hope has the power to heal and help in times of great anguish.

To hope, means to look forward to with desire and confidence, to have an expectation and a confidence. We speak of hope when we believe that something longed for will happen. It is our state of mind and a longing for a positive outcome in respect of events and circumstances in life. It can keep us going even in the toughest times. We need hope.

On one of our summer holidays to the forest of Dean, Gloucestershire we went into the Hereford Cathedral which was a beautiful retreat from the busyness of the day. Inside the cathedral was a huge, illuminated sign signifying hope. It was encouraging and lifted our spirits. Outside the cathedral was a statue with arms outstretched to heaven in an attitude of longing and supplication. I did not check to see the name of the artist or the title of the sculpture, but it just seemed to capture the emptiness of man and a longing and hopefulness for something more.

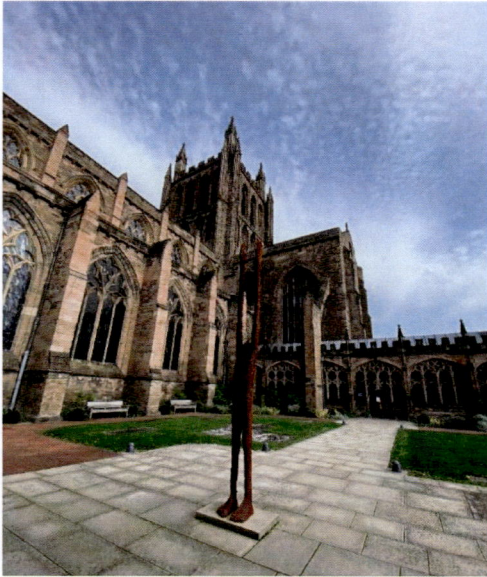

When we experience any time of difficulty or challenge, may we reach our arms to heaven and may we have hope.

Pray

When trouble darkens our world, give us light. When despair numbs our souls, give us hope. When we stumble and fall, lift us up. When doubts assail us, give us faith. When nothing seems sure, give us trust. When hopes fade, give us vision. When we lose our way, be our guide. That we may find serenity in Your presence, and purpose in doing Your will.

Knowledge and Wisdom

It is possible to collect large amounts of factual knowledge- through books, research, reading, and the Internet. We acquire facts, truths, and principles to build up our expertise and ability- or to add to a catalogue of qualifications. But we can still make a mess of things, make poor decisions, and go down wrong paths. Wisdom is always needed. We need wisdom to take the knowledge that we have, evaluate each new situation, use our experience, insight and lessons learned, and gain perspective before we think, speak and act. Knowledge is vital and good, but that knowledge needs to be used with discernment, judgement, and common sense. It takes a good dose of wisdom, experience, time, and patience to work out what is helpful, timely and appropriate. Wisdom. Discernment. Understanding. Let us ask God for this wisdom as Solomon did. Jesus is described as the source of all wisdom and knowledge.

If you need wisdom, ask our generous God, and he will give it to you. He will not rebuke you for asking. But when you ask him, be sure that your faith is in God alone. James 1 v 5-6

Fear of the Lord is the foundation of true wisdom. All who obey his commandments will grow in wisdom. Psalm 111 v 10 NLT

For God's secret plan, now at last made known, is Christ himself. In him lie hidden all the mighty, untapped treasures of wisdom and knowledge. Colossians 2 v 2-3 The Living Bible

The Spirit of the Lord will rest on him—the Spirit of wisdom and of understanding, the Spirit of counsel and of might, the Spirit of the knowledge and fear of the Lord—and he will delight in the fear of the Lord. He will not judge by what he sees with his eyes, or decide by what he hears with his ears; but with righteousness he will judge the needy, with justice he will give decisions for the poor of the earth. Isaiah 11v2-4

You are wisdom unimagined,
who could understand your ways.
Reigning high above the heavens,
reaching down in endless grace.

Bryan Brown / Aaron Keyes / Jack Anthony Mooring
Sovereign Over Us lyrics © Meaux Jeaux Music, Worshiptogether.com
Songs, Thankyou Music Ltd., Jack Mooring Music

Troubles

Jesus did not promise a trouble-free life. A lifetime of concerns, upsets, pressure, troubles, anguish, and conflicts is almost guaranteed and especially if you are part of a large family or community group. But we are encouraged to face these troubles with patience, insight, love and with the help of the Holy Spirit and in the power of God. If we have the right attitude towards these hurdles in the road, then we will never 'go under' but we will be able to travel through such difficulties and to use the experiences to help and support others. Paul and other early Christians experienced bucket loads of troubles and hardships but remained unswerving in their faith.

Paul's Hardships:

As far as we are concerned, we do not wish to stand in anyone's way, nor do we wish to bring discredit on the ministry God has given us. Indeed, we want to prove ourselves genuine ministers of God whatever we must go through—patient endurance of troubles or even disasters, being flogged or imprisoned; being mobbed, having to work like slaves, having to go without food or sleep. All this we want to meet with sincerity, with insight and patience; by sheer kindness and the Holy Spirit; with genuine love, speaking the plain truth, and living by the power of God. Our sole defence, our only weapon, is a life of integrity, whether we meet honour or dishonour, praise, or blame. Called "impostors" we must be true, called "nobodies" we must be in the public eye. Never far from death, yet here we are alive, always "going through it" yet never "going under". We know sorrow, yet our joy is inextinguishable. We have "nothing to bless ourselves with" yet we bless many others with true riches. We are penniless, and yet in reality we have everything worth having. 2 Corinthians 6 v 3-10 JBP

There are certain types of 'trouble' that can be crushing and cause great emotional turmoil, distress, and anguish. Trouble might be acute and painful, or it may be chronic and long lasting with little hope of reprieve. Paul knew all kinds of trouble- immediate and long term. The recent pandemic may leave many people with chronic ill health or mental health concerns. We may experience loss, grief, family tension, conflict, physical or mental ill health or a myriad of other things that we are unable to share. But the comfort and perhaps the remedy will be found in Christ.

The righteous cry out, and the Lord hears them; He delivers them from all their troubles. The Lord is close to the broken-hearted and saves those who are crushed in spirit. The righteous person may have many troubles, but the Lord delivers him from them all. Psalm 34 v 17-19

Our God is the Father of compassion and the God of all comfort, who comforts us in all our troubles, so that we can comfort those in any trouble with the comfort we ourselves receive from God. 2 Corinthians 1 v 3-5

PRAY For those who are carrying burdens and weights for others.

The storm may roar without me,
My heart may low be laid
But God is round about me,
And can I be dismayed?

From the hymn In heavenly love abiding

Integrity

"Integrity is doing the right thing even when no one is watching." C. S. Lewis

Whoever walks in integrity walks securely, but whoever takes crooked paths will be found out. Proverbs 10 v 9

When I was preparing teachers and volunteers for their weeks of volunteer teaching in China, there were several personal characteristics and qualities that I asked us all to be mindful of. Chinese colleagues and students, despite sometimes poor English, are extremely perceptive and trained 'people watchers.' Therefore, we needed to ensure that we were genuinely open, authentic, real, and sincere- all the time-even when perhaps we thought that we were not being observed in the classroom or in the community. Our Chinese colleagues would see through any insincerity and falseness. I encouraged us all to be as transparent, honest, and as open as possible, acknowledging mistakes, lack of knowledge, and letting them 'in' to the real person standing in front of them. One of my favourite words is integrity and it is a quality that I want to see grow in myself, and have always wanted to see developing in students, whether adult or child. Integrity is being consistent, trustworthy, accountable, and keeping to a personal set of values - all the time and even when things are tough, and no one is watching.

Jesus was recognized as a person of integrity. Those who opposed Jesus and were hostile to Him, knew that He was a person of truth and integrity, showed no partiality or deference to anyone, and was not easily swayed or diverted from His message or mission. They recognized that He spoke and taught the truth of God.

They sent their disciples to him along with the Herodians. "Teacher," they said, "we know that you are a man of integrity and that you teach the way of God in accordance with the truth. You aren't swayed by others because you pay no attention to who they are.   Matthew 22 v 16 NIV

Paul and his co-workers also knew that they had to live 'transparent' lives, as the world was watching. Paul experienced hard work, hardships, opposition, beatings, imprisonments, and distress. Yet, he remained faithful and true, refusing to put any stumbling block in the way of others.

As far as we are concerned, we do not wish to stand in anyone's way, nor do we wish to bring discredit on the ministry God has given us. Indeed, we want to prove ourselves genuine ministers of God whatever we must go through—patient endurance of troubles or even disasters, being flogged or imprisoned; being mobbed, having to work like slaves, having to go without food or sleep. All this we want to meet with sincerity, with insight and patience; by sheer kindness and the Holy Spirit; with genuine love, speaking the plain truth, and living by the power of God. Our sole defence, our only weapon, is a life of integrity, whether we meet honour or dishonour, praise, or blame.   2 Corinthians 6 v 7 JBP

These are the things you are to do: Speak the truth to one another. Judge with truth so there will be peace within your gates. Zechariah 8 v 16

Good judgement

There are lots of values that I long to see developing in our children and grandchildren-values that will help them to cope with the challenges of life. Strong qualities such as resilience, endurance, kindness, integrity, respect, self-esteem, self-confidence, and sound judgement. Good, sound judgement is important. We make hundreds of small decisions every day and some big, significant decisions during our lifetime, and so we need to have that ability to make correct, careful, considered decisions. It is more than just basic common sense, although that is essential. The old-fashioned word is 'being prudent.' The prudent person is shrewd, careful, weighs up the pros and cons, judges well, can be cautious, takes the long view, is a planner, reserves comments and words until they are needed and appropriate, and is able 'to read' situations and people with maturity and understanding. There is a great deal of support in schools now for teaching emotional intelligence, personal development, sound relationships, citizenship, and so forth.

The young David, even before the Goliath episode, was recognized as having many of these qualities.

In 1 Samuel 16 we find the troubled Saul seeking a close, trustworthy companion, a gifted musician and harp player, who would be able to relieve his dark moods. Saul's servants knew immediately who would fit the bill. That chosen candidate was the young boy, David. David's reputation had gone before him.

One of the servants said to Saul, "One of Jesse's sons from Bethlehem is a talented harp player. Not only that—he is a brave warrior, a man of war, and has good judgment. He is also a fine-looking young man, and the Lord is with him." 1 Samuel 16 v 18 NLT

Other translations used different phrases for 'good judgement,' such as 'prudent in matters', 'chooses his words carefully', 'a man of good presence', 'prudent in speech', and 'of good, solid judgement.'

David was taken into the royal household and would go on to play a key role in the kingdom. David had already been anointed by Samuel as king in Saul's place, would dramatically defeat the mighty Philistine, Goliath, and become a leader in Israel's army. As David's fortunes, stature, popularity, and reputation grew, Saul became more fearful of him. But Saul was not just afraid of David's growing wisdom, abilities, and successes. Saul was afraid of him because the Lord was clearly with him in all things.

And David went out wherever Saul sent him, and he prospered and behaved himself wisely; and Saul set him over the men of war. 1 Samuel 18 v 5

David acted wisely in all his ways and succeeded, and the Lord was with him. When Saul saw how capable and successful David was, he stood in awe of him. v 14-15

David had more success and behaved himself more wisely than all Saul's servants, so that his name was very dear and highly esteemed. v 30

PRAY Father God, we pray for our children, and our young men and women. We want them to be people of integrity, wise beyond their years in attitude, behaviour and speech, people of sound judgement and character. More than anything, we want them to know you and that you would be with them in all things.

Endurance

I love the word 'endurance.' I have had lots of challenges along life's way to help me begin to develop this value and quality. You may be familiar with the phrase 'when the going gets tough the tough get going.' 'Stickability', staying power, resolve, perseverance, and steadfastness, are perhaps key values or qualities that we need, if we are to mature and have the 'patient endurance' that is often referred to in the Bible.

Consider it a sheer gift, friends, when tests and challenges come at you from all sides. You know that under pressure, your faith-life is forced into the open and shows its true colours. So don't try to get out of anything prematurely. Let it do its work, so you become mature and well-developed, not deficient in any way. James 1 v 3 MSG

There is one sure thing in life and that is, that challenges, problems, setbacks, and difficulties will come and that we need the emotional stamina and stability to stand our ground and be able to deal with whatever the situation requires. Jesus does not promise a trouble-free life as a Christian, but He does want us to be secure, stable, and strong-strong in His love. There will be trials, disappointments, hurdles, obstacles, and problems a plenty, which will provide opportunities for this 'patient endurance. We would love God to fix our situation and remove all our problems. But he often calls on us to endure and promises to be with us and strengthen us as we do so.

William Carey was the father of the modern missionary movement, and he went to India in 1793. During his time there he faced a succession of problems and setbacks – but he kept going. He once said to his nephew, "If after my removal anyone should think it worth his while to write my life, I will give you a criterion by which you may judge its correctness. If he gives me credit for being a plodder, he will describe me justly. Anything beyond this will be too much. I can plod. I can persevere in any definite pursuit. To this I owe everything."

We also glory in our sufferings, because we know that suffering produces perseverance; perseverance, character; and character, hope. And hope does not put us to shame, because God's love has been poured out into our hearts through the Holy Spirit, who has been given to us. Romans 5 v 3-4

Take the old prophets as your mentors. They put up with anything, went through everything, and never once quit, all the time honouring God. What a gift life is to those who stay the course! You've heard, of course, of Job's staying power, and you know how God brought it all together for him at the end. That's because God cares, cares right down to the last detail. James 5 v 11 MSG

BEATITUDES

The 'Beautiful Attitudes' or the 'be'- attitudes of Jesus Matthew 5

Jesus had begun His teaching and healing ministry and in Matthew 5 and Luke 6, we find the account of Jesus being followed by the disciples, followers, and crowds, going high up on to the slope of a mountain, to a quiet place, sitting down and beginning to teach. In a traditional teaching pose, in front of a huge crowd, Jesus does not give a lecture, a treatise or a speech, but His value system- His statements of the characteristics of 'being', or the 'be'- attitudes. These 'beautiful attitudes' were intended to be seen in His followers, and each of us, and to be a true reflection of Him. As we consider each Beatitude in turn, I have added some personal thoughts based on each one, along with the words of Jesus in different versions of the Bible, which may prove to be more of a meditation on His amazing words. I trust that you may be challenged and blessed as you consider each of these blessings in turn.

The Golden Rule

"Do to others whatever you would like them to do to you. This is the essence of all that is taught in the law and the prophets. Matthew 7 v 12

This statement is often known as The Golden Rule. The Jews were familiar with something like this but always in the negative form. Only Jesus used the thought positively.

Blessed are the poor in spirit: for theirs is the kingdom of heaven

You're blessed when you are at the end of your rope. With less of you there is more of God and His rule. Matthew 5 v 3 MSG

What happiness comes to you when you feel your spiritual poverty! For yours is the realm of heaven's kingdom.

God blesses those people who depend only on Him. They belong to the kingdom of heaven. CEV

Jesus wants us to recognize and to understand who we really are and our need of Him. We are to recognize an emptiness that only He can fill. We are to see ourselves in the low place, willing to ask for and to accept help.

We are to see and admit to our weaknesses and to see others as better than ourselves. We are to be willing to be vulnerable, willing to be unseen, and adaptable to others. We are to be those who are happy to serve, without insisting on things being done our way, without needing our voice to be heard, and without taking the credit for things. We are to recognize that anything we 'do' will not earn us favour with Him but that everything is by His grace. This is the opposite of self-promotion, self-reliance, and seeking advantage over others. It is being content to be where God has put us, without having that inflated view of ourselves. This is a change that can only come gradually.

The Methodist Covenant Prayer

I am no longer my own but yours.
Put me to what you will,
rank me with whom you will;
put me to doing,
put me to suffering;
let me be employed for you,
or laid aside for you,
exalted for you,
or brought low for you;
let me be full,
let me be empty,
let me have all things,
let me have nothing:
I freely and wholeheartedly yield all things
to your pleasure and disposal.
And now, glorious and blessed God,
Father, Son and Holy Spirit,
you are mine and I am yours. So be it.
And the covenant now made on earth, let it be ratified in heaven.

Blessed are those who mourn, for they will be comforted

"You're blessed when you feel you've lost what is most dear to you. Only then can you be embraced by the One most dear to you. MSG

"How happy are those who know what sorrow means for they will be given courage and comfort! JBP

Grieving in all its forms and any kind of loss or sense of loss, not just the loss of a loved one, can cause overwhelming sadness and grief. It may be the loss of a relationship, job, health, physical or mental wellbeing, finance, prospects, career, or whole host of other life situations. Sadness, grief, sorrow, and loss of this kind, can cause a 'heart sickness' that feels as if it cannot be healed.

The prophet Jeremiah, when he considered the ruin of his people and the captivity of Judah, expressed his overwhelming sadness, intense sense of loss and sorrow, poignantly. *"Incurable sorrow has overwhelmed me, and my heart is sick within me"*. *"My sorrow is beyond healing; my heart is faint within me"*. *"There is no cure for my grief. My heart breaks for what I see and hear." Jeremiah: 8 v 18.* Jeremiah longed for hope and a healing balm.

God wants us to know that whatever the nature of our pain, sorrow, loss, and grief, we can experience His comfort, as He is the source of every comfort.

Praise be to the God and Father of our Lord Jesus Christ, the Father of compassion and the God of all comfort, who comforts us in all our troubles, so that we can comfort those in any trouble with the comfort we ourselves receive from God. 2 Corinthians 1 v 3-4

Jesus: Don't get lost in despair; believe in God, and keep on believing in Me. John 14 v 1 The Voice

"Don't let yourselves be disturbed. Trust in God and trust in me. John 14 v 1

Blessed are the meek, for they will inherit the earth

"You're blessed when you're content with just who you are—no more, no less. That's the moment you find yourselves proud owners of everything that can't be bought. Matthew 5 v 5 MSG

"Blessed (inwardly peaceful, spiritually secure, worthy of respect) are the gentle, the kind-hearted, the sweet-spirited, the self-controlled, for they will inherit the earth. AMP

Contentment is a beautiful word. I am told that the word contentment comes from the Latin word *contentus* which means 'held together' or 'intact, whole'. Contentment is a sense of being complete, of wholeness, accepting who you are, what you have and your situation. The ability to be satisfied despite circumstances.

In our western society we pursue goals, happiness, our desires, ambitions, financial gain, control, validation, success, and stuff. We look for external sources of happiness. We compare ourselves with others and with who they are and what they have. But perhaps contentment is about appreciation, the reality of the present and satisfaction.

A group of isolated nomads, high in the Himalayas of Eastern Bhutan, were shown images of various emotions and asked for their own words to describe each emotion. When asked for the word that described contentment one of them said "It's hard to translate it exactly, but the closest word is chokkshay, which is a very deep and spiritual word that means 'the knowledge of enough.' It was the idea that right here, right now, everything is just right as it is, regardless of what you are experiencing outside." Daniel Cordaro Research Anthropologist.

I need to know that 'I am enough'. I am who I am, and I will not compare myself with someone else. How whole do you feel inside? Of course, it is always possible to change and to grow as an individual. 'My situation is enough'. It may not be ideal, it may be challenging, it may be painful, but I can have an attitude of gratitude for the bits that are good. I can accept the reality of the present without kicking against it. I can be intentional about accepting my situation and choose to be content, while making any adjustments that are possible.

I want to be in this 'enough' place- held together, intact, whole, and content. If I can reach for this then I may become a gentler person, sweet spirited, self-controlled, kind, gracious, not brash or boasting, and my life will have a positive influence on others. If I can be at peace with myself and willing to wait and let God take control of my life and my circumstances, then I will have more of the meekness and contentment that He wants for me.

I have learned to be content, whatever the circumstances may be. I know now how to live when things are difficult, and I know how to live when things are prosperous. In general, and in particular, I have learned the secret of facing either poverty or plenty. I am ready for anything through the strength of the One who lives within me. Paul, Philippians 4

Blessed are those who hunger and thirst for righteousness, for they will be filled

"Happy are those whose greatest desire is to do what God requires; God will satisfy them fully! JBP

Babies and small children have a clear system of notifying parents and carers when they are hungry or thirsty and they need food, milk, or water. They cry, may become crotchety, irritable, and can clearly make their needs known. When our son was small, and even into teenage years, we never left home without an emergency pack of food and drink. This would consist of a cereal bar, apple, banana, and a drink and sometimes a chocolate bar as a treat. These emergency rations would accompany us to the cinema, park, and any outing from home as we attempted to avoid his rising irritability and reducing low blood sugar levels. By contrast, I cannot remember a time when I was hungry or thirsty. By building into my day a regular pattern of four meals with snacks and drinks in between whenever possible, I can maintain a good balance and satisfy my needs for nutrition and fluids. It is hard to imagine what it must feel like to be without food or water for days or even weeks, and to have to survive with minimal nutrition. Many in our world today are in this desperate position of being hungry and lacking clean water and it has been distressing recently to see the images of famine in Madagascar not caused by war but by climate change.

In this Beatitude, we are called to have a hunger and thirst for God and for His righteousness. I am to tune into the hunger pangs, the cues, that make me recognize my need of Him and so have an appetite and longing for Him. Sadly, often days go by, and I have missed the hunger cues and signals. I have been too busy, too focussed on other things and have not had a regular pattern of meals with Him- spending time with Him. So, my appetite has reduced and become dulled. Jesus promises me that if I come to Him, I will never be hungry and I will never be thirsty. I love this image from Isaiah of food stalls along the way and picnics on the hills as I travel with Jesus. I need to have my regular meals, but there are the emergency rations to hand too. I can be satisfied, supplied, enlivened, and I can be full. Nothing else will fully satisfy.

Pray

May I be childlike and cry out to you for help and for your presence.

May I be aware of your presence and nurture during the day, beginning and ending each day with you. May I be thankful for your constant care and provision.

They will never be hungry or thirsty. Sun and desert heat will not hurt them, for they will be led by one who loves them. He will lead them to springs of water. Isaiah 49 v 10

There'll be food stands along all the roads, picnics on all the hills— Nobody hungry, nobody thirsty, shade from the sun, shelter from the wind, For the Compassionate One guides them, takes them to the best springs. Isaiah 49 v 10 MSG

He satisfies those who are thirsty and fills the hungry with good things. Psalm 107 v 9

"I am the bread of life," Jesus told them. "Those who come to me will never be hungry; those who believe in me will never be thirsty. John 6 v 35

The people ate and were satisfied. Afterward the disciples picked up seven basketfuls of broken pieces that were left over. Mark 8 v 8

Blessed are the merciful, for they will be shown mercy

Blessed, content, sheltered by God's promises, are the merciful, for they will receive mercy. Amp

"You're blessed when you care. At the moment of being 'care-full,' you find yourselves cared for. MSG

He has showed you, O man, what is good. And what does the Lord require of you but to do justly, and to love kindness and mercy, and to humble yourself and walk humbly with your God? Micah 6 v 8 AMP

I am not sure if you have read the book Wonder by R.J. Palacio or its film, about 10 year old August Pullman and his journey through High School. August has a rare genetic disorder which has caused a severe facial difference and the book follows his journey through school after being home schooled and protected by his family. August meets with cruelty and bullying in school but also with acceptance and kindness and can survive and thrive through the kindness of friends. The book explores issues of difference and acceptance, friendship, prejudice and bullying but most of all kindness. Every month one of the Teachers, Mr Browne, chose a precept or ethos statement for the students to follow and one of my favourite ones was the following quotation: *When given the choice between being right or being kind, choose kind.* Dr Wayne W Dyer This book went on to inspire the 'Choose Kind' Movement based on the idea presented by the headteacher of the school in his graduation speech to the students. *"If every single person in this room made it a rule that wherever you are, whenever you can, you will try to act a little kinder than is necessary, the world would be a better place."*

Jesus calls us to compassion. We feel compassion and concern when we see and feel the distress and needs of others. But there is action associated with compassion and that action is mercy. When compassion takes action to relieve pain, distress or need then compassion becomes mercy. Mercy is a 'noun'-it's a mission, an act, or a kindness shown. But we are asked to go beyond this- we are asked to 'love' mercy and kindness- not just to do it occasionally but to 'love' it. We are asked to be kind and merciful not just when it is convenient or others are watching or to receive credit for it, but we are to live the way of compassion and mercy all the time. We are to care, to offer kindness, comfort, acceptance, and forgiveness. This is a life transforming, costly and generous way to live but this is the way of Jesus.

Do all the good you can,

By all the means you can,

In all the ways you can,

In all the places you can,

At all the times you can,

To all the people you can,

As long as ever you can.

John Wesley's Rule

Blessed are the pure in heart: for they shall see God

Blessed [anticipating God's presence, spiritually mature] are the pure in heart [those with integrity, moral courage, and godly character], for they will see God. AMP

You're blessed when you get your inside world—your mind and heart—put right. Then you can see God in the outside world. MSG

My husband and I have been to Chengdu, Sichuan Province, China, on several occasions, and we have had the dubious privilege of being taken to the Chinese Opera or restaurants where we have witnessed Bian Lian or the cultural art of 'face changing'. This 'face changing' skill in which the performers, rapidly change their face masks, multiple times, is unique to Sichuan Opera and there are only about 200 performers who are skilled in this art form. Using dance movements as a distraction, moving to quick rhythmic music (which sounds awful), each mask is quickly whisked away while the next mask is pulled down either by secret silk threads or silk or fine paper layers rapidly shaken from the side. How they do it is supposed to be top secret. Some performers can change as many as ten face masks in less than twenty seconds. Each mask is a different colour and signifies a different emotion or character. One performer, Jing Xu, after changing her many masks, finally, reveals her own face to the audience very briefly, before putting on her final actor's mask to receive applause.

I thought of the mask dance as I read the verse about being pure in heart-being authentic and real. We sometimes put on a mask, many different masks, or even a brave face. In the Beatitudes, Jesus is wanting us to set straight our core values – the crucial values that we will not compromise on. This beatitude is deeply challenging as it calls for integrity-the desire to do the right thing when no one is watching or when the choice to do the right thing is challenging, difficult or goes against what others are doing. It is about consistency, sincerity, trustworthiness, honesty and not hiding behind an artificial 'face' or pretence. It is about being genuine.

The promise that accompanies this beatitude is that we will see and experience more of God and that we will detect and see more of His hand at work around us. We will see more of the heart of God for ourselves and others. Father God sees our heart and our masks and loves us still. He is not fooled by the outward appearance, external observance and shallow words but sees into the heart. He wants to change us from the inside out. On many occasions Jesus challenged the Pharisees and called them 'stage players, 'pretenders' (hypocrites), -words that listeners would instantly recognize.

Since God has so generously let us in on what He is doing, we're not about to throw up our hands and walk off the job just because we run into occasional hard times. We refuse to wear masks and play games. We don't manoeuvre and manipulate behind the scenes. And we don't twist God's Word to suit ourselves. Rather, we keep everything we do and say out in the open, the whole truth on display, so that those who want to can see and judge for themselves in the presence of God. 2 Corinthians 4 v 1-2

Pray

Father, we can never lose your love. It is constant and unshakeable. I do not need to hide from you.

But I hide my thoughts, feelings, and concerns from others. Help me to be open and authentic with those closest to me. Your perfect love casts out fear.

Blessed are the peacemakers, for they will be called children of God

Blessed, spiritually calm with life and joy in God's favour, are the makers and maintainers of peace, for they will express His character and be called the sons of God. AMP

When you show people how to cooperate instead of compete or fight, that's when you discover who you really are, and your place in God's family. MSG

How joyful you are when you make peace! For then you will be recognized as a true child of God. TPT

This beatitude seems to be almost the litmus test of our true character and likeness to Jesus. We can demonstrate who we truly are and the quality of our hearts transformation and character, by the way in which we are recognized as peacemakers. So, this beatitude cuts me to the core. I frequently mess up! I say the wrong thing, and frequently use the silent treatment instead of walking towards a conflict or seeking resolution. So, I'm finding this beatitude deeply challenging! We are called to be to be peaceable but more than that we are called to be peacemakers. We are called to be the ones who intentionally and actively move towards the tension, problem, and source of conflict with the love and wisdom of Jesus. So, I am finding that this beatitude is causing me pain.

Jesus was a man of peace, but we also see Him in action in conflict situations. He was not afraid to walk towards it. At this time of Advent, we think of Jesus, who stepped into our world and our mess while we were strangers and enemies, as a reconciler and a peacemaker. Jesus came to bring us back into fellowship, reconciliation, and peace with the Father.

God was reconciling the world to himself in Christ, not counting people's sins against them. And he has committed to us the message of reconciliation." 2 Corinthians 5 v 19

Moreover, if He did that for us while we were sinners, now that we are men justified by the shedding of his blood, what reason have we to fear the wrath of God? If, while we were his enemies, Christ reconciled us to God by dying for us, surely now that we are reconciled, we may be perfectly certain of our salvation through his living in us. Nor, I am sure, is this a matter of bare salvation—we may hold our heads high in the light of God's love because of the reconciliation which Christ has made. Romans 5 v 11

"He made peace by the blood of the cross". Colossians 1 v 20

Blessed are the persecuted for theirs is the kingdom of heaven

"How enriched you are when persecuted for doing what is right! For then you experience the realm of heaven's kingdom. How blessed you are when people insult and persecute you and speak all kinds of cruel lies about you because of your love for me. So, leap for joy—since your heavenly reward is great. For you are being rejected the same way the prophets were before you." Matthew 5 v 10-12

During Covid lockdown periods last year we were not able to meet in our church building for a time, but for many Christians in the countries on the Open Doors World Watch List Top 50 countries where there is persecution, meeting in a designated church building is simply not an option. In many countries, to be a Christian is dangerous. Many Christians do not have the luxury of a building, as they meet covertly, in small groups, and often in the open at secret locations. In some countries, where there is persecution, increased surveillance measures are taken both inside and outside of their meeting places, or their buildings and churches have been closed or demolished by the authorities. Those becoming Christians, may be accused of bringing shame on their family, their community, their culture, and their heritage, and this may lead to the loss of entitlement to education, to employment, essential identity documents, a home and even to imprisonment and loss of life. Isolation is a common problem for many persecuted Christians and yet Jesus says that these people are blessed, that they are enriched, and that they should leap for joy that they have the privilege of suffering in this way. This is a very hard call!

A Chinese bookshop owner will be jailed for seven years for selling Christian books - mainly Bibles. Chen Yu, the owner of Wheat Bookstore was given a prison sentence, in Linhai City Court, in the Zhejiang province of eastern China. He had sold more than 20,000 books to 10,000 customers before being charged with "illegal business operation". In China, it's currently an offence to carry out religious activity without the express permission of authorities. Alongside his prison sentence, Chen Yu had to pay 200,000 yuan – approximately £23,000. The books sold by Chen Yu include those written by Pastor Wang Yi, who has been accused of "inciting subversion or state power". The Pastor was jailed for 9 years in 2019.Premier Christian News

Jesus acknowledges that by following Him and His way this will bring us into conflict with a culture and society that does not recognize His values. This testing of our faith, the lessons, and the rewards that persecution, conflict, and challenge bring are for now, in the present, but also for the person with his eyes on the future, the heaven that is to come.

"He is no fool who gives what he cannot keep to gain what he cannot lose" Jim Elliot A Christian Missionary who with 4 others, were killed in Ecuador in 1956.

Pray

We pray for those who are persecuted for their trust in you. Give them your peace, your strength, reassurance, joy, and hope. We pray for your church in China, India, Iran, North Korea, Nigeria, Israel, and the countries known to Open Doors. Thank you, Lord, that your church is not a building but the men and women who love and seek to serve and follow you.

Insults and false accusations

"Blessed are you when people insult you, persecute you and falsely say all kinds of evil against you because of me." Matthew 5 v 12 NIV

"Count yourselves blessed every time people put you down or throw you out or speak lies about you to discredit me. What it means is that the truth is too close for comfort, and they are uncomfortable." MSG

If someone makes any kind of allegation about a person, whether this relates to their personal, family, employment, or church life, then this undoubtedly causes emotional turmoil and acute distress. Whether a claim is false, unsubstantiated, and uncorroborated; a clear perspective, fairness and objectivity are often the first things to go. The person accused feels indignant, hurt, confused, fearful for their reputation, may seek to clear their name, and is often panicked and fearful by the situation that they find themselves in. They will be anxious about any consequences, even if they are confident and assured by others that they are innocent. Unfair treatment, malicious gossip, being side-lined, and unkindness, can cause deep unhappiness and stress. The consequences of insults and accusations can be painful and prolonged.

But here, Jesus is speaking of insults, false accusations, being 'put down,' belittled, isolated because of connection to Jesus and trust in Him. People may wish to discredit Him, but you are the nearest target. Jesus wants us to remain calm, to stand firm, avoid any thought of retaliation, and to quietly trust Him with any consequences. This very hard to do. But Jesus set the bar high in this respect. When He was falsely accused and endured blatant lies and allegations, He said nothing.

Then he was accused by the chief priests and religious leaders, but he remained silent. Pilate said, "Don't you hear these allegations?" But Jesus offered no defence to any of the charges, much to the great astonishment of Pilate. Matthew 27 v 12-14

Christ suffered for you, leaving you an example, that you should follow in his steps. He committed no sin, and no deceit was found in his mouth. When they hurled their insults at him, he did not retaliate; when he suffered, he made no threats. Instead, he entrusted himself to him who judges justly. I Peter 2 v 22-24

Salt and Light

You are the salt of the earth. You are the light of the world. You are light bearers-I've put you there on a hilltop.

Let me tell you why you are here. You're here to be salt-seasoning that brings out the God-flavours of this earth. If you lose your saltiness, how will people taste godliness? You've lost your usefulness and will end up in the garbage.

Here's another way to put it: You're here to be light, bringing out the God-colours in the world. God is not a secret to be kept. We're going public with this, as public as a city on a hill. If I make you light-bearers, you don't think I'm going to hide you under a bucket, do you? I'm putting you on a light stand. Now that I've put you there on a hilltop, on a light stand— shine! Matthew 5 v 13-16

My church is on a hillside, next to a major roundabout, in clear view of its local community and neighbours. The church is in a key position on the roundabout, with a significant foot fall in front of it, and with cars continually coming past on this major road intersection and getting a glimpse of what goes on inside. However, if we are to truly demonstrate the love of Jesus within our building, we cannot just be a building on a roundabout on the high ground at the top of a hill! So, how are we to be seen so that we are the salt and light that Jesus speaks of?

We are seeking to be His body within our community- His arms, legs, feet, lips and heart demonstrating His love so that all may come to Him. We are to be a welcoming and inclusive community of believers, attractive, winsome, loving, generous and so drawing others into the knowledge, love, and fellowship of Jesus. Each person has gifts, skills, talents, abilities, and temperaments that God intends for us to use to build up his body and His kingdom in this small corner. We should explore and recognize these God given gifts in ourselves and in each other so that together we can shine. May our fellowship be somewhere where each person is valued, each person is needed, and each person's unique gifts are used. Our little lights joined together will make a wonderful broad beam of light shining out like a lighthouse on the hill.

In his grace, God has given us different gifts for doing certain things well. So, if God has given you the ability to prophesy, speak out with as much faith as God has given you. If your gift is serving others, serve them well. If you are a teacher, teach well. If your gift is to encourage others, be encouraging. If it is giving, give generously. If God has given you leadership ability, take the responsibility seriously. And if you have a gift for showing kindness to others, do it gladly. Don't just pretend to love others. Really love them. Romans 12 v 6-9 NLT

Pray

We have so many different skills and talents.

Using these many gifts, may we work together , enjoying everyone's contribution,

to build your church, in faith, hope and love. In your grace, help us to use our creative skills for the benefit of all, and to build your Kingdom of justice and peace. Help us to bring out the 'God colours in our world and to shine for you.

SONGS OF SIGNIFICANCE

Songs of Significance: The Father sings over us

There are wonderful examples of worship songs in the Bible—Moses and Miriam, David and Solomon's many poems and songs, Deborah and Barak, Mary in the Magnificat, Paul and Silas singing in their prison cell, to name a few. Today we each may have our own favourite worship songs or hymns that speak eloquently and meaningfully to each of us in their different ways, but I want to begin a series with these amazing words from the prophet Zephaniah.

"The Lord your God is with you,
the Mighty Warrior who saves.
He will take great delight in you;
in his love he will no longer rebuke you,
but will rejoice over you with singing."
Zephaniah 3 v 17 NIV

Zephaniah was one of the last of the minor prophets speaking during the reign of King Josiah, a short while before the Babylonians conquered and carried away many from the land of Judah. Zephaniah's message was one of uncompromising doom and gloom. His was a message of God's judgement, to root out idolatry, corruption, and unfaithfulness. But then in a great crescendo of love comes the message that for those who will seek the Lord, trust Him, and be his people, God will sing over them with delight and joy. Our Father God rejoices in us and sings over us. He takes joy and delight in us His children and sings over us His songs of love. What an amazing thought.

For the Lord your God is living among you.
He is a mighty saviour.
He will take delight in you with gladness.
With his love, he will calm all your fears.
He will rejoice over you with joyful songs." NLT

I have heard so many songs
Listened to a thousand tongues
But there is one
That sounds above them all.
The Father's song
The Father's love
You sung it over me and for eternity

It's written on my heart.

Heaven's perfect melody
The Creator's symphony
You are singing over me
The Father's song.

Heaven's perfect mystery
The king of love has sent for me
And now you're singing over me
The Father's song.
Matt Redman, The Father's Love, Released June 20 2000

Songs of Deliverance Moses and Miriam

The Israelites, after leaving Egypt, had been guided by God to an area of desert near to the sea but Pharoah and his forces were in pursuit, and the people were terrified. Moses counselled them to be unafraid, to stand firm, and to see the salvation and deliverance of their God. "The Lord will fight for you; you need only to be still." During the night, the Angel of God, and the pillar of cloud, had moved into a strategic position between Pharoah's forces and the Israelites, so that Pharoah was unable to see the camp of the Israelites. Perhaps also, God in His kindness, was hiding the sight of the terrifying army from view so that the Israelites wouldn't continue to tremble, fear and be overwhelmed. "Throughout the night the cloud brought darkness to the one side and light to the other side." During the night, God placed the Egyptians in darkness, hiding them from view, while He was dividing the waters of the sea in preparation for the Israelites great deliverance. Without looking behind, the Israelites walked through the divided waters on dry ground, while the returning waters and waterlogged ground brought death to Pharoah's 600 best chariots, all his other chariots and riders, officers, and troops. All were lost. When the Israelites saw the mighty hand of God displayed against the Egyptians, the people put their trust in Him and in Moses.

Then Moses and the Israelites sang this song to the Lord:
"I will sing to the Lord,
for he is highly exalted.
Both horse and driver
he has hurled into the sea.
"The Lord is my strength and my defence
he has become my salvation.

He is my God, and I will praise him,
my father's God, and I will exalt him. Exodus 15 v 1-3

In your unfailing love you will lead
the people you have redeemed.
In your strength you will guide them
to your holy dwelling.   Exodus 15 v 12 -13

The Lord reigns for ever and ever. Exodus 15 v 18

Then Miriam the prophet, Aaron's sister, took a timbrel in her hand, and all the women followed her, with timbrel and dancing, singing their praises to God. What a celebration that was! However, after this dramatic deliverance and rescue, God was to lead them into the desert of Shur- where there was no water! It was not until they came to Elim and its twelve springs of water, that their thirst could be satisfied.

God guides us, His redeemed, with His unfailing love and His strength. He protects. When things are bleak and trying, it is easy to feel overwhelmed and preoccupied with the problems. They block out our view of everything else. Sometimes God will say do not look behind you- look ahead and go forward. Let us try to sing our songs of praise when things are going well and when we are in the hard place. Sometimes after the deliverance comes the desert and the drought!

I lift my eyes up
To the mountains
Where does my help come from?
My help comes from You
Maker of Heaven
Creator of the earth.

Oh, how I need You Lord
You are my only hope
You're my only prayer
So I will wait for You
To come and rescue me
Come and give me life.

Brian Doerksen

Deborah's victory song

Deborah's victory song in Judges 5 speaks of leaders, leadership, and followers, and praises God who gives the victory. It is about leaders who lead and who fulfil a role or have a task to fulfil, and followers who willingly follow. Deborah was a leader who was in touch with her God but who also had the personal and essential qualities of leadership. But I get ahead of myself. Here is the background to the victory song.

In Judges 4 and 5, we read, that once again, the Israelites were up against it! Jabin, the king of Canaan, and Sisera, the commander of his armies and 900 chariots, had been attacking and humiliating the Israelites for twenty years. The Israelites were oppressed, and their weapons removed from them, so that they had little chance to defend themselves, let alone to fight back.

It was at this time that Deborah came to prominence. Deborah was a prophet, a leader of Israel, and a judge who held 'court' under the Palm of Deborah, between Ramah and Bethel in the country of Ephraim. Deborah is described as a 'mother in Israel,' who possessed the calm wisdom of the Spirit in settling disputes and who was a person of some authority. Deborah also was in tune with the heart of God and was guided by Him in the matter of the assault plan on their enemies. Deborah knew the time and she also knew the place- around the river Kishon near Mount Tabor. The heavy chariots would be disadvantaged on the wet ground near the river. Deborah was confident too of God's deliverance.

"The Lord says, 'I will draw them to the Kishon River, and you will defeat them there.'" Judges 4 v 6-7.

Barak, reluctant to go, unless Deborah went with him too, was finally urged to go forward by her direct command.

Then Deborah said to Barak, "Now is the time for action! The Lord leads on! He has already delivered Sisera into your hand!" Judges 4 14 -16

On that day, Deborah, Barak and their ten thousand men defeated the enemy. Deborah and Barak sang their song of victory.

Then sang Deborah and Barak son of Abinoam on that day, saying, For the leaders who took the lead in Israel, for the people who offered themselves willingly, bless the Lord. Hear, O kings; give ear, O princes; I will sing to the Lord. I will sing praise to the Lord, the God of Israel. Judges 5 v 2-3

Following this battle the land had rest for forty years- until the next enemy, the Midianites, and the next warrior, Gideon, came into the picture.

Deborah was a true leader who could take the lead. But she needed others who were followers and who offered themselves willingly. It is interesting that in the hall of fame in Hebrews 11, it is Barak who is mentioned and not Deborah! Perhaps leaders sometimes accept that their efforts and work are not always recognized and recorded!

And what more shall I say? I do not have time to tell about Gideon, Barak, Samson and Jephthah, about David and Samuel and the prophets, who through faith conquered kingdoms, administered justice, and gained what was promised. Hebrews 11 v 32-33

Build Your kingdom here
Let the darkness fear
Show Your mighty hand
Heal our streets and land
Set Your church on fire
Win this nation back
Change the atmosphere
Build Your kingdom here
We pray

Come set Your rule and reign
In our hearts again
Increase in us we pray
Unveil why we're made
Come set our hearts ablaze with hope
Like wildfire in our very souls
Holy Spirit, come invade us now
We are Your Church
And we need Your power
In us.
Build Your kingdom Here, Rend Collective

David's Song of Praise

The Lord lives! Praise to my Rock! 2 Samuel 22 and Psalm 18:

The Lord is my rock, my fortress, and my saviour;
my God is my rock, in whom I find protection.
He is my shield, the power that saves me,
and my place of safety.
He is my refuge, my saviour,
the one who saves me from violence.
I called on the Lord, who is worthy of praise,
and he saved me from my enemies.

David is looking back on his life as warrior, leader, and king, and in gratitude to his God, sings this amazing song of praise for all that God has helped him to be and to achieve. God has saved him from his enemies, including Saul, and preserved his life. Psalm 18 is almost identical to 2 Samuel 22 and may have been repeated or added to towards the end of David's life. David sings his song of praise and thanks to his God- his rock, fortress, deliverer, shield, strength, stronghold, saviour, refuge, support, lamp, and light for his way. David looks back with gratitude and the titles for his God and His place in his life just pour out from his lips.

There is one aspect of his praise song that shone out to me. Many times, in his life, David was a fugitive, needing to run away and hide. When he fled from Saul, he needed to hide out in rocks, caves, and mountains, constantly moving for fear of his life. He must often have felt trapped, closed in, and in a tight place without a place of safety. "Hell's ropes clinched me tight; death traps barred every exit."

In my distress (when seemingly closed in) I called upon the Lord and cried to my God; He heard my voice out of His temple (heavenly dwelling place), and my cry came before Him, into His (very) ears. Psalm 18 v 6 AMP

But God would lead him to a wide space, a wide-open field, a large, an open place with wide paths, where he could move freely. 2 Samuel 22 v 20 is translated in the following ways.

He stood me up on a wide-open field. I stood there saved—surprised to be loved! MSG

He brought me forth also into a large place. NIV

When I was fenced in, you freed and rescued me because you love me. CEV

He brought me out to wide-open spaces; he pulled me out, because he is pleased with me. CEB

The Lord supported me, He led me to a place of safety. NLV

He was pleased with me, so he rescued me. He took me to a safe place. ERV

Many people can feel trapped and hemmed in by their circumstances. They are cornered, in a tight place, fenced in, unable to move, physically, mentally, emotionally, financially, and in a myriad of ways. But God wants us to have space where we can move freely, safely and thrive. God wants us to be in that spacious, safe place. The enemy would have us backed into a tight corner, up against the wall, but God wants us to be free.

"We are hedged in (pressed) on every side [troubled and oppressed in every way], but not cramped or crushed; we suffer embarrassments and are perplexed and unable to find a way out, but not driven to despair; we are pursued (persecuted and hard driven), but not deserted [to stand alone]; we are struck down to the ground, but never struck out and destroyed." Paul 2 Corinthians 4 v 7-9

Pray

For those who may feel hemmed in, or isolated and lonely. The Lord hears those who call out to Him.

A song of sorrow by Babylon's rivers

You may well remember the Boney M song 'By the Rivers of Babylon' which was famous in 1978 and became one of five top selling singles at that time. It had originally been written by Brent Dowe and the lyrics and themes are based on the experience of the exiles in Babylon in the sixth century B.C. and Psalm 137.The song also contain those wonderful words from Psalm 19 v 4. It is an unusual song in that the words are from scripture. I remember using the song in school and using the B side of the single also, 'Brown girl in the ring'.

By the rivers of Babylon, there we sat down
Yeah, we wept, when we remembered Zion
When the wicked
Carried us away in captivity
Required from us a song
Now how shall we sing the Lord's song in a strange land.

Psalm 137 (NIV)
By the rivers of Babylon, we sat and wept when we remembered Zion.
There on the poplars we hung our harps,
for there our captors asked us for songs,
our tormentors demanded songs of joy;
they said, "Sing us one of the songs of Zion!"
How can we sing the songs of the Lord while in a foreign land?
If I forget you, Jerusalem, may my right hand forget its skill.
May my tongue cling to the roof of my mouth if I do not remember you,
if I do not consider Jerusalem my highest joy.

The Psalm and the song capture the experience of the exiles who had been deported in several waves from Judah to Babylon. This was a watershed moment for the exiles and the Jewish nation. They had been deported, dispersed and their opportunity for central worship at the Temple had gone. The Temple in Jerusalem would be destroyed, their worship disrupted, their culture absorbed into another, a new language learned and their whole identity as a nation deeply affected. This was a song of captivity in a time of sorrow, instability, and an uncertain future. Jerusalem had signified covenant, temple, security, the familiar and God's presence. But how could they sustain their worship and faith for a period of more than fifty years in exile away from their homeland?

Many would feel a longing for the old ways and the familiar. They were without their Temple worship and routines. How can we sing our songs of worship? They had no song left in them. But they did not break their harps. They hung their harps on the trees and refused to sing for the entertainment of their captors. However, there was hope and many kept that hope alive. Prayers, sabbath observance and community continued and grew strong. Meeting together continued but in smaller groups and with family worship becoming important. Their deep relationship with their God continued. While they were in exile, new ways would be found to build up their faith and to worship together.

The Boney M song ends with the words from Psalm 19 v 14, a psalm of David.

Let the words of my mouth and the meditation of my heart
Be acceptable in Your sight,
O Lord, my strength, and my Redeemer.

For the exiles, God continued to be their strength, their rock, and their firm foundation. God was their Redeemer who would bring them back to their promised land. The Temple and the walls would be rebuilt.

Pray

May we never stop singing. May we continue to sing, fellowship, worship and connect- but in fresh new ways.

Songs of Joy and Rejoicing- Nehemiah

When the people of Israel had been taken into Babylonian captivity by Nebuchadnezzar, they were unable to sing their songs of praise and joyful hymns.

Beside the rivers of Babylon, we sat and wept
as we thought of Jerusalem.
We put away our harps,
hanging them on the branches of poplar trees.
For our captors demanded a song from us.
Our tormentors insisted on a joyful hymn:
"Sing us one of those songs of Jerusalem!"
But how can we sing the songs of the Lord
while in a pagan land? Psalm 137

But when the exile was over and more than 42,000 people had returned to their homelands, including their 200 singers, the time was ready to rebuild and to sing again. The city walls of Jerusalem had been rebuilt in record time and now was the time for the dedication of the walls with rejoicing, praise, and thanksgiving. Nehemiah had arranged for two large thanksgiving choirs to lead the people in praise and worship. The Levites, in addition to their other responsibilities, were professional worship leaders and singers, responsible for songs of praise and thanksgiving and would lead the people in this session of worship and praise. They had been brought together from all the regions and the surrounding areas of Jerusalem. For this celebration, the instruments were also brought out-the harp, the lyre, horns, trumpets, flutes, tambourines, drums, cymbals, and bells. This was to be some celebration!

Also, on that day they offered great sacrifices and rejoiced because God had given them great joy; the women and children also rejoiced, so that the joy of Jerusalem was heard from far away. Nehemiah 12 v 43

The worship and praise were for everyone-priests, Levites, leaders, men, women, and children- everyone was included. This celebration of praise was meant to be heard by everyone in and around Jerusalem. But it was not just the songs, the music, the instruments, and the words that would be heard. It was the sheer joy of the singing that would impact and affect the listeners. The joy of Jerusalem would be heard. This worship and praise would speak powerfully to others.

Be filled with the Holy Spirit, singing psalms and hymns and spiritual songs among yourselves, and making music to the Lord in your hearts. And give thanks for everything to God the Father in the name of our Lord Jesus Christ. Ephesians 5 v 19-20

Sing to the Lord a new song;
sing to the Lord, all the earth.
Sing to the Lord, praise his name,
proclaim his salvation day after day.
Declare his glory among the nations,
his marvellous deeds among all peoples.   Psalm 96

We have a new song to sing. We trust and pray that it will be heard by the community around us.

Song of Mercy and Salvation Mary

In Luke chapter one we read that the Angel visited Mary in her hometown of Nazareth, with the announcement of the birth of the child, Jesus, her child. Mary was a young woman, formally engaged or 'betrothed' to Joseph, with formal arrangements and promises of marriage in place which could not be broken or cancelled. We read that Mary fully accepted the role that God had given to her with trust and grace. Mary acknowledged that God was with her, that she had been chosen and that she was blessed. Mary, at an early stage in the narrative, went to the hill country of Judaea, to her cousin Elizabeth, who was in her sixth month of pregnancy, and that Mary went 'with haste,' making a journey of over eighty miles, to be with her relative. Elizabeth greeted Mary and with the inspiration of the Spirit, blessed Mary with some astounding prophetic words.

Mary then declared the following amazing words, which are often referred to as The Magnificat or Mary's song. I love The Message version in which Mary says, "I'm dancing the song of my Saviour God." Mary's song is one in which she continually points to the goodness, mercy, blessing and power of her God. Mary, recognizing her own need and Israel's need of a saviour, focuses on her Lord and His never-ending mercy.

"Oh, how I praise the Lord. How I rejoice in God my Saviour! For he took notice of his lowly servant girl, and now generation after generation forever shall call me blest of God. For he, the mighty Holy One, has done great things to me. His mercy goes on from generation to generation, to all who reverence him. How powerful is his mighty arm! How he scatters the proud and haughty ones! He has torn princes from their thrones and exalted the lowly. He has satisfied the hungry hearts and sent the rich away with empty hands. And how he has helped his servant, Israel! He has not forgotten his promise to be merciful. For he promised our fathers— Abraham and his children—to be merciful to them forever." Luke 1 v 46- 55 TLB

God's promise is to show mercy. This never-ending mercy, compassion and kindness are for everyone who will turn to God and reverence Him. May we always approach God's throne of grace with confidence, so that we may receive mercy and find grace to help us in our time of need-and then sing and dance for joy.

His mercy flows in wave after wave on those who are in awe before him. Luke 1 v 50 MSG

He embraced his chosen child, Israel; he remembered and piled on the mercies, piled them high. It's exactly what he promised, beginning with Abraham and right up to now. Luke 1 V 55 MSG

Hallelujah!
Sing to God a brand-new song,
praise him in the company of all who love him.
Let all Israel celebrate their Sovereign Creator,
Zion's children exult in their King.
Let them praise his name in dance;
strike up the band and make great music! Psalm 149v 1 MSG

Great is Thy faithfulness, O God my Father
There is no shadow of turning with Thee
Thou changest not, Thy compassions, they fail not
As Thou hast been, Thou forever will be
Great is Thy faithfulness
Great is Thy faithfulness
Morning by morning new mercies I see
All I have needed Thy hand hath provided
Great is Thy faithfulness, Lord, unto me.
Thomas O. Chisholm (1923)

Songs at Midnight Paul and Silas

About midnight Paul and Silas were praying and singing hymns to God, and the other prisoners were listening to them. Acts 16 v 25

Paul and Silas had arrived in Philippi, a major city, and a Roman outpost. Outside the city gates near the river, a small group of mainly women, met for prayer. Paul and Silas joined with the group, which included Lydia, a worshipper of God. Lydia was an influential businesswoman, a seller of purple dyes and cloth, and after listening to Paul, she became a Christian, along with her household. Paul and Silas stayed on in Philippi, and each Sabbath, joined the group meeting by the river.

On one occasion, when they were going to the place of prayer, they were confronted by a female slave who had a spirit of divination by which she could predict the future. She had earned a great deal of money for her slave owners by this fortune-telling. She would constantly follow Paul shouting out, "These men are servants of the Most High God, who are telling you the way to be saved." This happened day after day, until Paul rebuked the spirit, and the woman was released and restored. However, her owners, realizing that their source of income was gone, took hold of Paul and Silas, dragged them through the marketplace and took them to the city magistrates. "These men are Jews and are throwing our city into an uproar by advocating customs unlawful for us Romans to accept or practice," they declared. The Magistrates ordered Paul and Silas to be stripped, beaten with rods, publicly flogged, and then thrown into prison. The jailer was given special orders to guard them carefully and so he put them into the inner, deepest cell, with their feet fastened in the stocks.

But at midnight, Paul and Silas were praying and singing hymns to God while all the prisoners listened to their songs of praise and worship. A violent earthquake occurred, shaking and breaking up the very foundations of the prison. The prison doors were flung open, the prisoners' chains were released, and most of them escaped. However, Paul and Silas remained where they were. The jailer, after fearing for his own life, "called for lights, rushed in, and trembling all over, fell at the feet of Paul and Silas. He led them outside, and said, "Sirs, what must I do to be saved?" And they replied, "Believe in the Lord Jesus and then you will be saved, you and your household." Acts 16 v 29-30 JBP

Paul shared the good news of Jesus with the jailer and his household. "There and then in the middle of the night he (the jailer) took them aside and washed their wounds and he himself and all his family were baptised without delay. Then he took them into his house and offered them food, he and his whole household overjoyed at finding faith in God. Acts 16 v 34 JBP

For Paul and Silas there were highs and lows in Philippi. Lydia and her household, the jailer and his household and no doubt many others, became Christians and formed the first church in Philippi. But Paul and Silas had also endured abuse, hostility, prejudice, beatings, flogging and the maximum-security 'hole in the ground' in the prison. But still, they could pray, sing, and praise their God. Their songs were also songs of witness. Where there could have been groans, cries of pain and misery, complaints of unjust treatment and abuse, there were songs of joy and praise.

How are we with highs and lows? Do we kick against the trials?

For Paul and Silas this was a shared experience. They endured this trial and low place together. The one would encourage and support the other. When things are rough, or the trial extreme, then it is good to have someone standing at your side. We are not meant to do this on our own.

Two people are better off than one, for they can help each other succeed. If one person falls, the other can reach out and help. But someone who falls alone is in real trouble. Likewise, two people lying close together can keep each other warm. But how can one be warm alone? A person standing alone can be attacked and defeated, but two can stand back-to-back and conquer. Three are even better, for a triple-braided cord is not easily broken. Ecclesiastes 4 v 9-12 TLT

Pray

For those who may be going through trials and challenges. May they know that they are not alone.

May we learn to be people of praise and joy, and to be thankful, even in the dark times.

The New Song of the Redeemed Revelation

When he, (the Lamb), had taken the book, the four living creatures and the twenty-four elders prostrated themselves before the Lamb. Each of them had a harp, and they had golden bowls full of incense, which are the prayers of the saints. They sang a new song, and these are the words they sang, "You are worthy to take the scroll, and to open its seals; for you were slain and have redeemed us to God by your blood out of every tribe and tongue and people and nation and have made us kings and priests to our God; and we shall reign on the earth."

Then in my vision I heard the voices of many angels encircling the throne, the living creatures and the elders. There were myriads of myriads and thousands of thousands, crying in a great voice, "Worthy is the Lamb who was slain to receive power and riches and wisdom, and strength and honour and glory and blessing!"

Then I heard the voice of everything created in Heaven, upon earth, under the earth and upon the sea, and all that are in them saying, "Blessing and honour and glory and power be to him who sits on the throne, and to the Lamb, for ever and ever!" The four living creatures said, "Amen", while the elders fell down and worshipped. Revelation 5 v 8-13 JBP

I sing for joy

He put a new song in my mouth, a hymn of praise to our God. Many will see and fear the Lord and put their trust in him. Psalm 40 v 1-3 NIV. He taught me how to sing the latest God-song, a praise-song to our God. Psalm 40 v 3 MSG

"A new song, always new; keep up the freshness of your praise. Do not drivel down into dull routine.... We have new mercies to celebrate, therefore we must have new songs." C H Spurgeon

Phil and I used to sing together at events such as youth meetings, coffee bars, church services, outreach events, beach missions, and even at the Leeds Town Hall on one occasion. On the beach missions at Paignton, Douglas and Peel on the Isle of Man, Leysdown on the Isle of Sheppey,

Llandudno and Bangor in Wales, and many other places we were regularly used to try to draw a crowd, so that when a good crowd had assembled, then the main speaker could step forward and take over. Phil remembers one occasion, on a very cold and dismal evening on the promenade of a seaside resort, we were singing 'Go tell it on the mountain,' and other songs to draw in a crowd, when the preacher said, "You may as well do, as there is no crowd tonight!" We loved singing and during our late teenage years and early married life, before children came along, we enjoyed using our gifts in this way. Music was and still is very important-especially to Phil.

Why do we sing in worship? God wants us to sing. God seeks our praise and worship, and He wants it to be fresh and new. He is a creative God and He wants to give us new songs to sing. When we worship, the songs should take us away from ourselves, so that our thoughts, prayers, praise, and worship turn to God. Worship songs should help us re-focus, touch us deeply, and connect us with those who join in with the song. The best songs are the memorable ones-they come to us when we need them the most-in the middle of the night or when we are struggling with a problem or a challenge. Our songs can also a powerful testimony to others, as the psalm says, some may hear the words and the music, be curious and seek to know more about the source of the song.

He taught me how to sing the latest God-song, a praise-song to our God. More and more people are seeing this: they enter the mystery, abandoning themselves to God. Psalm 40 v 3 MSG

Let the message about Christ, in all its richness, fill your lives. Teach and counsel each other with all the wisdom he gives. Sing psalms and hymns and spiritual songs to God with thankful hearts. Colossians 3 v 16 NLT

The whole earth is filled with awe at your wonders; where morning dawns, where evening fades, you call forth songs of joy. Psalm 65v 8 NIV

Sing to the Lord a new song;
sing to the Lord, all the earth.
Sing to the Lord, praise his name;
proclaim his salvation day after day.
Declare his glory among the nations,
his marvellous deeds among all peoples. Psalm 96 v 1-3 NIV

NAMES OF GOD

El Shaddai: Nothing is impossible

When Abram was ninety-nine years old, the Lord appeared to him and said,

"I am God Almighty; walk before Me [with integrity, knowing that you are always in My presence], and be blameless and complete in obedience to Me." Genesis 17 v 1-2 AMP

I'm establishing my covenant between me and you, a covenant that includes your descendants, a covenant that goes on and on and on, a covenant that commits me to be your God and the God of your descendants. And I'm giving you and your descendants this land where you're now just camping, this whole country of Canaan, to own forever. And I'll be their God." MSG

Abram, at the age of 75, had been called by God to leave Haran, a place of security and stability, and to step out into an uncharted, unknown land, but a promised land, even though that land was currently occupied by other tribes. God had promised Abram a land, a blessing and a nation that would come from his union with Sarai. Believing God's promises, Abram had become a tent dweller, an alien, a stranger with a nomadic lifestyle, travelling south, with no permanent base or land of his own. The chapters in early Genesis read a little bit like his travelogue. Abram's journeys with family and flocks would take him hundreds of miles from Ur of the Chaldeans (now Iraq). But now aged ninety-nine years of age and with Sarai, Hagar, the thirteen-year-old Ishmael, (his child with Hagar), and all his company, God once again speaks directly to Abram, revealing yet more of His character, His promises, His blessings, and His purpose.

God reveals Himself as- The Lord or Yahweh (the One who was always there) and El Shaddai the Almighty, the 'nothing is impossible for Him' God, all sufficient One, the life giver, who longs to pour out His blessing on His children. God promises an everlasting covenant with Abram and with his descendants. God promises a child for Sarai with the hope of future generations of families from their union. God gives a change of name to Abram and Sarai. Abram (exalted father) becomes Abraham (father of a multitude), and Sarai (my princess) becomes Princess. God promises fruitfulness, possession of the land of Canaan and His constant presence. God is the promise keeper, the covenant making God, the One who is longing to bless.

Abraham's God is also our God. We are always in His presence, and He longs to bless. We can hold fast to that Name.

The name of the Lord is a strong tower;

the righteous run into it and are safe. Proverbs 18 v 10 RSV

Those who love me, I will deliver;
I will protect those who know my name.
When they call to me, I will answer them;
I will be with them in trouble;
I will rescue them and honour them.
With long life I will satisfy them
and show them my salvation.
Psalm 91 v 14-16

The God who sees me

She (Hagar) gave this name to the Lord who spoke to her: "You are the God who sees me," for she said, "I have now seen the One who sees me." That is why the well was called Beer Lahai Roi (well of the Living One who sees me.) Genesis 16 v 13-14

Phil, Sam, and I have a tracker on our mobile phones called 'find my phone' so that wherever we are we can locate each other if needed. This has been useful when we have needed to collect Sam from an event at school or a visit away from school, as we can note his exact location and check how far away he is. We know where he is. We can see his location exactly.

Hagar, Sarah's handmaid, was pregnant, in distress, vulnerable and alone, and was running away from an intolerable situation of abuse and family tension to a desert place where she could not be found. She was running away 'from something' that she could not handle or see a way out of, and which was overwhelming, with no prospect of a good resolution. But God had His eyes on her. God knew exactly where she was and saw into her future and that of her son, Ishmael. God did not need a tracker. He always knew where she was and her dilemma. He had always seen her.

The angel of the Lord asked her "Hagar, slave of Sarai, where have you come from, and where are you going?" v 8

Hagar was running away 'from something' but had no idea where she was 'going to' next. She was locked into her present situation and her perception of it and could not see the path ahead that God had for her. Hagar's vision was restricted. But God knew the whole story-beginning, middle and end.

Hagar was instructed to go back to the situation that she had fled from, but now with a clearer vision and specific promises. Hagar had become aware of, she had 'seen' the overwhelming love and care of God, had been given a glimpse of her future and that of her child, and had her eyes opened to the loving nature of her God. "You are the God who sees me." That's because she said, "I have now seen the One who sees me." Genesis 16 v 13 Hagar could now see more of her God and His watchful care over her life. She now saw the One who saw her.

In life, there is nothing that can separate us from the love of Christ and His care for us. No distress, anguish, hostility, pain, relationship breakdown, trauma, separation, or anything else is ever hidden from the eyes of our God. He sees and cares. He may not remove the anguish or pain immediately. We may have to return to it as Hagar did. But He sees and because we see Him and His nature of love, then we are sustained, and we are held in that love.

Psalm 33
The Lord looks from heaven;
He sees all the sons of men.
From the place of His dwelling He looks
On all the inhabitants of the earth;
He fashions their hearts individually;
He considers all their works.

Behold, the eye of the Lord is on those who fear Him,
On those who hope in His mercy,
To deliver their soul from death,
And to keep them alive in famine.
Our soul waits for the Lord;
He is our help and our shield.
For our heart shall rejoice in Him,
Because we have trusted in His holy name.
Let Your mercy, O Lord, be upon us,
Just as we hope in You. NIV

Father God:

Your watchful gaze is always there. You see me at all times and in all places. Help me to turn my gaze to you and look for you every day. When I want to run, then call me back, and remind me of who You are and who I am in You.

The Lord will provide: Jehovah Jireh

Then Abraham looked up and glanced around, and behold, behind him was a ram caught in a thicket by his horns. And Abraham went and took the ram and offered it up for a burnt offering instead of his son. So, Abraham named that place The Lord Will Provide. And it is said to this day, "On the mountain of the Lord it will be seen and provided." Genesis 22 v 13-14

The account of Abraham's obedience to God and his willingness to give Isaac as an offering in the mountainous region of Moriah, is a disturbing and perplexing one. Abraham is requested by God to sacrifice Isaac, the child of promise, blessing, and hope, and his precious, longed for only child, whom he dearly loves. But in the account, we see the God who sees, who anticipates the need for a substitute, and who provides.

I love the way in which Abraham responds to the call of God and the Angel with the simple "Here I am." Clearly it was not uncommon for Abraham's friendship and walk with God to be a personal one, and secure in that relationship, he could follow God's principles and patterns and know what he was to do. Abraham had trusted God with each step of his journey from Haran and even now, in this most testing of places and situations, Abraham knew and trusted that God's promise to bless still held true.

Sometime later, God tested Abraham. He said to him, "Abraham!" "Here I am, "he replied. Genesis 22 v 1

Abraham did not dither, but acted straight away, taking care of the practical details himself (preparing the firewood and saddling the donkey) instead of giving these ordinary, even menial jobs to the servants, and he sets off with Isaac to Moriah. Abraham tells Isaac that 'God will provide Himself the lamb' and assures the servants that 'we will come back to you'. Just as the dreadful deed was about to be completed, the Angel stays his hand, and Abraham again responds to the voice.

But the angel of the Lord called out to him from heaven, "Abraham! Abraham!" "Here I am," he replied. V 11

Abraham turned around to see a ram caught by its horns in a thicket, rendering the feisty, frightened animal more easily caught. God had provided the substitute for the sacrifice and once again assured Abraham of His promises to bless, to multiply and for his descendants to be conquerors in the promised land.

The lessons that I take away from this account are that God sees all my circumstances and situations and that He is there in the small details. The account helps me to learn how to trust in the tough and testing places in life, and to know that God wants to bless my life as I walk with Him and listen to His voice. And above everything, God has provided a living sacrifice for me- the gift of his own Son to die in my place so that I can walk free.

The next day John saw Jesus coming toward him and said, "Look, the Lamb of God, who takes away the sin of the world! This is the one I meant when I said, 'A man who comes after me has surpassed me because he was before me.' John 1 v 29-30

For God loved the world so much that he gave his only Son so that anyone who believes in him shall not perish but have eternal life. God did not send his Son into the world to condemn it, but to save it. John 3 v 16-17

"I am who I am": Yahweh

God said to Moses, "I AM WHO I AM. This is what you are to say to the Israelites: 'I am has sent me to you.' God also said to Moses, "Say to the Israelites, 'The Lord, the God of your fathers—the God of Abraham, the God of Isaac, and the God of Jacob—has sent me to you.' "This is my name forever, the name you shall call me from generation to generation. Exodus 3 v 14-16

We read in Exodus chapter 3 of how God dramatically attracts the attention of Moses, calling him by name, from the fire of the burning bush. God declares to Moses that He has seen the slavery, misery, and distress of His people. God promises to bring them out of their pain, oppression, and suffering and lead them to a place of abundance and freedom in the land of promise. Moses is to be the agent of that journey to freedom.

More significantly, God reveals to Moses and to His people His true name and character. He is the 'I Am', Yahweh, the one who saves, the deliverer, and who brings freedom. This name is to be the name by which they are to call Him, call to Him, and know Him. The name Yahweh assures them that He was there before the beginning of time, and that He seeks to always be in relationship with His people. Moses is to speak with the elders and the people and to reveal the name- *"Yahweh, God of your ancestors—the God of Abraham, the God of Isaac, and the God of Jacob. This is my eternal name, my name to remember for all generations."*

The task given to Moses is to appear before the Egyptian Pharoah, with the request for him to release the people of Israel, his slave community, for three days, so that they may go to the wilderness to worship the God of their ancestors. God knows that the request will not be granted and that because of Pharoah's refusal, God Himself will raise His hand against the Egyptians until they release the Israelites to freedom. Moses knows that his journey will be under the banner of the name of Yahweh, the 'I Am who I Am," the God who is ever present, the Saviour, the deliverer.

Our Saviour Jesus is Yahweh, the name that was given to Him before his birth. When Gabriel came to Mary with the announcement of the birth of a son, she was told very clearly that His name was to be 'Jesus', 'Yahweh saves.'

You will conceive and give birth to a son, and you will name him Jesus. He will be very great and will be called the Son of the Most High. The Lord God will give him the throne of his ancestor David. And he will reign over Israel forever; his Kingdom will never end!" Luke 1 v 31-33

Jesus also uses the title 'I AM'. Jesus answered, "I tell you the truth, before Abraham was even born, I am!" John 8 v 58 NLT

"Abraham—your 'father'—with elated faith looked down the corridors of history and saw my day coming. He saw it and cheered." The Jews said, "You're not even fifty years old—and Abraham saw you?" "Believe me," said Jesus, "I am who I am long before Abraham was anything." That did it—pushed them over the edge. They picked up rocks to throw at him. But Jesus slipped away, getting out of the Temple. John 8 v 56-59 MSG

If you wish to read more then I have included the whole of Psalm 103 here. I was going to select a snippet from it but found it impossible! The whole Psalm of David is amazing, and I could not bring myself to choose out a section. It is worthy meditating on every phrase within the Psalm.

Psalm 103 A Psalm of David TLB

I bless the holy name of God with all my heart. Yes, I will bless the Lord and not forget the glorious things he does for me. He forgives all my sins.

He heals me. He ransoms me from hell. He surrounds me with loving-kindness and tender mercies. He fills my life with good things! My youth is renewed like the eagle's! He gives justice to all who are treated unfairly. He revealed his will and nature to Moses and the people of Israel.

He is merciful and tender toward those who don't deserve it; he is slow to get angry and full of kindness and love. He never bears a grudge, nor remains angry forever. He has not punished us as we deserve for all our sins, for his mercy toward those who fear and honour him is as great as the height of the heavens above the earth. He has removed our sins as far away from us as the east is from the west. He is like a father to us, tender and sympathetic to those who reverence him. For he knows we are but dust and that our days are few and brief, like grass, like flowers, blown by the wind and gone forever.

But the loving-kindness of the Lord is from everlasting to everlasting to those who reverence him; his salvation is to children's children of those who are faithful to his covenant and remember to obey him!

The Lord has made the heavens his throne; from there he rules over everything there is. Bless the Lord, you mighty angels of his who carry out his orders, listening for each of his commands. Yes, bless the Lord, you armies of his angels who serve him constantly. Let everything everywhere bless the Lord. And how I bless him too.

I am the Lord who heals you

The Israelites, released from their captivity in Egypt, have experienced God's dramatic delivery at the Red Sea and the destruction of their pursuing enemies, they have been guided, and protected by the pillar of fire and cloud, and have seen the powerful hand of God displayed, putting their trust in Him and in His servant Moses. In exuberant celebration and praise, Miriam and the women have danced and led the people in an outpouring of thanksgiving and praise to God for His mercy and salvation. After this celebration, Moses has led the people into the wilderness of Shur, an inhospitable desert, travelling for three days and thirty-three miles, where they discover that there is no water. Even the water at the oasis of Marah is spoiled and bitter. The people's rejoicing, dancing and words of praise now become moans, murmurs and complaints against Moses and God. They demand water but the water provided is bitter. Moses cries out to God and is directed to the God solution- a specific tree and its wood that when thrown into the pool of water at the oasis which will make the bitter water sweet again. The thirsty people will be satisfied.

It was there at Marah that the Lord set before them the following decree as a standard to test their faithfulness to him. He said, "If you will listen carefully to the voice of the Lord your God and do what is right in his sight, obeying his commands and keeping all his decrees, then I will not make you suffer any of the diseases I sent on the Egyptians; for I am the Lord who heals you." After leaving Marah, the Israelites travelled on to the oasis of Elim, where they found twelve springs and seventy palm trees. They camped there beside the water. Exodus 15 v 25-27 NLT

The provision of water at Marah was a time and a place of testing and trust. Their trust and obedience were also connected to a promise. If they would listen to God's voice, depend on Him, and follow His instructions, then He would protect their physical wellbeing and their health. God also reveals another new name and aspect of His character-Jehovah Rophe- the God who heals. Unfortunately, the people would continue to grumble and rebel on their journey- in as many as ten other occasions. Their murmuring and complaints would arise again, but God would be faithful to them. God is more than faithful. God led the people to Elim, where there were twelve springs of water and seventy palm trees and there they camped by the waters. Here they would find rest, refreshment, shelter, and safety. God's provision was over and above! But God would continue to test and to teach His people.

God, the One who heals, provided a greater source for our healing and salvation. Jesus died for us and because of His crucifixion on a Roman wooden cross we are now healed and restored. Jesus also promises living water for us

"He himself bore our sins" in his body on the cross, so that we might die to sins and live for righteousness; "by his wounds you have been healed." 1 Peter 2 v 24

Jesus answered, "Everyone who drinks this water will be thirsty again, but whoever drinks the water I give them will never thirst. Indeed, the water I give them will become in them a spring of water welling up to eternal life." John 14 v 13-14

He heals the broken-hearted and binds up their wounds. Psalm 147 v 3

And it came to pass, on a certain day, as he was teaching, that the Pharisees and doctors of the Law sat by, which were come out of every

town of Galilee, and Judea, and Jerusalem, and the power of the Lord was in him, to heal them. Luke 5 v 17

Pray

When things go well, I can praise and dance. When things are tough or I am tested and tried, I grumble and moan. In every situation, help me to trust in your faithfulness and provision.

Today, I pray for those who need your healing- in body, mind, spirit, and soul. You heal the broken hearted.

Names of God: Yahweh Nissi
The Lord my Banner

The Israelites, under God's direction, have now moved on to Rephidim, but once again the people's complaints continue. There is no water. Moses is instructed to strike a rock with the rod, the staff of God, which had been given to him, and water gushes out to satisfy the thirst of the people. But now the Israelites face their first great battle- the Amalekites. Joshua is instructed to take a group of handpicked fighting men into battle, while Moses, Aaron and Hur go to the top of the hill to intercede and pray for victory. Once more the rod of God becomes an important symbol and rallying point for the men. The rod can be seen from a distance almost like the flags and banners of warriors and armies. While ever the rod in Moses' hands was held high then the battle went well. That rod was the symbol of God's personal and powerful involvement in the lives of His people. The outstretched arms of Moses and his prayers were an appeal for God to intervene yet again in this urgent situation.

The Amalekites came and attacked the Israelites at Rephidim. Moses said to Joshua, 'Choose some of our men and go out to fight the Amalekites. Tomorrow I will stand on top of the hill with the staff of God in my hands.'

So, Joshua fought the Amalekites as Moses had ordered, and Moses, Aaron and Hur went to the top of the hill. As long as Moses held up his hands, the Israelites were winning, but whenever he lowered his hands, the Amalekites were winning. When Moses' hands grew tired, they took a stone and put it under him, and he sat on it. Aaron and Hur held his hands up – one on one side, one on the other – so that his hands remained steady till sunset. So, Joshua overcame the Amalekite army with the sword.

Then the Lord said to Moses, 'Write this on a scroll as something to be remembered and make sure that Joshua hears it, because I will completely blot out the name of Amalek from under heaven.'

Moses built an altar and called it The Lord is my Banner. He said, 'Because hands were lifted up against the throne of the Lord, the Lord will be at war against the Amalekites from generation to generation. Exodus 17 v 8-16 NIV

The cross of Jesus is our banner and our rallying point. The' Lord is our banner' is how we are identified. The cross is the symbol of God's protection and victory.

His banner over me is love. Song of Solomon 2 v 4

In that day the Root of Jesse will stand as a banner for the peoples; the nations will rally to him, and his resting-place will be glorious. In that day the Lord will reach out his hand a second time to reclaim the surviving remnant of his people Isaiah 11 v 10-11

You have given a banner to those who fear you, that it may be displayed because of the truth. Psalm 60 v 4

The Names of God:
Yahweh Shalom The Lord is Peace

The Israelites had lost sight of their God and for seven years God had allowed them to suffer at the hands of the Midianites. Although they were living in the land of promise they were living as a defeated, harassed, and oppressed people. They were living in fear, hiding in holes, caves, and safe places in the mountains like frightened animals. Their enemies, the Midianites, Amalekites, and other tribal people groups repeatedly invaded their land, stealing their crops and possessions and deliberately ruining everything that remained. The Israelites were an impoverished, powerless, and overpowered people, who felt abandoned by their God. For those seven years they had no peace.

The People of Israel, reduced to grinding poverty by Midian, cried out to God for help.

But God was about to step into their circumstances. He had prepared a man who would step forward, even though he felt that he had no authority, status, position or claim to be so chosen. That man was Gideon.

God had selected this 'mighty warrior' and would promise to be with him. Gideon would save his people using only three hundred men so that it was clear to all that the victory only belonged to God.

The angel of the Lord appeared to Gideon. He said, "Mighty warrior, the Lord is with you." Judges 6 v 11-12

The Lord turned to him and said, 'Go in the strength you have and save Israel out of Midian's hand. Am I not sending you? 'Judges 6 v 14

Even before battle plans were drawn up, Gideon prepared an offering and an altar, giving praise that God Himself and His Angel had appeared, that God was with him and his people, and that He would step into their desperate plight. After Gideon's battle with the Midianites, there was peace for forty years.

So, Gideon built an altar to the Lord there and called it The Lord Is Peace. To this day it stands in Ophrah of the Abiezrites. Judges 6 v 24

Thus, Midian was subdued before the Israelites and did not raise its head again. During Gideon's lifetime, the land had peace forty years. Judges 8.v 28

There may be times when we feel fearful, defeated, harassed, overwhelmed, and frustrated. We may ask with Gideon, 'where is God in all this?' and 'where are His wondrous works that others have spoken of? But our Prince of Peace longs for us to be well, to be whole, to be fulfilled and complete and to have His peace. He wants us to know His shalom.

Do not be anxious about anything, but in every situation, by prayer and petition, with thanksgiving, present your requests to God. And the peace of God, which transcends all understanding, will guard your hearts and your minds in Christ Jesus. Philippians 4 v 6-7

He will keep in perfect peace all those who trust in Him, whose thoughts turn often to the Lord! Trust in the Lord God always, for in the Lord Jehovah is your everlasting strength. Isaiah 26 v 3-4

Pray

Lord, I come before you ready to bring my worries, anxieties, and fears. I want to claim Your promise of blessings of peace and strength in my life. Bring a peace into my soul that passes all worldly understanding and make me a light for others to see Your strength.

Yahweh Tsuri: The Lord my Rock

I remember going to Brimham Rocks with our grandson, Sam when he was young, and being slightly horrified as he leapt around on the massive outcrops of rock, climbing to rather worrying heights with the confidence of a mountain goat. Rocks are regarded as places of safety, security, and these permanent fixtures can be seen as symbols of permanence, and dependability. David found himself in some tough situations- encounters with wild mountain beasts, persecuted by Saul, facing warriors in battle, and hiding in the mountains. There was one thing that he was sure of and that was that his God was his rock. David knew from experience that whatever he was going through, God was his place of refuge-his rock.

Praise be to the Lord my Rock,
 who trains my hands for war,
 my fingers for battle.
He is my loving God and my fortress,
 my stronghold and my deliverer,
my shield in whom I take refuge,
 who subdues peoples under me.
Psalm 144 v 1-2 David

Truly my soul finds rest in God;
 my salvation comes from him.
Truly he is my rock and my salvation;
 he is my fortress; I will never be shaken.
Psalm 62 v 1-2 David

"There is no one holy like the Lord;
 there is no one besides you;
 there is no Rock like our God.
1 Samuel 2 v 2 Hannah

We can have this same assurance that God will be our rock if we build our lives on Him. Jesus is the living stone, the precious cornerstone and as living stones we are being joined to Him.

"Therefore, everyone who hears these words of mine and puts them into practice is like a wise man who built his house on the rock. The rain came down, the streams rose, and the winds blew and beat against that house; yet it did not fall, because it had its foundation on the rock. Matthew 7 v 24-25 Jesus

As you come to him, the living Stone—rejected by humans but chosen by God and precious to him— you also, like living stones, are being built into a spiritual house to be a holy priesthood, offering spiritual sacrifices acceptable to God through Jesus Christ for in Scripture it says: See, I lay a stone in Zion, a chosen and precious cornerstone, and the one who trusts in him will never be put to shame. 1 Peter 2 v 4-6

My hope is built on nothing less
Than Jesus' blood and righteousness
I dare not trust the sweetest frame
But wholly lean on Jesus' name.

On Christ the solid rock I stand
All other ground is sinking sand
All other ground is sinking sand

When darkness veils His lovely face
I'll rest on His unchanging grace
In every high and stormy day
My anchor holds within the veil.

Edward Mote (1834)

The Lord our Righteousness

"Behold, listen closely, the days are coming," says the Lord,
"When I will raise up for David a righteous Branch;
And He will reign as King and act wisely
And will do those things that accomplish justice and righteousness in the land.
"In His days Judah will be saved,
And Israel will dwell safely;
Now this is His name by which He will be called;
'The Lord Our Righteousness.'
Jeremiah 23v 5-6 AMP

For many people, their longing and hope is to live a Godly and righteous life, but that way of living tends to escape them again and again. We all fall short and cannot hope to reach the standard that God desires for us. We fall and we fail and when we try to earn our way to God and trust in our good works and attempts at right living, we have a habit of failing miserably. But Jesus, by His grace alone and by His death for us, has made a way. He is the Lord our Righteousness. It is all about grace. God's plan in Christ was that righteousness could only come by faith -not through the law or striving and actions. It is God's grace and His grace alone.

Now we are seeing the righteousness of God declared quite apart from the Law (though amply testified to by both Law and Prophets)—it is a righteousness imparted to, and operating in, all who have faith in Jesus Christ. (For there is no distinction to be made anywhere: everyone has sinned, everyone falls short of the beauty of God's plan.) Under this divine system a man who has faith is now freely acquitted in the eyes of God by his generous dealing in the redemptive act of Jesus Christ. Romans 3 v 21-22

For those of us who have trusted in Christ and seek to follow Him, He promises to lead us into paths of righteousness. God wants us to be hungry to follow Him and His righteousness. Then we will be filled.

He restoreth my soul: he leadeth me in the paths of righteousness for his name's sake. Psalm 23v 3

Blessed are those who hunger and thirst for righteousness for they will be filled. Matthew 5 v 6

Paul encouraged the young Timothy to pursue righteousness and a Godly life along with those wonderful qualities of faith, love, perseverance, and gentleness. May we long for and seek these gifts and qualities.

But you, Timothy, are a man of God; so, run from all these evil things. Pursue righteousness and a godly life, along with faith, love, perseverance, and gentleness. Fight the good fight for the true faith. Hold tightly to the eternal life to which God has called you, which you have declared so well before many witnesses. 1 Timothy 6 v 5-6

Ish - My Husband

On that day, says the Lord, you will call me "my husband," and no longer will you call me "my Baal (Master)." For I will remove the names of the Baals from her mouth, and they shall be mentioned by name no more. And I will take you for my wife forever; I will take you for my wife in righteousness and in justice, in steadfast love and in mercy. I will take you for my wife in faithfulness, and you shall know the Lord. Hosea 2 v 16 & 19-20 RSV

I find that the Book of Hosea is a very challenging book to read, and The Message version is perhaps not the version to read in this instance. Hosea, the prophet to Israel, was instructed by God to take a faithless, adulterous woman, Gomer, as his wife, knowing that she would continue to be unfaithful and bring him shame and distress. But Hosea and his marriage to Gomer was to be a living parable, a picture story, of the faithfulness, compassion, and love of God for His people despite everything that they may do to turn from God, to rebel, and to cause self-inflicted pain into the bargain. The Hosea story illustrates that although we are often faithless like Gomer, that God is constant and forever faithful. He is our 'husband.' Wherever we go and whatever we do we can know that God will pursue us and bring us back into His love. His love will not let us go. Not ever.

For your Maker is your husband— the LORD Almighty is his name—
the Holy One of Israel is your Redeemer;
he is called the God of all the earth.
The LORD will call you back as if you were a wife deserted and distressed
in spirit— a wife who married young, only to be rejected," says your
God.
"For a brief moment I abandoned you,
but with deep compassion I will bring you back.
In a surge of anger I hid my face from you for a moment,
but with everlasting kindness I will have compassion on you,"
says the LORD your Redeemer.
Isaiah 54 v 5-8

And you husbands, show the same kind of love to your wives as Christ showed to the Church when he died for her to make her holy and clean, washed by baptism and God's Word so that he could give her to himself as a glorious Church without a single spot or wrinkle or any other blemish, being holy and without a single fault. Ephesians 5 25-27

Oh, love that will not let me go
I rest my weary soul in thee
I give thee back the life I owe
That in thine ocean depths its flow
May richer, fuller be.

Oh, cross that liftest up my head
I dare not ask to fly from thee
I lay in dust's life's glory dead
And from the ground there blossoms red
Life that shall endless be.

George Matheson, (1842-1906).

Abba Father

But while he was still a long way off, his father saw him and was filled with compassion for him; he ran to his son, threw his arms around him, and kissed him. Luke 15 v 20 NIV

One of the most familiar and well-loved parables of Jesus, 'The Prodigal Son,' should perhaps be more aptly renamed 'the parable of the loving Father.' As I read Luke 15 again, it struck me that the audience Jesus was addressing with this well-known set of parables, was a motley collection of tax collectors, sinners, Pharisees, and Teachers of the Law. Each member of His audience could perhaps and should, see themselves portrayed in this story as either the prodigal or the bad humoured, proud, older brother. What Jesus was highlighting in the story was the compassionate, loving Father who loved both of his sons desperately and went out to seek them.

The prodigal should rightly have been cut off permanently from family, community, and locality for bringing such disgrace on the father. The elder brother, by refusing to enter the house and greet his brother, had insulted his father, his father's status in the family and his wishes. Both sons had abused their father. Yet the father had kept a lookout for the younger son, had publicly run towards him in the road and had thrown his arms around him. The father had left the welcome party in honour of his returning, lost son, to seek out the older brother and to draw him in.

Jesus, in the story, was highlighting the 'abba' love of the Father of God. The many names of God that were known by his people were now superseded by this one supreme name 'Abba-Father.' It is as if Jesus is saying this is the name by which God is to be known. Their identity, and ours, is as a child of the Father, whether we are saint or sinner. In John's Gospel, Jesus refers to 'Father' 156 times. Jesus wanted this audience of the self-righteous and the sinner to be aware of the love of the Father for each of them- a unique and generous father love. Abba Father is seeking out and waiting for those who will return.

My sheep listen to my voice; I know them, and they follow me. I give them eternal life, and they shall never perish; no one will snatch them out of my hand. My Father, who has given them to me, is greater than all no one can snatch them out of my Father's hand. I and the Father are one. John 10 v 27-30

As a father has compassion on his children,
so the Lord has compassion on those who fear him;

for he knows how we are formed,
he remembers that we are dust.   Psalm 103 v 13-14

Praise be to the God and Father of our Lord Jesus Christ, the Father of compassion and the God of all comfort, who comforts us in all our troubles, so that we can comfort those in any trouble with the comfort we ourselves receive from God. 2 Corinthians 1 v 3-4

This, then, is how you should pray: Our Father in heaven, hallowed be your name, your kingdom come, your will be done, on earth as it is in heaven. Matthew 6 v 9-11

I have heard so many songs
Listened to a thousand tongues
But there is one
That sounds above them all.
The Father's song
The Father's love
You sung it over me and for eternity
It's written on my heart.

Heaven's perfect melody
The Creator's symphony
You are singing over me
The Father's song
Heaven's perfect mystery
The king of love has sent for me
And now you're singing over me
The Father's song.

The Father's Song Matt Redman
The Father's Song lyrics © Capitol Christian Music Group, Capitol CMG Publishing, Sony/ATV Music Publishing LLC

SEASONS – ADVENT

Light in the darkness

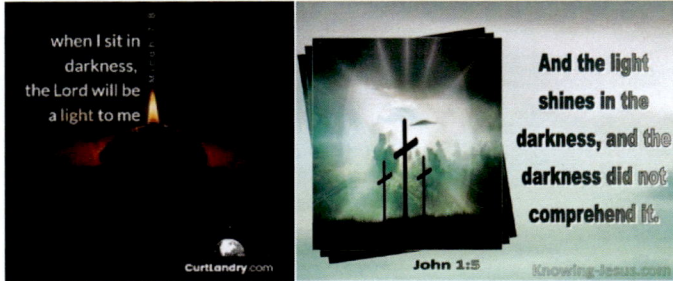

Do not rejoice over me, O my enemy;
when I fall, I shall rise;
when I sit in darkness,
the Lord will be a light to me.
Micah 7 v 8-11

At this time of year, it is dark and dismal. The mornings and the evenings are dark, our internal clocks and emotions, are struggling with long, cold, and dreary days despite the many festivals of light which celebrate the splendour of fireworks, colour, candles, and illuminations. We have made our advent rings and during Advent we are preparing our hearts and minds for the Coming, the Advent of Jesus. It is a time of hope and expectation. We may be sitting in darkness, but we have hope that the Light is coming. Many people may feel to be in a dark place at this time. But there is hope, that even if we feel as if we are sitting in darkness or stumbling our way ahead in the dark, that Jesus has promised to be our light. In the darkest of rooms, the smallest of candles can bring a shaft of light allowing us to see more clearly.

The people who sat in darkness have seen a great light, and for those who sat in the region and shadow of death, light has dawned. Matthew 4 v 16

By the tender mercy of our God, the dawn from on high will break upon us, to give light to those who sit in darkness and in the shadow of death, to guide our feet into the way of peace. Luke 1 v 79

You light a lamp for me. The Lord, my God, lights up my darkness. Psalm 18 v 28

Again, Jesus spoke to them, saying, "I am the light of the world. Whoever follows me will never walk in darkness but will have the light of life." John 8 v 12

I have come as light into the world, so that everyone who believes in me should not remain in the darkness. John 12 v 46

Pray

As we light a candle on the Advent ring, remember:

Lighting a candle is a symbol: of love and hope, of light and warmth. Our world needs them all.

Lighting a candle is a parable: It gives light to others. Christ gave Himself for others. He calls us to give ourselves.

Lighting a candle is a prayer: When we have gone, it stays alight, and the prayers that we have offered, continues.

Lighting a candle is for each of us: You're here to bring light, bringing out the God colours in the world. God is not a secret to be kept. Now that I've put you there on a hilltop, on a light stand- shine! Keep open house; be generous with your lives. By opening to others, you'll prompt people to open up to God, this generous Father in heaven. Luke 18 v 14-16

It is winter in Narnia," said Mr. Tumnus, "and has been for ever so long.... always winter, but never Christmas."
The Lion, the Witch and the Wardrobe by C.S.Lewis

Waiting

Waiting can be hard, long, and frustrating. I could not begin to add up the number of hours that I have spent in my lifetime to date, waiting- waiting for the birth of a child; waiting at the doctors, clinic, hospital; waiting at the school gate, activity club, holiday club, church hall; waiting for the production or concert to begin; waiting for exam results, decisions after interviews; waiting for the much needed holiday, or for news etc.

Waiting involves the expectation or hope that something will happen, being in readiness for its beginning or coming, and waiting with patient anticipation during the indeterminate period before the arrival or completion of the expected hope.

In Luke's account of the birth and ministry of Jesus, there is a lot of waiting by a lot of people- Zechariah, Elizabeth, Mary, Simeon, and Anna. But while their wait was longed for, anticipated, and prayed for, there would be others around them whose lives were not impacted by the waiting, and whose living carried on without this waiting, concern, readiness, or preparation. The waiting was for a longed-for Saviour and even when He arrived as an infant, there would be many years of waiting before the commencement of His ministry.

Zechariah and Elizabeth had prayed for and longed for a child. In their old age, Gabriel was sent to them with the news of the birth of their child, John. But the angel said to him: "Do not be afraid, Zechariah; your prayer has been heard. Your wife Elizabeth will bear you a son, and you are to call him John. Luke 1 v 13

Gabriel was also sent to the young Mary with news of the promised Saviour that she would bear. It could have been a troubling and anxious wait as she no doubt faced the questions and quizzical looks of neighbours and villagers. But she would take comfort in the company of her cousin Elizabeth as they waited together.   *Mary stayed with Elizabeth for about three months and then returned home. Luke 1 v 56*

Simeon, a righteous and devout man, living in Jerusalem, was *"waiting for the consolation of Israel, and the Holy Spirit was on him. It had been revealed to him by the Holy Spirit that he would not die before he had seen the Lord's Messiah". Luke 2 V 25-26* Simeon was led to the Temple by the Holy Spirit, at the exact time that Joseph and Mary arrived with the eight-day old infant, Jesus at the Temple for the ceremony of purification and circumcision. Simeon's long wait was at an end.

Anna, an 84-year-old, widow, and prophet who worshipped daily at the temple in Jerusalem, was also waiting, as were other worshippers, hoping for God's intervention in Israel. *She never left the temple but worshiped night and day, fasting and praying. Coming up to them at that very moment, she gave thanks to God and spoke about the child to all who were looking forward to the redemption of Jerusalem. Luke 2 v 37-38*

From infant to child to man, John and Jesus waited until the time was right for them to begin their ministries and appearances on the world's stage. And the child (John) grew and became strong in spirit, and he lived in the wilderness until he appeared publicly to Israel. Luke 1 v 80 Jesus was about thirty years old before he began his ministry. Luke 3 v 23

Jesus came into Galilee, proclaiming the Gospel of God, saying, "The time has come at last—the kingdom of God has arrived. You must change your hearts and minds and believe the good news." Mark 1 v 15

Waiting and perfect timing. God's timing is precise, and perfect. He steps in at the right time-the 'Kairos' time - "the appointed time in the purposes of God."

Strength will rise as we wait upon the Lord
We will wait upon the Lord, we will wait upon the Lord
Strength will rise as we wait upon the Lord
We will wait upon the Lord, we will wait upon the Lord.
Our God, you reign forever
Our hope, our strong Deliverer.
Chris Tomlin based on *Isaiah 40 v 31*

Come, Thou long expected Jesus
Born to set Thy people free;
From our fears and sins release us,
Let us find our rest in Thee.

Charles Wesley / R. H. Pritchard / Tom Howard, Come Thou Long Expected Jesus lyrics © Capitol Christian Music Group, Capitol CMG Publishing, DistroKid, Peermusic Publishing, Universal Music Publishing Group, Warner Chappell Music, Inc

Do not fear, for I am with you

One of the most popular Bible verses shared, bookmarked, and highlighted most often in the Bible is *Isaiah 41:10: "So do not fear, for I am with you; do not be dismayed, for I am your God. I will strengthen you and help you; I will uphold you with my righteous right hand."*

Do not yield to fear, for I am always near. Never turn your gaze from me, for I am your faithful God. I will infuse you with my strength and help you in every situation. I will hold you firmly with my victorious right hand.' MSG

This verse has helped many people who have been searching for answers during times of stress, loneliness, and difficulties. Through hardships and uncertainty, people have continued to seek God and to turn to the Bible for strength, peace, and hope.

In Luke and Matthew's Christmas accounts we read of many times when fear might have taken hold of individuals- Zechariah, Mary, Joseph, the shepherds, and the wise men. But reassurance and the knowledge of God's presence and purpose was given to each one so that they might not be fearful, terrified, or dismayed. In each circumstance they were given the reassurance of God's presence and specific guidance for each situation.

Zechariah *Then there appeared to him an angel of the Lord, standing at the right side of the altar of incense. When Zechariah saw him, he was terrified; and fear overwhelmed him. But the angel said to him, "Do not be afraid, Zechariah, for your prayer has been heard. Your wife Elizabeth will bear you a son, and you will name him John." Luke 1 v 11-13*

Mary *"Don't be frightened, Mary," the angel told her, for God has decided to wonderfully bless you! Very soon now, you will become pregnant and have a baby boy, and you are to name him Jesus. Luke 1 v 30-31*

Joseph was given reassurance and peace about the disturbing news that he had been given concerning Mary.

"While he was thinking about this, an angel of the Lord appeared to him in a dream and said, "Joseph, descendant of David, do not be afraid to take Mary to be your wife. For it is by the Holy Spirit that she has conceived. She will have a son, and you will name him Jesus—because he will save his people from their sins." Matthew 1 v 20. Joseph would later be guided by an angel of the Lord in a dream telling him to take Jesus and Mary to safety in Egypt. *"After Herod died, an angel of the Lord appeared in a dream to Joseph in Egypt and said, "Get up, take the child and his mother, and go back to the land of Israel, because those who tried to kill the child are dead." Matthew 2v 19-20 God's protection and care was constant.*

Shepherds *In that region there were shepherds living in the fields, keeping watch over their flock by night. Then an angel of the Lord stood before them, and the glory of the Lord shone around them, and they were terrified. But the angel said to them, "Do not be afraid; for see—I am bringing you good news of great joy for all the people: to you is born this day in the city of David a Saviour, who is the Messiah, the Lord. Matthew 2v 8-11*

The Wise Men having been warned in a dream not to return to Herod, left for their own country by another road. Matthew 2 v8. They could have been fearful of the wrath of King Herod and of being pursued by his soldiers, but they had the reassurance that God would protect them.

So, whenever we are fearful, dismayed, anxious, concerned, worried, troubled we can turn our gaze to Him and have the reassurance that God will be with us. The answer to fear is love- perfect love casts out fear.

Love came down at Christmas,
Love all lovely, love divine;
Love was born at Christmas,
Star and angels gave the sign.

Worship we the Godhead,
Love incarnate, love divine;
Worship we our Jesus:
But wherewith for sacred sign?

Love shall be our token,
Love shall be yours and love be mine,
Love to God and to all men,
Love for plea and gift and sign.

Christina Rosetti (1830-1894)

Pray

For those who may be dismayed or fearful this week.

For those for whom Christmas is very difficult perhaps because of loss, stress, busyness, family pressures, or loneliness.

Mary, Did You Know?

A King size bed

Then Mary said, "Here am I, the servant of the Lord; let it be with me according to your word." Then the angel departed from her. Luke 1 v 38

During Advent, we may consider how we can listen and respond to God, and so here we think about Mary's response to the message of the angel. What could have been Mary's response to the Angel's news?

Mary could have resisted the message of the Angel and therefore God's will for her and for us. She was accepting a life changing role with its many consequences for her. Her way ahead was unknown. Joseph, her family, and her community could reject her. How could she possibly explain what was to happen to her?

Perhaps Mary could have accepted the will of God but with resignation. Mary may not have been completely happy with the situation but what else could she do? She had been chosen, she had found favour, and as a young woman of very low social status in the cultural climate of her time, what choice would she have?

Mary could commit her future to God and trust that He could redeem any situation that she found herself in. That even as a pregnant teenager facing the gossip of the community, that God would work things out in good time.

Or Mary, as these words might indicate, might rejoice at the commission that she has been given- not just being willing to accept this role but trusting herself, her future, and the unknown, completely to her God, whatever the outcome may be. She is the servant of God, willingly submitting herself to the future that God was giving to her, not knowing any of the consequences, unable to see that in the future 'that a sword would pierce her own heart' but trusting her God completely. This is trust and faith indeed.

Pray

Father, sometimes life is hard, and I kick against the demands and the course of my life. I would like things to be easy, comfortable, convenient, and straightforward, knowing the direction and purpose of the path in front of me. But life is uncertain, unpredictable, difficult and I cannot see the road in front of me. But you have promised a light for my path and not a crystal ball into the future. Help me to trust you one step at a time, not with resignation but with gladness and trust that you know the end from the beginning. Your purpose for me is true and good.

Mary, did you know that your baby boy
Would one day walk on water?
Mary, did you know that your baby boy
Would save our sons and daughters?
Did you know that your baby boy
Has come to make you new?
This child that you delivered, will soon deliver you
Mary, did you know that your baby boy

208

Would give sight to a blind man?
Mary, did you know that your baby boy
Would calm the storm with his hand?
Did you know that your baby boy
Has walked where angels trod?
When you kiss your little baby
You kiss the face of God
Mary, did you know?
Mary, did you know?
Is Lord of all creation?
Mary, did you know that your baby boy
Would one day rule the nations?
Did you know that your baby boy
Is heaven's perfect Lamb?
That the sleeping child you're
Holding is the great, I Am
Mary, did you know? (Mary, did you know?)

Mary's Treasure Store of Precious Words

But Mary treasured up all these things and pondered them in her heart. Luke 2 v 19

Mary kept all these things to herself, holding them dear, deep within herself. MSG

There were many things that Mary was told about her new baby Son.

From Joseph: she was told that her Son was Holy Spirit conceived and that He was to be called "Jesus— 'God saves'—because He will save His people from their sins."

From the shepherds she learned: that His birth was a joyful event, meant for everyone, worldwide. That He was Saviour, Messiah, and Master.

"Don't be afraid. I'm here to announce a great and joyful event that is meant for everybody, worldwide: A Saviour has just been born in David's town, a Saviour who is Messiah and Master.

From Simeon, who took the tiny 8-day old child into his arms at His naming day Mary learned that He was salvation in person, a God revealing light to the non-Jewish nations and the glory of God's people Israel, a sign from God Himself, and a 'heart revealer.' Mary was also told of soul and heart pain that would be waiting for her in her future.

"Sovereign Lord, now let your servant die in peace,
as you have promised.
I have seen your salvation,
which you have prepared for all people.
He is a light to reveal God to the nations,
and he is the glory of your people Israel!"

And to Mary directly: *"This child is destined to cause many in Israel to fall, and many others to rise. He has been sent as a sign from God, but many will oppose him. As a result, the deepest thoughts of many hearts will be revealed. And a sword will pierce your very soul."*

Mary and Joseph *"were speechless with surprise at these words."*

At the very time Simeon was praying, Anna, the Prophetess broke into an anthem of praise to God and talked about the child to all who were waiting expectantly for the freeing of Jerusalem.

Some years later, Mary would hear from the Scholars from the East, the title, the King of the Jews and the words of Micah referring to the Messiah (by their report from the very lips of Herod.) She would witness these great men kneeling in worship before her child opening their luggage and presenting their gifts of gold, frankincense, myrrh. These scholars had searched records, documents, scriptures, and prophecies, and had then followed the star to worship her child.

"Where can we find and pay homage to the new-born King of the Jews? We observed a star in the eastern sky that signalled his birth. We're on pilgrimage to worship him."

So, Mary privately treasured all these words. She stored them away in her heart and mind as she watched her Son, Jesus growing into manhood.

We have treasure that we can store in our hearts and share. We are not to keep it to ourselves. We have the knowledge of Jesus, God's Son, Emmanuel, the Wonderful Counsellor, the Prince of Peace who has come to bring salvation. The shepherds shared news of a Saviour for the whole world- for everyone- good news that must be treasured but also shared.

For God, who said, "Let there be light in the darkness," has made this light shine in our hearts so we could know the glory of God that is seen in the face of Jesus Christ. We now have this light shining in our hearts, but we ourselves are like fragile clay jars containing this great treasure.

Insecurity and a refugee status

Veiled in flesh the Godhead see
Hail the incarnate Deity
Pleased as man with man to dwell
Jesus, our Emmanuel!

Jesus was born into very humble, insecure and at times frightening circumstances. Israel was enduring a tyrannical Roman rule. Mary had taken a very precarious journey to Bethlehem, in the final month of her pregnancy and had delivered her baby, with perhaps minimal support, in very basic and perhaps unsanitary conditions. Shepherds, those common working men, had visited Mary and the child Jesus, shortly after His birth, but with those wonderful and surprising messages from the Angels. When sacrifice was offered at the Temple for this first born, male child, the sacrifice was one that was the bare minimum, one that would be given by a family of very modest means - a pair of turtledoves or two young pigeons. Being warned in a dream to escape from Herod and his anger, the family would escape to Egypt, leaving hurriedly, in the middle of the night, and remain there as strangers, foreigners and refugees in a strange land, because Herod's intention was to search for and destroy the child.

So, Joseph got up and took the Child and His mother while it was still night and left for Egypt.

When once again, Joseph was instructed in a dream to return to his homeland, after two years as a refugee family, he took Mary and Jesus back to the land of Israel. It was with great wisdom and foresight, knowing that Herod Archelaus was ruling in place of his father Herod the Great, and realising that Jesus could still be in danger, that he took his family, again warned by God in a dream, to Nazareth, in the region of Galilee. Roman soldiers were billeted just outside of Nazareth and Nazarenes were treated with suspicion and caution by other Jews because of this. Jesus was once called 'Jesus the Nazarene' in an insulting, derogatory way. But this move would perhaps keep Jesus safe.

And so, the infant Jesus, the Lord's salvation, Emmanuel, God with us, the One who would save His people from their sins, the Messiah, the

Anointed, the Ruler and Shepherd of His people Israel, the Light in the darkness was born in simple circumstances.

He left the glory of heaven and emptied Himself of everything to be our Saviour.

May we truly acknowledge Him to be our Lord and Saviour and trust Him with whatever uncertainties, problems, unexpected challenges and fears may come our way into a new year. He can handle it.

Christ Jesus, who, though He was in the form of God, did not count equality with God a thing to be grasped, but emptied himself, taking the form of a servant, being born in the likeness of men. And being found in human form he humbled himself and became obedient unto death, even death on a cross. Therefore, God has highly exalted him and bestowed on Him the name, which is above every name, that at the name of Jesus every knee should bow, in heaven and on earth and under the earth, and every tongue confess that Jesus Christ is Lord, to the glory of God the Father. Philippians 2 v 7-11.

In the bleakness of a Bethlehem stable love was born. A love that was undeserved and that was for all. May we reflect His love and grace in how we respond to others, to the needs of our community and our world.

Epiphany The Journey of the Maji

The journey of the Maji was a major expedition, travelling from the East to the land of Israel, in their search for a new king. It was a considerable move, a location shift, an uncertain and arduous journey of unknown timing and length. The Maji- those scholars, astrologers, or kings from the region of Persia, Eastern Syria, or the borders of India, faced a long and perhaps dangerous journey. They would travel light, with essential goods only, packed on horse and camel. It would be a long, uncomfortable, and exhausting journey, in their search for a special child, in a land many miles away. The Maji had observed a special star in its rising, signifying the birth of a new king, and their journey, their relocation, was to search for this new, special king, to pay homage, to give gifts and to worship him.

After hearing the king, they went their way; and behold, the star, which they had seen in the east, went on before them, continually leading the way, until it came and stood over the place where the young Child was. Matthew 2 v 9

They kept going. They kept moving forward. The Maji's followers, friends may have thought them crazy to undertake such a journey-the cost, the distance, the inconvenience, the hazards, and the uncertainty. The routes and resting places of their journey would be unfamiliar, hazardous, and strange. The Maji would experience confusion at Herod's palace as the child was not to be found there, and yet the star was still present. But they kept moving. *The sight of the star filled them with indescribable joy. v 10* In spite of the hardships they kept travelling towards the child.

Guidance by star and dream

The Maji were sensitive and responsive to God's leading by signs, star, and dream. The voices in their heads and around them could have told them that they were stupid, unwise, and that of course Herod should be trusted not to harm the child who would be king. Or the Maji could have turned back at that point. But their instincts, the quiet prompting of God, told them to follow their research, the rising, leading star, and the dream's instruction. This was faith and trust indeed. Their journey home may have been a longer route, but still they followed the dream's instruction and the guidance of God.

They returned to their own country by another route because God had warned them in a dream not to go back to Herod. v 12

The new year will hold many new challenges and joys for us. There may be people to feel stuck, immobilized, isolated, lost and confused, with relationships seemingly on hold. The message of the Maji may be to keep moving forward following the promptings and leading of the Holy Spirit as we continue to look for Jesus. We don't have to feel stuck, and stationary. Let us step forward with hope into a new year and keep moving forward towards the light of Jesus.

As with gladness men of old
Did the guiding star behold;
As with joy they hailed its light,
Leading onward, beaming bright;
So, most gracious God, may we
Evermore be led to thee.
William C Dix (1837 - 1898)

A Prayer for the Year ahead

I arise today
Through a mighty strength:
God's power to guide me,
God's might to uphold me,
God's eyes to watch over me;
God's ear to hear me,
God's word to give me speech,
God's hand to guard me,
God's way to lie before me,
God's shield to shelter me,
God's host to secure me.
(First Millennium - Bridgid of Gael)

The Journey Of The Magi by T.S. Eliot

"A cold coming we had of it,
Just the worst time of the year
For a journey, and such a long journey:
The ways deep and the weather sharp,
The very dead of winter."

And the camels galled, sore-footed, __refractory__,
Lying down in the melting snow.
There were times we regretted
The summer palaces on slopes, the terraces,
And the silken girls bringing sherbet.
Then the camel men cursing and grumbling
And running away, and wanting their liquor and women,
And the night-fires going out, and the lack of shelters,
And the cities hostile and the towns unfriendly
And the villages dirty and charging high prices:
A hard time we had of it.

214

At the end we preferred to travel all night,
Sleeping in snatches,
With the voices singing in our ears, saying
That this was all folly.

Then at dawn we came down to a temperate valley,
Wet, below the snow line, smelling of vegetation;
With a running stream and a water-mill beating the darkness,
And three trees on the low sky,
And an old white horse galloped away in the meadow.
Then we came to a tavern with vine-leaves over the lintel,
Six hands at an open door dicing for pieces of silver,
And feet kicking the empty wine-skins.
But there was no information, and so we continued
And arriving at evening, not a moment too soon
Finding the place; it was (you may say) satisfactory.

All this was a long time ago, I remember,
And I would do it again, but set down
This set down
This: were we led all that way for
Birth or Death? There was a birth, certainly,
We had evidence and no doubt. I had seen birth and death,
But had thought they were different; this Birth was
Hard and bitter agony for us, like Death, our death.
We returned to our places, these Kingdoms,
But no longer at ease here, in the old dispensation,
With an alien people clutching their gods.
I should be glad of another death.

SEASONS – EASTER

The donkey - "It's for Jesus"

When they were approaching Jerusalem and had come to Bethphage and Bethany on the slopes of the Mount of Olives, he sent off two of his disciples with these instructions, "Go into the village just ahead of you and as soon as you enter it you will find a tethered colt on which no one has yet ridden. Untie it and bring it here. If anybody asks you, 'Why are you doing this?', just say, 'The Lord needs it, and will send it back immediately.'" So, they went off and found the colt tethered by a doorway outside in the open street, and they untied it. Some of the bystanders did say, "What are you doing, untying this colt?", but they made the reply Jesus told them to make, and the men raised no objection. So, they brought the colt to Jesus, threw their coats on its back, and he took his seat upon it. Mark 11 v 1-7

Jesus would have made this journey to Jerusalem many times over the years and so he would have had several contacts and friendships in the area during these visits. Jesus was thoroughly prepared for this, His final visit to Jerusalem, and was carefully setting the stage for the journey to the cross. The timings, events and preparations were securely in His hands. Yet Jesus was still training His disciples, delegating essential tasks, and involving them in His Kingdom work. By sharing the specific details of the colt of Bethphage, He was building and growing the disciple's faith and trust in Him. He was telling them what would happen, and it did happen exactly as He said it would.

Jesus and the disciples had always travelled on foot on their journeys, but now Jesus sends off two of His disciples to collect a donkey, his chosen method of transport for this very public entry into Jerusalem. Jesus delegates this task with a very clear set of instructions and even the words to say. If anyone approached them or asked them what they were doing, they were to simply say that "the Lord needs it." That simple statement was sufficient for the owner to release the donkey to them immediately and to satisfy the bystanders that this was not something that they should be concerned about!

The disciples just needed to say the words, "It's for Jesus." It is these few simple words that have struck me quite forcibly- "It's for Jesus." We may need to regularly review what we do and what we give to make sure that everything that we do, and give is for Him. We can often establish our worth by what we accomplish, by what we achieve, by what we can earn and by what we can control. So, at times we need to take a rain check, and look at our heart, our motives, and our life in Christ. We need to make sure that what we are doing 'is for Jesus' and that 'He needs it.'

I warm to the owner of the donkey. He had an open hand and as soon as the request for the donkey was made there was not a second thought in his mind. Without hesitation he released the colt to the disciples. Sometimes when your heart finds something that you need to do, and you know that it is the right thing to do, you need to do it straight away. It's not a good idea to dither! Or the moment may well pass. Sometimes if you pause and wait then the 'moment', the gift, the challenge escapes us and goes.

"Shout and cheer, Daughter Zion!
Raise your voice, Daughter Jerusalem!
Your king is coming!
a good king who makes all things right,
a humble king riding a donkey,
a mere colt of a donkey.
I've had it with war—no more chariots in Ephraim,
no more war horses in Jerusalem,
no more swords and spears, bows, and arrows.
He will offer peace to the nations,
a peaceful rule worldwide,
from the four winds to the seven seas.
Zechariah 9 v 9-19

Jesus entered the city on a humble donkey, as a man of peace and not the conquering, triumphant, warrior leader that many in Jerusalem were perhaps hoping for. May we be people of peace too.

A Celtic Prayer

I place my hands in yours Lord.
I place my hands in yours.

I place my will in yours Lord.
I place my will in yours

I place my days in yours Lord.
I place my days in yours

I place my thoughts in yours Lord.
I place my thoughts in yours

I place my heart in yours Lord.
I place my heart in yours

I place my life in yours Lord.
I place my life in yours.

Cloaks and Branches

Then they brought the colt to Jesus and threw their garments over it, and he sat on it. Many in the crowd spread their garments on the road ahead of him, and others spread leafy branches they had cut in the fields. Jesus was in the centre of the procession, and the people all around him were shouting, "Praise God! Blessings on the one who comes in the name of the Lord! Blessings on the coming Kingdom of our ancestor David! Praise God in highest heaven!" So, Jesus came to Jerusalem and went into the Temple. After looking around carefully at everything, he left because it was late in the afternoon. Then he returned to Bethany with the twelve disciples. Mark 11 v 7-11

I love the extravagance of the praise, honour, and acknowledgement that the disciples and the crowds gave to Jesus as He entered Jerusalem. Clothing and cloaks were thrown on to the colt to make a saddle for the coming king and then branches, leaves and clothes were thrown down on to the floor in front of the colt as a wonderful red carpet for Jesus and the colt to walk on as He made His triumphal entrance into the city. There was noise, shouts, singing and cries of 'hosanna'. The noisy procession was exuberant, loud, colourful, exciting, noisy, liberating, and joyful. There was no self-consciousness or inhibition. Bystanders joined in with the noise and the celebration.

I wonder how I would have reacted had I been at the scene on this occasion. I believe that I am probably known as a person of quiet restraint and self-control, of calmness and of considered action and purpose, a person of few words but of quiet intent and timely conversation. Would I have taken off my outer clothes in extravagant worship and thrown them to the floor and cut branches from the local trees and bushes to wave with happy abandon, and raised my voice in praise and adoration at the coming of the king? Would I have thrown caution to the wind, thrown off my inhibitions and self-consciousness, with no regard for the comments of others around me and simply joined in this cacophony of praise and worship? Or would I have been the quiet bystander, embarrassed and uncertain as to whether to join in with the crowd?

Praise in worship is a strange thing. Sometimes the large worshipping gathering makes it easier to praise, to raise the hands, to move and to sing the fast-paced worship songs. Sometimes I need to be in the large crowd- and the larger the better sometimes. I can be anonymous, concealed and feel safe in the crowd with a palm branch in my hands.

The real test of worship would follow shortly after this day's event as the crowd gathered and clamoured for the death of Jesus. There would be those people in the crowd that day who would be shouting for Barabbas and for Jesus to be crucified. They would forget their cries of Hosanna and would instead shout 'crucify'. Would I have stood my ground and shouted for the Saviour King when those around me were all clamouring for His death? Would my voice then have been the loudest? Jesus, my Jesus! That would be praise and worship indeed.

Sometimes they strew His way,
And His sweet praises sing;
Resounding all the day
Hosannas to their King

Then "Crucify!"
Is all their breath,
And for His death
They thirst and cry.

My song is love unknown, Samuel Crossman, written in 1664

Pray

May my life during the week match my worship words on Sunday. Help me in my heart to realize that what I do each day is an integral part of my worship. I want to honour you with my heart, soul, mind, and strength every day of my life.

Easter Reflection- the right people, the right places, the right timing and the right opportunity

Christ is risen. He is risen indeed. On this first week after Easter Sunday, perhaps we should remind ourselves each new day- I am loved, I am forgiven, I am redeemed, I am chosen, I am a child of God, and I am special. Let this be our anthem each day. As I have been reading through the accounts at the end of the Gospels, I have thought about some of the famous and not so familiar characters and the roles that they had to play in those last significant days.

There are times in life when things seem to come together perfectly- even if not easily. You are in the right position, in the right place, at the right time and with the right opportunity for something of significance to happen. I love the words that were spoken to Esther when she was given the royal position in the King's household- a position that would lead to the saving of her people. *"And who knoweth whether thou art come to the kingdom for such a time as this?" Esther 4 v 14 KJV*

In the Easter accounts there are people in the right place, at the right time, with the right facilities or wealth or opportunity, who take significant steps in Jesus's journey to the cross and after His death. There was the man who made available his guest room for the final Passover meal. Simon of Cyrene, of North Africa, a strong man, coming home from work, was available to take over the cross bearing for Jesus. A Roman Captain, at the foot of the cross and standing guard over the proceedings, made his first faith declaration, "This has to be the Son of God!" Joseph of Arimathea, a high-ranking Jewish official, and a member of the Sanhedrin, risked his position and reputation to publicly identify with a criminal and to request of the Roman Governor, Pilate, that he should be allowed to take the body of Jesus from the cross and place it for burial in his wealthy tomb. The burial shroud had already been purchased. This was his significant moment in time. Nicodemus, another wealthy, influential Jew, brought expensive burial spices with which he could anoint and bury the body of Jesus. Working together, Joseph and Nicodemus, risking much, placed the body of Jesus in the cave tomb, not knowing that this was not the end of the Jesus story. The lives of each of these men would never be the same again. Key people at key moments in time, for such a time as this.

Jesus directed two of his disciples, "Go into the city. A man carrying a water jug will meet you. Follow him. Ask the owner of whichever house he enters, 'The Teacher wants to know, where is my guest room where I can eat the Passover meal with my disciples?' He will show you a spacious second-story room, swept and ready. Prepare for us there." The disciples left, came to the city, found everything just as he had told them, and prepared the Passover meal. Mark 14 v 12-16

There was a man walking by, coming from work, Simon from Cyrene, the father of Alexander and Rufus. They made him carry Jesus' cross. Mark 15 v 21

But Jesus, with a loud cry, gave his last breath. At that moment the Temple curtain ripped right down the middle. When the Roman captain standing guard in front of him saw that he had quit breathing, he said, "This has to be the Son of God!" Mark 15 v 37-39

Joseph of Arimathea, a highly respected member of the Jewish Council, came. He was one who lived expectantly, on the lookout for the kingdom of God. Working up his courage, he went to Pilate and asked for Jesus' body. Pilate questioned whether he could be dead that soon and called for the captain to verify that he was really dead. Assured by the captain, he gave Joseph the corpse. Having already purchased a linen shroud, Joseph took him down, wrapped him in the shroud, placed him in a tomb that had been cut into the rock, and rolled a large stone across the opening. Luke 23 v 50-53

Nicodemus, the man who had come to Jesus at night, came too, bringing a hundred pounds of embalming ointment made from myrrh and aloes. Together they wrapped Jesus' body in a long linen cloth saturated with the spices, as is the Jewish custom of burial. John 19 v 39-40

Pray

Jesus, my life is in your hands. My time is in your hands.

May I be in the right place, at the right time so that I may serve.

Help me to be sensitive to your Spirit so that I know when to act, when to be still, when to speak, when to be silent, and always to willingly follow you.

We are family. Christ is Risen

Jesus said to her, "Mary!" At this she turned right round and said to him, in Hebrew, "Master!" "No!" said Jesus, "do not hold me now. I have not yet gone up to the Father. Go and tell my brothers that I am going up to my Father and your Father, to my God and your God." John 20 v 16-17

After Jesus's resurrection and this first meeting with Mary, Mary is commissioned to go to the disciples, to give them the news that Jesus is alive, but not yet ascended to His Father. Mary, the first witness to the resurrection, becomes the first one to testify to the resurrection, and was invited to do something very specific, and to go with a clear, specific message.

But Jesus did not ask her to go to His disciples. Jesus asked her to go to His brothers with the message that He is going 'to my Father and your Father, to my God and your God.' The disciples, the followers, the friends, the men and women who have travelled with Jesus for the past three years, are now called His family- they are his brothers and sisters and God, His Father is also now their Father. They are family.

Mary did as Jesus asked and went with the message," He is risen." But sadly, the gathered disciples did not believe her at this point. That, however, would soon change when Jesus Himself would come to them with His message of peace. They thought that Mary's account was an 'idle tale' and something perhaps that she had imagined in her distress. Jesus Himself later appears to his friends, His brothers, who were meeting together in fear and trepidation in a locked and secure room.

As followers of Jesus, we are His family too. Jesus has invited us into His family. He speaks to us personally as He did to Mary, calling us by name. She could not mistake His voice as His call was personal, loving, and gentle. Jesus tells her who she is -she is Mary.

May we have that sense of belonging to His family and sharing life with our brothers and sisters in the faith. We are in this together.

While he was still talking to the crowds, his mother and his brothers happened to be standing outside wanting to speak to him. Somebody said to him, "Look, your mother and your brothers are outside wanting to speak to you." But Jesus replied to the one who told him, "Who is my mother, and who are my brothers?"; then with a gesture of his hand towards his disciples he went on, "There are my mother and brothers! For whoever does the will of my Heavenly Father is brother and sister and mother to me." Matthew 12 v 46-50

All honour to God, the God and Father of our Lord Jesus Christ; for it is his boundless mercy that has given us the privilege of being born again so that we are now members of God's own family. Now we live in the hope of eternal life because Christ rose again from the dead. 1 Peter 1 v 3

We are family. In a church family we have brothers, sisters, mothers, fathers, aunties, uncles, nephews, nieces, cousins, grandparents-all related together because Jesus has chosen us to be in His family. Let us connect, contribute, communicate well and care for one another.

Jesus, you have called us by name, and you want us to be connected as family. Being in a family is sometimes tough. There are tensions, challenges, disappointments but also joys and celebrations. As you gave your peace on that resurrection day may we know your peace. As you breathed your Holy Spirit on that first day may we know the love and power of your Holy Spirit in our lives and in our church.

Remembering-Just as He told you

If you are a little like me, you may sometimes half listen to what someone is saying or perhaps misinterpret or misread a significant message. This is not a good thing to do and is certainly not 'active listening'. It is easy to 'fit' a message into what we think it should be based on experience or logic. In the days leading up to His death, Jesus had explained to His disciples and followers that He would be betrayed, killed but would rise again from death. On Easter Sunday, it was Mary and the women at the tomb who were the first to 'remember' what Jesus had told them about resurrection, and for this to truly impact their lives.

The men said to them, 'Why do you look for the living among the dead? He is not here; he has risen! Remember how he told you, while he was still with you in Galilee: "The Son of Man must be delivered over to the hands of sinners, be crucified and on the third day be raised again." 'Then they remembered his words. Luke 24 v 2-8

Then Jesus appeared to the gathered disciples in Jerusalem and said to them, 'This is what I told you while I was still with you: everything must be fulfilled that is written about me in the Law of Moses, the Prophets and the Psalms.' Then he opened their minds so they could understand the Scriptures. Luke 24 v 44-45

Jesus had tried to prepare them for this very moment and now, the truth, the reality and the impact of His resurrection was dawning on the disciples and followers. They were remembering and their minds would begin to be opened to understand the scriptures. They were at the beginning of a journey of remembering and discovery, mulling over all that they had heard, weighing everything up and absorbing what they had seen, heard, and received, with the help of His Holy Spirit. Their memories and accounts would be carefully compiled and written down for the benefit of others and eventually for us. The purpose of their Gospel accounts was that others might hear, understand, and have life in His name.

But these are written that you may believe that Jesus is the Messiah, the Son of God, and that by believing you may have life in his name. John 20 v 31

We have a wonderful gift in our hands- the Bible. Even with poor memories, we can be continually reminded of God's words and meet with the living Jesus. The Holy Spirit is there to help us to understand and to remember. The young Timothy was advised to keep on searching the scriptures.

You must go on steadily in all those things that you have learned and which you know are true. Remember from what sort of people your knowledge has come, and how from early childhood your mind has been familiar with the holy scriptures, which can open the mind to the salvation which comes through believing in Christ Jesus. All scripture is inspired by God and is useful for teaching the faith and correcting error, for re-setting the direction of a man's life and training him in good living. The scriptures are the comprehensive equipment of the man of God and fit him fully for all branches of his work. 2 Timothy 3 v 14-17

PRAY

Jesus, I want to be still and listen for Your still, small voice.

Please speak to me through your word, the Bible.

As You speak to me, please show me want you want me to be and to do.

So often I come to you with lists and demands.
Like a tornado I spew them out as commands.
To the next task, I move on with my day
Completely missing what you might have to say.
The noise of the world clogs my ears
And clouds my mind with fog and fears.
I need you to clear my senses, O Lord!
Give me a heart in tune with your Word.
May I be ever eager to hear your voice;
May listening continually be my choice.

A Prayer of willingness to Listen by Rachel Mojo.

A Breakfast Barbecue on the Beach

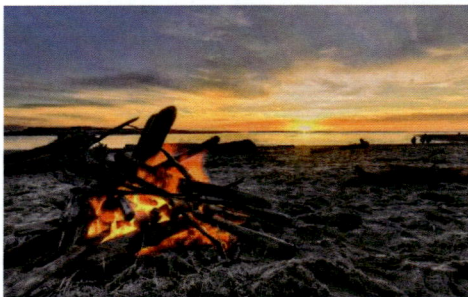

When they landed, they saw a fire of burning coals there with fish on it, and some bread. Jesus said to them, 'Bring some of the fish you have just caught. 'So, Simon Peter climbed back into the boat and dragged the net ashore. It was full of large fish, 153, but even with so many the net was not torn. Jesus said to them, 'Come and have breakfast.' None of the disciples dared ask him, 'Who are you?' They knew it was the Lord. Jesus came, took the bread, and gave it to them, and did the same with the fish. John 21

After the crucifixion of their Jesus, the disciples were perhaps feeling confused, disillusioned, defeated, empty and so had gone back to the boats and their fishing nets in one of their known fishing locations. They had returned to the familiar, the safe, to where they felt confident- and yet their nets were empty. They had been on the open water all night but had caught nothing. As morning light was breaking, a figure on the shoreline called out to them.

We are now back at the beginning- to where Jesus first called them, with their fishing boat on the shoreline. They were invited to let down their nets on the other side of the boat. What madness is this? They are experienced fishermen. Yet these experienced sailors and fishermen obeyed and hauled in a huge catch of fish. Then Jesus invites them to" come and have breakfast". At this point, the penny has dropped! They know that this is the risen Jesus. There is no mistake. His barbecue was ready, the fish were cooked and there was fresh bread to share. Jesus was ready to serve this simple meal to His disciples. "Jesus took the bread and gave it to them and so also with the fish". (This action is so very reminiscent of His serving them bread at the last supper and of the feeding of the 5,000 with the bread and fish). So, the disciples and Jesus settled down to a hearty and welcoming breakfast, sharing time together and enjoying being in one another's presence. This was a simple meal with friends- His disciples.

What a wonderful image this portrays. Jesus is saying 'Come and be with me.' He had made provision for them, but Jesus also asked them to bring some of the fish that they had just caught with His help. He wanted them to contribute to the meal.

Jesus then called Peter to one side. There was no reprimand or judgement. But there was restoration, commissioning, and a new hope. I love the charcoal fire image. Peter had denied Jesus three times over a charcoal fire but here Peter was given the opportunity to declare three times his love for Jesus again, next to a charcoal fire.

Jesus invites us to come, rest, eat, be with Him. He has what we need and can sustain us. He has prepared things for us and for us to do. We can enjoy His presence. We cannot do this on our own.

But Jesus also asks us to bring what we have. Bring that to the meal as well. Add it to the feast that He has prepared. May we bring whatever we have.

Pray

Jesus- you are the Risen Lord and Saviour. You invite us to come to you. We come with our worries, our troubles, our mess, our mistakes, our regrets, and our failures. You can provide for us, but you also invite us to bring to you what we have. May we enjoy your presence and be able to declare our love for you.

Gracious and holy Father, give us wisdom to perceive you,

Diligence to seek you, patience to wait for you,

eyes to behold you, a heart to meditate on you,

and a life to proclaim you,

through the power of the Spirit of Jesus Christ our Lord.

A Prayer of St Benedict

Feed my sheep. Feed my lambs

When they had finished breakfast, Jesus said to Simon Peter, "Simon son of John, do you love me more than these?" He said to him, "Yes, Lord; you know that I love you." Jesus said to him, "Feed my lambs."A second time he said to him, "Simon son of John, do you love me?" He said to him, "Yes, Lord; you know that I love you." Jesus said to him, "Tend my sheep." He said to him the third time, "Simon son of John, do you love me?" Peter felt hurt because he said to him the third time, "Do you love me?" And he said to him, "Lord, you know everything; you know that I love you." Jesus said to him, "Feed my sheep." John 21 v 15-17

The television listings recently have been full of programmes such as 'Spring-time on the farm,' 'Our Yorkshire Farm, 'The Yorkshire Vet'' and Kate Humbles, 'Escape to the Farm' when we have been delighted by the sight of the birth of new lambs, calves and goats coming into the world and witnessing the care and commitment of the farmers during their busy and often challenging lambing season. We have had a wonderful insight into the life of the farmer.

We have just enjoyed a break away in North Yorkshire and had the pleasure of crossing the North Yorks Moors and visiting resorts such as Staithes and Whitby on the East coast. Along the way we have seen farms, fields, and moors, full of new lambs and sheep. On one quiet road across the moor, the car was brought to a sudden stop, by a sheep and her lamb in the middle of the road with the small lamb choosing to suckle from its mother. We waited patiently until the lamb was fully satisfied and the car was able to continue with its journey. Fortunately, the road was not too busy, and our car and a second car were content to wait for the feeding session to finish, when the sheep and her lamb were ready to move on. So, I have been reminded of this significant moment in Peter's life when the fisherman became a shepherd to care for and nurture the lambs and sheep of Jesus, the Chief Shepherd.

When the Risen Jesus invited His disciples to share His breakfast on the beach, Jesus called Peter to one side, and in a moving conversation, gave space for Peter to make his three-fold confession of love for Him. Jesus then gave Peter his three-fold commission to ministry. Peter's failures, short comings, defeat, denial, his assessments of himself in comparison with other disciples, were now to be put in the context only of his love for Jesus, inadequate as it was, and Jesus's complete knowledge of Peter's heart. Peter was forgiven, loved, restored, re-engaged and now newly commissioned. Peter was to care for those followers, present and future, who needed care, nourishment, protection, comfort, and strength, and he was to give them his concern and love- as a shepherd cares for the sheep.

God has given each of us a commission - to care, to nurture and to love. It is a huge and a costly task.

And so I am giving a new commandment to you now—love each other just as much as I love you. Your strong love for each other will prove to the world that you are my disciples." John 13 v 13-14

"I am the Good Shepherd and know my own sheep, and they know me, just as my Father knows me and I know the Father; and I lay down my life for the sheep. I have other sheep, too, in another fold. I must bring them also, and they will heed my voice; and there will be one flock with one Shepherd".

My sheep recognize my voice, and I know them, and they follow me. I give them eternal life and they shall never perish. No one shall snatch them away from me, for my Father has given them to me, and he is more powerful than anyone else, so no one can kidnap them from me. I and the Father are one." John 10

Pray

You know our hearts. You know our motives, thoughts, struggles, inadequacies, defeats -like Peter- and yet you love us with a love that we cannot fully comprehend. You have called us by your grace. You have called us to be family and to join in your work. May we find the purpose for which you designed us. May we listen for your shepherd's voice and follow.

The Transformation of Peter

When the Council saw the boldness of Peter and John and could see that they were obviously uneducated non-professionals, they were amazed and realized what being with Jesus had done for them! And the Council could hardly discredit the healing when the man they had healed was standing right there beside them! Acts 4 v 13-14 TLB

They couldn't take their eyes off them—Peter and John standing there so confident, so sure of themselves! Their fascination deepened when they realized these two were laymen with no training in Scripture or formal education. Acts 4 v 13-14 MSG

I am sure that like me, you will have had times when you felt that you were not qualified to undertake a task or role, that you did not have the right credentials, experience or character traits required, and that quite frankly, you were out of your depth. So, I have been continuing to think about Simon Peter and how he was changed from fisherman, sailor, to disciple to defeated failure and betrayer, to shepherd of the early church, and then on to being the gifted teacher of the scriptures, evangelist, preacher, and apostle that we see in the book of Acts. This is some transformation.

At the Feast of Pentecost, seven weeks after the death of Jesus, Peter stepped forward to preach to a gathered crowd, after the coming of the Holy Spirit, and on this single occasion, 3,000 people committed their lives to Christ. This first amazing sermon by Peter must have been inspirational and was certainly gifted with references to other scriptures from the Prophet Joel, Psalm 16, Psalm 110 and with other references to Old Testament teachings. This was Peter the fisherman and not Peter the trained, educated Jewish scholar.

Then Peter preached a long sermon, telling about Jesus and strongly urging all his listeners to save themselves from the evils of their nation. And those who believed Peter were baptized—about three thousand in all! They joined with the other believers in regular attendance at the apostles' teaching sessions and at the Communion services and prayer meetings. Acts 2 v 40-42

At the Beautiful Gate of the Temple, Jerusalem, Peter was instrumental in the healing of a man lame from birth and who would have been familiar to all those who had attended Temple worship over many years. Peter, who at one time may have been over-confident, proud, and independent, now reflects all of the glory and credit for the man's instantaneous healing, back to His Lord, refusing to take any credit to himself, claiming only the faith that had been given to him by God Himself.

"Jesus' name has healed this man—and you know how lame he was before. Faith in Jesus' name—faith given us from God—has caused this perfect healing. Acts 4 v 10

Jesus saw something in Peter. He saw the potential of this man, despite any flaws in his character. Jesus saw what Peter could become. Jesus would later call Peter 'the rock' on which He would build His church. Peter went on to teach and build up the church, especially in Jerusalem among Jewish Christians.

The message perhaps for the Christian is to never feel inadequate, useless, untrained, lacking formal education and academic qualifications. If God has a purpose for you and you only, and called you to a task, then He will equip and provide for that task. Our God sees the potential that you have, to become what He would love you to be, and to do the things that He has for you to do. We are all unfinished works. We are not there yet. There is stuff that He will need to deal with.

Pray

You see into the centre of our being. You see our potential. You have graced us with different skills and talents. Using our gifts, may we work together each in our own special way valuing everyone's contribution. May we be grounded in faith, hope and love.

The Fisherman's Ring worn by the Pope

The Fisherman's Ring, the Pope's ring, which has the image of Peter fishing from his boat, was used to seal official documents signed by the Pope. Since at least the Middle Ages it has been a tradition for Catholics meeting the Pope to show their devotion by kissing the ring.

Now I get it! They're speaking my language!

"They're speaking our languages, describing God's mighty works!" Acts 2 v 11 MSG

"We are from these different countries, but we can hear these men in our own languages! We can all understand the great things they are saying about God."

The Feast of Pentecost was perhaps the best attended Jewish festival in Jerusalem with Jews and visitors from all corners of the world, sharing many languages, gathering for the Feast. The disciples and followers of Jesus had also gathered, possibly in the Temple Courts area for the festival, as they waited for the promised Holy Spirit. When the Holy Spirit came, the disciples and followers were first aware of the sound- a loud, audible sound like a powerful, gale force wind filling the whole building. This was followed by flames of fire settling upon the head of each one present. As the Holy Spirit moved among them, disciples and followers began to speak out their praises and worship to God in spoken languages that they had never learned, as the Spirit came them power. The crowds, attracted first by the sound of the strange wind, began to gather round, then hearing words of praise and thanksgiving in their own native tongues and languages, from the mouths of a motley collection of uneducated Galileans.

The disciples were speaking out to all within earshot, the wonderful works of God. They were praising their God, proclaiming His goodness, communicating, and delivering their praise in such a dramatic way, that their hearers were astounded at what they were hearing- because they were now tuned in and hearing this, each one in their own native language.

The lovely phrase 'now you're speaking my language' means 'now I see what you're getting at' now I can understand what you're saying' and even' I think that we are on the same page!' Now I can see it!

So often when we are talking about Jesus and our Christian faith, we are not talking the same language as our listeners. We are not on the same page, and so it is not surprising that 'they don't get it!' Some years ago, a book called *The Five Love Languages. How to express Heartfelt Commitment to your Mate* by Gary Chapman, became an instant best seller. The book outlines five different ways (words of affirmation, quality time, receiving gifts, acts of service and physical touch) that we can express, receive, and experience love. The author believed that it was important to know your 'love language and that of your partner to make sure that you were communicating in the way that you can receive the message. He also believed that love could get' lost in translation' when couples speak different love languages.

The crowd in Jerusalem got the message very clearly. The worship and praise were in their 'first' language, their 'heart' language, their 'love' language.

"There are Parthians, Medes, and Elamites; there are men whose homes are in Mesopotamia, in Judea and Cappadocia, Pontus, Asia, Phrygia, Pamphylia, Egypt, and the parts of Africa near Cyrene, as well as visitors from Rome! There are Jews and proselytes, men from Crete and men from Arabia, yet we can all hear these men speaking of the magnificence of God in our native language."

After Peter's clear presentation of the gospel message of salvation, to the crowd, three thousand individuals that day were added to their group. They had heard, 'got it' and responded in faith.

Pray

Forgive me when my words of praise and thanks are feeble or non-existent.

Help me so that my words and my life may speak of you in ways that can be understood.

Give me the words to say so that they are clear, simple and do not confuse. Help me to tune into the way that others are thinking, feeling and speaking so that I can bring your grace and love.

The Emmaus Road

Jesus was present and quietly available. It was a safe encounter. He gently questioned. "What are you so concerned about?" "What things?" He listened and gave space for more to be shared – for their story to be told.

As our daughter Charlotte was making her final journey, we had the privilege of being supported during those few hours, by a wonderful nurse in the ICU. She was quietly strong and gently efficient as she moved around the bedside attending to the needs of her patient and to our own. She came close and spoke when needed and graciously moved away giving space but a quiet confident presence. With one of her final questions "What do you want us to do?", she gave us the space and control to make decisions. She was unhurried and walked alongside us on that difficult road that we had to share with Sam, our very small grandson, barely 6 years old. What he would remember of this time would be so crucial and significant. When the time was right for Sam to see his mummy for the last time, before she passed on, the nurse had beautifully combed and styled Charlotte's hair, washed and folded her hands to enclose a bible text that we had had quickly scribed on a small piece of paper, and removed every sign and object of the instruments and tubes that had been there to help to support life. The time was precious even though the pain and grief were real.

There are so many gifted, experienced, and skilled Nurses, Doctors and Care Workers who are supporting and being family to those who are on their final journey in this life, in the Care Home and the wards in Hospital and Hospice. There are so many family members who are not able to be with their loved one at this end point and whose grief and pain is heightened because of it.

As counsellors, friends, colleagues, and neighbours, may we walk gently alongside the other. May we be quietly available, giving space for their story to be told and offering the gift of listening. May we offer that safe space, coming near when needed but then silently and intuitively stepping back into the background. The needs of the 'other' overwhelm our own needs for a short time but may we have the gift of listening beyond the spoken words and the quiet presence that will bring the presence of Jesus to the conversation.

Where do you pitch your tent?

I have lost count of how many Scouts camping trips our grandson has completed. As he is becoming more experienced with pitching his tent, he is discovering that there are key factors that need to be considered. The most crucial of these is the location- location, location, location. He is learning that he needs to pitch the tent on level, dry, solid ground away from the prevailing wind, but where there is a natural windbreak, perhaps from the trees, and away from any hazards. Pitching the tent on a hillside is to be avoided, and it is an advantage to choose a place where there are local amenities and resources nearby. But perhaps the most important thing is that the tent is secured. However, the tent is only a temporary dwelling, and our grandson is always very keen to get back home to his more permanent structure.

In Peter's sermon in Acts 2 v 26-28 MSG we read,

I saw God before me for all time.
Nothing can shake me; he's right by my side.
I'm glad from the inside out, ecstatic;
I've pitched my tent in the land of hope.
This comes from Peter's Pentecost sermon to the crowds, and he uses David's prophetic words in Psalms, which refer to Jesus. As I read Peter's sermon, the phrase that leapt out to me was the one referring to Jesus, by David, that 'He had pitched his tent toward hope'. Jesus knew that death was not the end for Him and that He was heading to the land of hope. I too want to pitch my tent toward hope. There is a future home waiting for me. When Phil and I were married, many, many years ago now, I remember the Minister at the wedding ceremony advising us to choose carefully when we were pitching our tent! He was referring to our home, our friends, our support network, and our church. We were to pitch our tent wisely.

Paul, who was a tent maker and knew all about tents, knew that his life here was only temporary and that there was a permanent home prepared for him and for all who believed. Our permanent home, our inheritance was guaranteed, and that guarantee is the Holy Spirit living within us. We are 'in Christ' and have the promised Holy Spirit as the guarantee of all that Jesus has secured for us. As it is an inheritance, we do not have to work for this. It is something that is given and cannot be earned.

And because of what Christ did, all you others too, who heard the Good News about how to be saved, and trusted Christ, were marked as belonging to Christ by the Holy Spirit, who long ago had been promised to all of us Christians. His presence within us is God's guarantee that he really will give us all that he promised; and the Spirit's seal upon us means that God has already purchased us and that he guarantees to bring us to himself. This is just one more reason for us to praise our glorious God. Ephesians 1 v 13-14

As believers 'in Christ' we are sealed by the Holy Spirit. We have God's seal upon our lives and His seal is the guarantee of purchase- our purchase. It is a guarantee, a first instalment, His promise to come for us, a small taste of our inheritance, and a mark of hope. It demonstrates that our home here is only temporary- we are camping under canvas until we are ready for our permanent dwelling place. But I don't often live as if my life here is temporary. It is easy to accumulate and to fill the tent with 'stuff'. Do you remember the old Jim Reeves song?

This world is not my home
I'm just a-passing through
My treasures are laid up
Somewhere beyond the blue.
The angels beckon me
From heaven's open door
And I can't feel at home
In this world anymore.
James Travis 'Jim' Reeves (Aug 20,1923-July 31 1964)

So, let us keep pitching our tent towards hope just as Jesus did. We have a wonderful inheritance that He has secured for us and in the meantime, Jesus wants us to have an abundant life that is full of joy. May we be happy campers.

Essential equipment: The Holy Spirit

You're the witnesses. What comes next is very important: I am sending what my Father promised to you, so stay here in the city until he arrives, until you're equipped with power from on high. Luke 24

Our grandson is a senior Scout and has been on many camps and expeditions over the years with both Cubs and Scout groups. One key element of the preparation for any of these events is the extensive equipment and kit list that he is provided with. He has done expeditions, walks and camps on many occasions now, so he knows the value of carefully checking and ticking off the items on the lists as he adds them to the rucksack. He recently completed a two-day expedition, setting off with the 65-litre rucksack which carried everything- sleeping bag, map, orientation gear, radio, food, spare clothes, that he would require for two days away from home, come storm. rain, or shine. In July he will attend a seven-day camp in the Lake District and will be provided with an even more extensive kit, food, and clothing list, so that he is prepared for whatever he and the scout group may experience. (A brief aside from the adult here. On the very short weekend camps we have learned to skip the soap, wash bag and towel. They are never used anyway! A toothbrush is the only essential hygiene kit.)

Jesus, after His resurrection, had spent time with His disciples and followers over a period of forty days. He had appeared to them at different times, had eaten with them and had continued to talk with them about the kingdom. This was a time of 'unquestionable demonstrations' of His presence and 'infallible proofs' given to them by their Saviour. While He had spent time with them in Jerusalem, the disciples had been given a clear command not to leave the city. They were to wait. This would be a scary thing for the disciples. Jerusalem was now a place of danger and betrayal for them and for any who had been seen with Jesus. They were hiding in small rooms, behind locked doors and keeping a very low profile. The High priests and the religious leaders had engineered a plan, a cover up, involving a bribe of a significant amount of money to the guards, who had witnessed both angel and empty tomb stone.

Meanwhile, the guards had scattered, but a few of them went into the city and told the high priests everything that had happened. They called a meeting of the religious leaders and came up with a plan: They took a large sum of money and gave it to the soldiers, bribing them to say, "His disciples came in the night and stole the body while we were sleeping." They assured them, "If the governor hears about your sleeping on duty, we will make sure you don't get blamed." The soldiers took the bribe and did as they were told. That story, cooked up in the Jewish High Council, is still going around. Matthew 28 v 11-15 MSG

So, the disciples had to wait. They were to wait for what had been promised. They were to wait until they were empowered, equipped and ready for action. They were to wait for the Holy Spirit. They were to wait until they were "clothed (fully equipped) with power from on high." Acts 1 v 4-5

Jesus would not send them out into a hostile city unless and until He had properly equipped them for everything that they would need and that they would experience.

Perhaps they grew impatient while they waited. For how long would they need to wait? What and who were they waiting for? Jesus referred to the Holy Spirit, as 'He' and 'Him' and so would they know Him instantly? So many questions must have flooded their minds. But they waited. Their work, their mission could not begin until they were equipped.

Pray

Thank you that I am clothed with your salvation.

Thank you that you provide everything that I need to trust in you and to follow.

Thank you that you prepare the way ahead for me.

Forgive me when I rush on without map or compass.

Help me to trust you more.

Fill me with your Holy Spirit, so that I am ready for anything that you purpose for me.

Amen

Spirit of the Living God,
Fall afresh on me.
Spirit of the Living God,
Fall afresh on me.
Melt me, mould me,
Fill me, use Me,
Spirit of the Living God,
Fall afresh on me.
Daniel Iverson (1926)

Breathe on me, breath of God:
fill me with life anew,
that I may love as you have loved
and do as you would do.

Breathe on me, breath of God,
until my heart is pure,
until my will is one with yours
to do and to endure.

Breathe on me, breath of God;
fulfil my heart's desire,
until this earthly part of me
glows with your heavenly fire.

Breathe on me, breath of God;
so shall I never die,
but live with you the perfect life
of your eternity.
Edwin Hatch (1835 - 1889)

Life among the Believers Acts 2

The believers continued to devote themselves to what the apostles were teaching, to fellowship, to the breaking of bread, and to times of prayer. United in purpose, they went to the Temple every day, ate at each other's homes, and shared their food with glad and humble hearts. They were praising God and enjoying the good will of all the people. Every day the Lord was adding to their number those who were being saved.

In Acts chapter 2 we read about the phenomenal growth of the early church. They did not have a building to meet in! But what they did have was connection, attachment, contact, inter dependence, affiliation, regular communication, and hospitality. They built relationships around meeting in the temple court area and their homes, sharing food and prayer. They developed relationships, vital links, and bonds that others saw and wanted to connect in with.

If you listen to most testimonies of how people come to faith there is almost always a connection with a person- a friend or group of friends, who were thought of as different, attractive, had something special, cared for others and showed an inexplicable love.

Today there are lots of opportunities and ways of sharing and connecting so that we can support each other and reach out to other people. There are many new ways to connect, in home groups, hospitality in gardens and homes, in sharing food and meals, picnics in the park, café style church, warm spaces, letters and phone calls of support.

Connection, Communication and Contact are so important.

PRAYERS

A Circle Prayer for the new year

He surrounds me with loving-kindness and tender mercies. Psalm 103

Circle us, Lord with your presence.

Father, you surround us with your loving-kindness and tender mercies.

We can never leave your presence. If we go up to heaven you are there. If we go to the farthest ocean, you are there. You are always there.

Circle us, Lord with your grace and forgiveness.

Forgive us all that is past- for harsh words, for unkind thoughts, for past mistakes and wrong decisions. For hurts, losses, and griefs that we have known in the past year. Forgive us.

Circle us, Lord. Circle our families and friends with your presence and your peace.

Be with those who have lost loved ones.

Be with those who are fearful and anxious.

Bring strength to those with health concerns.

Bring hope to those who are frustrated or in despair.

Bring comfort to those living alone.

Circle us, Lord. Circle us with your guidance and grace.

Be with our families, those that we care about and those that we are responsible for.

Be in the workplace and the home.

Protect us in the decisions that we face.

Where there is change and uncertainty may we be strong.

Safeguard our homes and our relationships.

When things are tough and the way is unclear, then be our guide.

Circle us, Lord. Circle us with your wisdom and protection.

For countries where there is fighting and civil war that has caused the displacement of people.

We do not know what to do and the news is disturbing. We pray for those in a position to make changes. Guide them well.

Circle us, Lord. Circle our church and each person with the joy of your Salvation

Keep our eyes fixed on Jesus.

Help us to be sharers of your good news.

Circle us, Lord. Circle us with your blessing as we enter this new year.

Show us those people who need our help and your Gospel.

May we point others to the love, peace, hope and joy that can be found in you.

The supremacy of the Son of God

Sometimes I need to be reminded of who Jesus really is and lift my eyes up to Him.

The Son is the image of the invisible God, the firstborn over all creation. For in him all things were created: things in heaven and on earth, visible and invisible, whether thrones or powers or rulers or authorities; all things have been created through him and for him. He is before all things, and in him all things hold together. And he is the head of the body, the church; he is the beginning and the firstborn from among the dead, so that in everything he might have the supremacy. For God was pleased to have all his fullness dwell in him, and through him to reconcile to himself all things, whether things on earth or things in heaven, by making peace through his blood, shed on the cross. Colossians 1 v 15-20

Jesus you are Creator

You created all things- the beauty of the heavens and the natural world. When you saw the wonders of your creation, and all that you had made, you declared that it was very good. Your creation declares your glory.

We are in awe of the sights, sounds and wonders of this world.

Colossians says that "Jesus, The Son, is the image of the invisible God, the firstborn over all creation. For in him all things were created: things in heaven and on earth, visible and invisible, whether thrones or powers or rulers or authorities; all things have been created through him and for him.

Jesus you were there at the beginning. We give thanks and praise for your creation. You are with us now.

Jesus Christ the same yesterday and today and for ever.

Jesus, you are Lord overall

We confess that we have not cared for your world, and we are sad. We have squandered resources and there is inequality. We are witnesses to disasters, poverty, hunger, drought, flood, climate change and more.

We are selfish, and self-sufficient. Show us that we are part of your whole. Show us our need to be family, to be community, and to be together.

God who is one, make us one with you, one with your creation and one with each other.

Show us what it means to act justly, to love mercy and to walk humbly with our God.

Jesus Christ the same yesterday and today and for ever.

Jesus you are the lord of compassion

As you looked out over the city of Jerusalem, you longed to gather your children together, as a hen gathers her chicks under her wings. You saw people as sheep without a shepherd.

As you look out over our world today, your heart is torn for the suffering and torment that you see there.

Yet in the horror, war and displacement, we see humanity, compassion and generosity.

We pray for your people there and ask that they may know that they are not alone. We pray for safety, security, rest, and hope for your people. We pray for those who are mourning. We pray for those displaced and for the agencies bringing relief, safe exit to new countries and new homes.

Jesus Christ the same yesterday and today and for ever.

Jesus you are the head of your body the church

You call us to work together. We are your disciples. May we worship you, share your life and reflect your love. You are the God of connection and community. Help us to let go of 'me and mine' and build a community of 'us and ours.' Help us to love our neighbours – our neighbours in foreign places and our neighbours here. May we grow in compassion and use whatever gift we have in the service of others.

Jesus Christ the same yesterday and today and for ever.

Jesus, you have called us to be in this place.

As we serve and reach out to others in our small corner may we reflect your love.

We pray for new opportunities. We pray for the new Mums and Toddler Group. We pray for a clear vision in all these ventures.

Jesus Christ the same yesterday and today and for ever.

Jesus, you call us to follow you. We commit ourselves again to follow. Thank you that you accept us as we are and that you are changing us into your image, your likeness. Forgive us when we mess up. Show us what we need to lay down and what we need to pick up. Help us to see the opportunities to share your love and your peace, whether small or large. Help us to see your footsteps and to follow.

Jesus Christ the same yesterday and today and for ever.

The Lord's Prayer

Our Father, who art in heaven, hallowed be thy name;

Father God, help us to see and worship you for who you are. Take your rightful place in our hearts and lives. We thank you that you are our Father and that we are your children because of Jesus- your son, the one with whom you are well pleased. We are your children too because of what Jesus has done for us. We are family and heirs with Christ. We thank you that we belong to a family of Christians around the world, belonging together in Jesus. You are the father of us all and we are all your children.

thy kingdom come; thy will be done; on earth as it is in heaven.

We thank you that you are a God of compassion, justice, and mercy. There are wrongs and evils in our world that must break your heart and so we pray for Christians in parts of the world where there is persecution, torment, war, and suffering. May your kingdom come to these places. We pray especially for Christians in Ukraine and for those who have found safety in neighbouring countries. The news is distressing as we hear reports from Iran, China, Hong Kong, and Ukraine. We pray for the peacemakers. Help us to see your hand at work in these places. May we find your will for our lives, for our church here, and in the wider world. Your will is good and so help us to do things your way and in your time. Help us to live a life that reflects you and your kingdom.

Give us this day our daily bread.

Today we want to be thankful for all that you have given to us. You are a loving and generous Father, and we can bring every aspect of our lives to you. We pray for those we may know who may lack basic things. We pray for the many agencies in our city that are trying to bridge the gap and bring practical and financial help to individuals and families. We pray for those supporting individuals and families who have relocated here from other countries.

And forgive us our trespasses, as we forgive those who trespass against us.

Father God we ask for your forgiveness for all that we have done wrong. For the times when we have spoken, thought, and acted in harsh and unloving ways that do not reflect you. We are sorry. Help us to let go of all that is wrong and hurtful, and not to harbour any bad feeling. May we be generous with our love and our forgiveness and help us to love each other as you love.

And lead us not into temptation; but deliver us from evil.

Father we are weak, and it is easy to be led away from our focus on you. We ask for your protection and strength. We pray for those who are going through testing times, who are struggling with loss of any kind, ill health, or isolation. Would you encourage and comfort them, and step into each situation. Surround us all with your love and protection.

For thine is the kingdom,

the power and the glory,

for ever and ever. Amen

You are the same yesterday, today and forever. You never change and you are sovereign over all things. May we put you in your rightful place and work for your kingdom here- in our families, our church, our work, our community, and our city.

Say the Lord's Prayer together:

Our Father, who art in heaven, hallowed be thy name.

thy kingdom come; thy will be done; on earth as it is in heaven.

Give us this day our daily bread.

And forgive us our trespasses, as we forgive those who trespass against us.

And lead us not into temptation; but deliver us from evil.

For thine is the kingdom, the power and the glory, for ever and ever. Amen.

Trinity Sunday Prayer

We can often be troubled by blurred or distorted vision when we look at ourselves, when we look at other people and situations, and in our Christian walk. The change is gradual and sometimes imperceptible. Let us come to the throne of grace and pray for wisdom to see clearly- to be aware of needs in our world, and to spend time in the spaces to bring people and situations that we know of, to God.

Father God, you see all things, all people, all nations.

Help us to open our eyes, so that we can see others as you see them and see you at work in our world.

We pray for those who may be in a dark place.

We ask for your light to shine on those whom we know, who are in distress, worried, or despairing in any way.

We pray for those who may feel sad, crushed, overlooked, or burdened.

We pray for those who are struggling with upheaval, and change, that your grace and peace will be with them.

We pray for those who have experienced loss of any kind.

Your word says that when I sit in darkness the Lord will be a light for me.

Father, Son, and Holy Spirit show your love and your light.

We pray for your light to shine in earth's darkest places.

We pray for those who are persecuted or silenced because of their faith.

We pray for those who have lost their employment, their home, or their opportunity of education because of their faith or their gender.

We ask you to be with those who are falsely imprisoned, in refugee camps and centres.

We pray for Christian communities persecuted in many places far and wide-in Nigeria, Afghanistan, Somalia, Eritrea, Pakistan, and India and many more.

Your light can shine in the darkest of places.

Father, Son, and Holy Spirit show your love and your light.

We pray that your light will shine in our world's war torn and desperate places.

For families in Ukraine and Russia- families who are separated, displaced and on the move. We pray for those who do not have even a temporary home or safe place. We pray for our linked churches in Romania who are offering space, rest, and hope.

We ask for your healing love for those individuals, and communities within communities, where there is rejection, hostility, and danger.

Father, Son, and Holy Spirit show your love and your light.

We pray for your light to shine in those places in our world where the good news of salvation, is not known and heard. We ask for courage for those Christians and their organisations who are helping to share your light and the good news of Jesus.

Father, Son, and Holy Spirit show your love and your light.

We pray for your light to shine in this place and in our city.

Show us how we can shine for you in this community.

We pray for those who feel that their light is flickering or in danger of going out. Encourage and strengthen them.

Open our eyes to see you at work in each other and in our place of worship.

Father, Son, and Holy Spirit show your love and your light.

THE WRITER

Jane Coates has been married to Phil for fifty-two years and they have four adult children and six grandchildren. They have always lived in Leeds which is their hometown also.

Jane has a degree in Psychology and 3 postgraduate qualifications. She is a qualified and experienced Social Worker (CQSW) with an additional qualification in Psychiatric Social Work (Cert PSW) She has worked as a Child Protection Worker for the NSPCC, the Family Therapy Team at St. James's University Hospital, Leeds and as a generic Social Worker also in Leeds.

It was difficult to continue a career in social work with four young children in the family and so Jane completed a P.G.C.E. Primary in 1990 and was a primary school teacher in Leeds for the next 27 years, teaching in several 'central' Leeds Primary schools. Most of Jane's teaching was with challenging children, many of whom had behavioural, social, family, and emotional difficulties, in addition to learning difficulties, and many with English as an additional language (EAL). She had Leadership and Senior Management responsibilities at her last school, a challenging inner-city school, for six and a half years. After leaving full time paid employment, Jane volunteered at a local school for a further 5 years which was a joy. This was a teaching post with all the enjoyment of teaching and supporting small children but without the extra pressures of assessment, planning, and the many other additional burdens that seem to surround today's teachers.

Jane gained CELTA and TEFL qualifications which enabled her to teach English to adults whose first language is not English. Jane went on to teach in Bangladesh, and Kolkotta, India, on short volunteer projects with BMS World Mission. Jane spent three months working in Luanda, Angola, West Africa also with BMS World Mission, supporting and developing pre-school education projects. Jane has taught with Amity, a Chinese Christian Organisation in China, on their intensive Summer English Courses, for eleven consecutive summers, supporting groups of Chinese Teachers of English with their English language and teaching skills. These 3- and 4-week Amity programmes were always based in rural and remote areas of China where the support of native English speakers with a qualified teacher and an excellent volunteer team was greatly valued. Jane has led teams of volunteer teachers to several Provinces in China-Sichuan, Hebei, Jiangsu, Anhui, Gansu, Inner Mongolia, and Guanxi Autonomous Region.

After retiring from teaching, Jane did not retire but became the Pastoral Care Coordinator, a volunteer role, at her local Baptist church, where she has been a member for the past 43 years. Jane leads a team of Pastoral Care Workers.

Jane is a wife, a mother, a grandmother, a homemaker, a volunteer, and has lots of other essential roles. Her encounter with Jesus began when she was a teenager and His faithfulness, grace and love has been with her, her husband, and their family throughout these many years. The journey has not always been easy and there have been challenges, and unexpected twists and turns in the road.

Trust in the Lord with all your heart;

do not depend on your own understanding.

Seek his will in all you do,

and he will show you which path to take.

Proverbs 3 v 5-6 TLT

You chart the path ahead of me and tell me where to stop and rest. Every moment you know where I am. You both precede and follow me. Psalm 139 v 3 and 5 TLB